THE 8 VALUES OF
HIGHLY PRODUCTIVE COMPANIES

Creating Wealth from a
New Employment Relationship

Dr Tim Baker

First published in 2009
Australian Academic Press
32 Jeays Street
Bowen Hills Qld 4006
Australia
www.australianacademicpress.com.au

National Library of Australia Cataloguing-in-Publication entry

Author:	Baker, Tim.
Title:	The 8 values of highly productive companies: creating wealth from a new employment relationship / Tim Baker.
ISBN:	9781921513206 (pbk.)
Notes:	Bibliography.
Subjects:	Industrial relations.
	Organizational change.
	Industrial management.
	Corporate culture.

Dewey Number: 658.315

Cover photograph by Andrea Rinarelli.

Cover and text design by Andrea Rinarelli of Australian Academic Press, Brisbane.

Dr Baker emphasises the values of highly productive companies and provides, in this latest publication, a practical application of the model that managers can use from Day 1 in the workplace to achieve improved productivity. As a student of his work, I can recommend the principles outlined in *The 8 Values of Highly Productive Companies,* and the understanding his work provides of the employer–employee relationship in contemporary management structures today. This is compulsory reading if you want to add value to your management activities and build successful productive organisations in both the private and public sector.

Alastair Dawson, BA, MBA, FAIM, MAICD
Chief Executive Officer, Rockhampton Regional Council

Since purchasing our business 5 years ago, and using Dr Tim Baker as our external organisation development consultant, we have seen a trebling of our turnover, a 5% increase in profit and practically no staff turnover. Many of the practices that Tim put in place within our business are written about in the book. Tim's management training has been a major contributor to our success. I recommend this book to all business managers.

Terry Cubit
Managing Director, Queensland Thermo King

Every company, team, and individuals, has to rethink how we are engaging our employees and ourselves at the workplace to stay competitive and productive. In *The 8 Values of Highly Productive Companies,* Tim delivers a practical model and change process on aligning the changing needs and interests of individual and organisation. Tim has worked with several multinational companies in Singapore and all of them have found the model extremely useful and insightful in preparing them to further enhance their psychological contract with their workforce.

Dr Tan Bee Wan, PhD
Executive Chairman, Integrative Learning Corporation Pte. Ltd.

To create value organisations need values-based management. This book based on Dr Baker's prior research on eight values of employee–employer relationship should be of great practical significance to modern managers.

Professor Milind Sathye
Deputy Head of the School of Business and Government, University of Canberra

Tim Baker writes frankly on the most important challenge facing businesses today: How to work together collaboratively, honestly and respectfully to gain the greatest value from our most important resource — our people. From TQM to Self-Directed Work Teams the failure of management techniques to deliver on their promises can be explained and predicted by this work. If you think you are doing it right, think again and read this book. And then consider: Can we solve the environmental challenges of our world if we do not resolve the human relationship challenges of our workplaces?

Dr Roxanne Zolin
Associate Professor, Queensland University of Technology

The 8 Values of Highly Productive Companies is an inspiring book with great practical value. Tim provides much more than smart ideas, he draws on his real world consulting experience and his academic knowledge to make a convincing case for a values approach to management which can enhance the productivity and sustainability of organisations.

Professor Hitendra Pillay
Queensland University of Technology, Brisbane, Australia

Through a refreshingly selective mix of reference material and his own experiences Dr Tim Baker has produced a comprehensive guide to managing our most important business resource — 'our people'. The book has helped me to create a workplace environment where the staff are genuinely valued, appreciate each other and are proud of the business and their own achievements.

Mark Bunt
General Manager, Epicentre Trading, Brisbane, Australia

Tim's book is a 'must-have' in any manager's library. With scholarly thoroughness and contemporary case studies, you will learn of current trends in the workplace of the new millennium.

Sergio Carlo Maresca FAIM
International best-selling author of *Breakaway!* and *Focus! or Fold!*

Tim has managed to extract a concise understanding from the latest research on the new work area and influences. The chapter on 'Them and Us' provides an insightful background and by itself provides excellent guidance for practitioners. An excellent read for organisation specialists.

Hermias C. Hendrikse
Director of Organisation Effectiveness, Etisalat, United Arab Emirates

This book provides a new millennium understanding of the workplace environment and how to implement this paradigm shift in employee–employer relations. With this knowledge the reader will be equipped to rationalise behavioural trends and move to the forefront of organisational practice to create a company with exceptional human capital and productive value.

Steve Settle
Company Director and Senior Business Manager, Brisbane, Australia

Dr Baker's book presents 21st century leadership in a form that all managers should read. In today's world of cross-functional project teams and assignments, employers and employees need to operate with a strong values based relationship contract, guiding continuous learning and value creation. Such a partnership is the key to meeting the goals of employees and organisational flexibility and knowledge management.

Bob O'Connor
Director Corporate Education, Queensland University of Technology

This user-friendly, well-laid out book is a must read for anyone, such as academics, students, professionals, and managers, who are interested in obtaining a better understanding of the radical changes in workplace relationships between the employer and employee. Using an 8 values-based framework, Tim provides a road map to guide the reader through the process (including pitfalls) in handling the transition from the traditional relationship to the dynamics of the contemporary workplace. At the end of each chapter, using reflective questions, case studies, summary of key points, Tim helps to reinforce the concepts explored in the book and provides an excellent reality check.

Bill Synnot
Co-author of *The Toolbox for Change: A Practical Approach*

Excellent … A much needed resource for today's airline industry management and employees!

Captain Saravanan
Airline Pilot, Singapore Airlines, Singapore

This book is certain to make a significant contribution to improving staff retention, recruitment and productivity of companies in a climate of accelerated change and uncertainty. Read and enjoy this very interesting book.

Brent D. Peterson, PhD
Author of *Fake Work: Why People Are Working Harder Than Ever but Accomplishing Less, and How to Fix the Problem*

In *The 8 Values of Highly Productive Companies*, Tim Baker has provided an excellent model, useful for any organisation wishing to improve their productivity and effectiveness to accomplish significant improvement that will transfer directly to the bottom line. Dr Baker provides the guidance, plus sufficient background to understand why the guidance makes sense and will work, so that leaders can immediately put his ideas to work. The results will not be instantaneous, but signs of those results will appear in very short order. He points out many of the hurdles getting in the way of companies becoming highly productive, and provides clear solutions for overcoming those hurdles. In short, this is a book for organisational leaders to begin actuating positive results while they continue to learn more about to achieve those positive, bottom line results.

Joel S. Finlay, Ph.D., RODC
Editor, Organization Development Journal
President, KSYC Production Industries
United States of America

With its practical approach and its focus on creating highly productive companies, Tim Baker's book is a welcome addition to the management literature. It is a valuable resource for all of those who wish to deepen their knowledge and understanding of how people and organisations behave, and it provides the tools which will enable them to develop their skills in fostering enhanced individual and organizational performance. Written in an easily accessible style, it offers a route map for organizational transformation.

Professor Marie McHugh
Vice Chair British Academy of Management
Department of Management, University of Ulster
United Kingdom

Dr Tim Bakers book, apart from being useful, sensible and practical has a thought-provoking, contemporary relevance.

Commissioner Bob Atkinson
Queensland Police Service

I dedicate this book to my
darling wife Carol and my two beautiful
daughters Georgie and Portia.

■

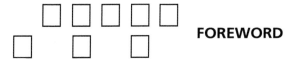

FOREWORD

I am delighted to write this foreword to *The 8 Values of Highly Productive Companies*. Dr Tim Baker has written a ground-breaking book to assist managers in changing the culture of their organisations. All you need to do is read the book and then apply and use the principles Tim presents.

My international consulting work has brought me in contact with Tim. I have known him for 3 or 4 years and have become familiar with his consulting practices and personal philosophies regarding organisational change and learning organisations. He has served many companies through consulting assignments in various parts of the world, such as Saudi Arabia, India, Singapore, Taiwan, the Philippines, Indonesia, Finland, Canada and soon the United States. Tim has helped some of the world's largest multinational companies, including Nokia, Unilever, Boeing, SAP, IBM, Volvo, Singapore Airlines, Al Safi, and many more over the past decade. From a practical perspective, Tim understands the needs and interests of modern organisations and their employees from an international perspective.

Excellent research solves the practical needs of organisations. *The 8 Values of Highly Productive Companies* is based on Tim's doctoral research. This research provides a proper map of the new world of work. A precisely updated map leads us to our destination; an inadequate and old map just causes confusion. If you don't read this book you might be using an old and imprecise map of the world of work. Get the right map, read this book!

In 2007, Tim's doctoral thesis won an outstanding doctoral award from Emerald/EFMD — one of the world's most reputable international publishers of management research. The eight values are based on Tim's research. As Tim points out in this book, the employment relationship is currently going through the most significant change since the Industrial Revolution and mangers need a conceptual but practical understanding of what is happening between leaders and employees.

Much of the frustration between management and labour in the workplace is the result of a lack of alignment between the employees and the changing needs and interests of people and organisations. This book is not only a timely addition to management ideas, but it will be of enormous practical benefit to managers and management researchers seeking to serve their companies.

The 8 Values of Highly Productive Companies is divided into three parts: Part I paints a picture of the new world of work and the need to develop a new employment relationship. Part II introduces the 'New Employment Relationship Model', consisting of eight values: Flexible Deployment, Customer Focus, Performance Focus, Project-Based Work, Human Spirit and Work, Commitment, Learning and Development, and Open Information. These are explained in terms of their benefits to the contemporary employee and employer and provide practical advice on how they can be implemented. Part III covers how this model can be implemented in an organisational setting.

My recent book (co-authored with Gaylan Nielson), *Fake Work: Why People Are Working Harder Than Ever but Accomplishing Less, and How to Fix the Problem* and the research upon which it is based suggests that Tim has the right ideas. For organisations to be successful, employee work must be aligned to the organisation's strategy.

This book is certain to make a significant contribution to improving staff retention, recruitment and productivity of companies in a climate of accelerated change and uncertainty. Read and enjoy this very interesting book.

Brent D. Peterson, PhD
United States of America

Dr Brent D. Peterson has an international reputation in the fields of organisational development and change management. Dr Peterson has facilitated more than 3,000 corporate workshops and learning interventions. His clients range from Nike, Alaska Pipeline, and Kodak to British Petroleum, Volvo, Fuji Film, and NASA. Dr Peterson is author or co-author of more than 20 books dealing with learning and development. He earned a PhD degree in organisational behaviour at Ohio University.

CONTENTS

This book is for managers interested in creating a productive workplace culture.

Instead of helping, most current human resource development (HRD) approaches are hindering — and in so doing — damaging businesses in the current climate of accelerated change and uncertainty. I expose this HRD fraud in Part I of *The 8 Values of Highly Productive Companies: Creating Wealth from a New Employment Relationship.* Part II discusses the New Employment Relationship Model consisting of eight core values. This model is the foundation for creating a workplace culture suited for the 21st century. The requirements of employer and employee have profoundly changed over the past 25 years, but traditional HRD has not kept pace with these shifting priorities.

Despite the rhetoric, current HRD practices — at the very least — are holding businesses and workers back from realising their full potential. These traditional programs come and go. Approaches such as process re-engineering, self-directed work teams, downsizing, and rightsizing and so on, are replacing each other because they are ineffective and unsustainable attempts at meeting the necessities of organisations operating in this rapidly changing global environment. Conventional HRD is obsessed with competencies, skills development, and implementing and following processes and procedures. These strategies are essentially about doing, applying or improving something within the business; they do not question the underlying assumptions of the conventional employment relationship.

What organisations need now — more than ever — is a different approach that confronts the mindsets employer and employee have of their relationship. *The 8 Values of Highly Productive Companies: Creating Wealth from a New Employment Relationship* promises to do this. It is difficult to argue with the notion that changing people's thinking is the cornerstone for changing their behaviour.

Most of the popular management books assume that people are ready and willing to change their behaviours and practices. Long-established HRD practices place too much emphasis on behaviour modification and too little on changing the way people think. Implementing innovative organisational practices with conventional thinking is ultimately futile. One step forward, two steps back, as they say.

The psychological contract has radically and irreversibly changed since the latter part of the last century. Prior to this revolution in the workplace, the traditional employment relationship had dominated industry since the birth of the Industrial Revolution. For more than 200 years, the employment relationship has been constant, predictable, and arguably a successful blueprint for the individual and organisation. Most existing HRD practices have either based their approach on this conventional 'them and us' relationship, or fail to take into account the shifting sands of the psychological contract.

Even the label 'human resource' is a hangover from a bygone era. The term implies that employees are the property of organisations in much the same way as technical resources are owned by the business. Yet most employees really do not see themselves as organisational resources, at the beck and call of employers. Now younger workers are likely to consider themselves as free agents who happen to temporarily work in a particular organisation in exchange for certain benefits and conditions. This book exposes the myth that the existing HRD industry is helpful. It is not.

The 8 Values of Highly Productive Companies: Creating Wealth from a New Employment Relationship promises to help managers navigate their way through this tumultuous time in our history. By using the roadmap outlined in the book, managers have at their disposal a unique methodology that benefits both their organisation and the individuals working in it. Part III shows how you can positively alter the culture of a workplace for the well-being of both parties in the employment relationship.

This book is timely against a backdrop where most organisations are struggling to adapt or survive to the new emergent international marketplace. On the other hand, employees are becoming increasingly disillusioned with corporate practices that fail to take into account their changing needs and interests. It is therefore sensible to consider a new way forward for HRD.

Enjoy.

Dr Tim Baker

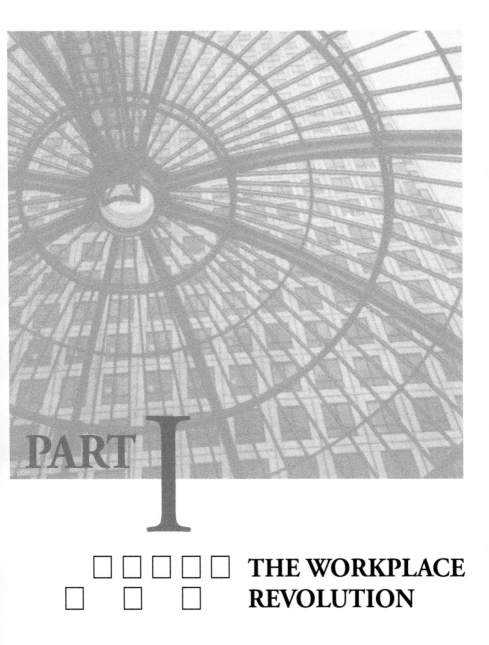

PART I

THE WORKPLACE REVOLUTION

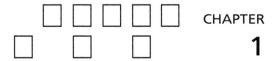

1

The End of 'Them and Us'

The traditional employment relationship has been an important and successful centrepiece of industry since the dawn of the Industrial Revolution, yet the relationship has been under strain lately because the marketplace has changed dramatically in the last 25 years.

The employment relationship as we know it is a relic of the last century. Yet most of today's companies are still operating on the values of the traditional employment relationship. Companies functioning from the traditional 'them and us' relationship between management and labour are unlikely to survive in a 21st century marketplace that is increasingly volatile and unpredictable. This phenomenon is in direct contrast to the marketplace of the 20th century, which was characterised as relatively stable and predictable. There were, of course, a few exceptions, such as the Great Depression and the stock market crash of 1987, but these were extraordinary episodes in an otherwise steady commercial environment. The traditional employer/employee relationship functioned effectively in a stable and conventional marketplace. But this long-established employer/employee relationship — the one we have all experienced first-hand in our working life — is entirely unsuitable for the current times; it is causing more harm than good to employers and employees.

Globalisation and the heightened competition this invites has challenged organisations to be more responsive to fluctuations in market conditions and trends. To remain competitive, organisational leaders have applied a multitude of strategies with limited success. Many of these approaches (advocated in the popular management literature) only 'tinker at the edges' of organisational transformation; they do not get to the 'heart of the matter'. A lot of the recommendations in these well-meaning books fail to address (or even question) the validity of the traditional employment relationship in the current environment.

At the same time, this 'new economy' (Robinson, 2000) has also radically changed the employment needs of workers. For instance, the traditional employment relationship values job security, formal qualifications, and organisational loyalty. These values have been rapidly replaced by employability, continuous learning, and independence respectively. Contemporary thinking employees are unlikely to have these needs met working in a company that assumes the values of the traditional employment relationship. Conversely, the manoeuvrability requirements of the modern company are unlikely to be met by employees who embrace traditional values in the employment relationship. Today, tension and frustration is a common consequence of the nonalignment between the needs and interests of individuals and organisations.

On the other hand, there are many productive gains for modern organisations and contemporary employees from a new employment relationship. From the employers' perspective, apart from the capacity for greater responsiveness and flexibility to meet the needs of an increasingly volatile marketplace, several other benefits are evident. Some of these include an increased capacity to find and keep good staff, higher morale and employee engagement levels, greater and more sustainable productivity, and improved customer responsiveness; all critical factors for any thriving enterprise.

The Workplace Revolution

For these reasons, employees and employers need a radically different kind of relationship from the one that has existed for over 200 years. Managers, employees, trade union officials, and human resource personnel must change their thinking about the employer/employee relationship. This is easier said than done. There are many pressures to retain the traditional employment relationship, yet the costs of retaining a 'them and us' dichotomy between employee and employer are too high for both entities. So it is not surprising that there is currently an explosion of interest in the changing relationship between employees and employers among academics and human resource development (HRD) practitioners (e.g., Beaumont & Harris, 2002; Grimmer & Oddy, 2007; Guest & Conway, 2002; Maguire, 2002; Nelson & Tonks, 2007). However, until recently, a lack of credible research on organisations about the employment relationship has hampered progress. Much of the previous research on the employment relationship has identified what this new relationship should consist of, without also examining what employees and employers actually expect (Kissler, 1994; Shore & Tetrick, 1994; Sims, 1994). Most modern management books paint an overly optimistic picture of organisations and their willingness to embrace the values of a new employment paradigm. These superficial accounts should be challenged. What we need is more rigorous

CASE STUDY

Organisational Transformation at the Chicago Tribune

Popular research-based books such as *In Search of Excellence, A Passion for Excellence, Reinventing the Corporation, The 100 Best Companies to Work for in America, Creating Excellence, Change Masters, and Leaders* have documented that increasing numbers of corporations have undergone a transformation in both culture and performance. Many of the values, beliefs, and norms that seemed essential in establishing and building the reputations of successful companies are now being challenged, to the extent that many consider a systematic transformation of those variables necessary for companies to remain viable.

The *Chicago Tribune*, one of the largest and most prominent newspapers in the United States, underwent such a transformation. The event that triggered the *Tribune's* transformation was the 1985 strike involving all five of the production union locals at the newspaper's printing facility in downtown Chicago.

In addition to contract matters, the primary issues sparking the strike were control over recruitment and selection and transfers. The key *Tribune* production managers, who had long believed that these issues were crucial to their ability to combine knowledge technology with advanced, socially responsible management, responded swiftly to the walkout. They sought to fill all vacant positions without hiring any of the persons on strike. Within days they brought in a small core of qualified machine operators and press operators, either by transferring them on temporary assignment from the other *Tribune* operation centres across the country or by recruiting them through strategically placed advertisements from other newspapers. For several weeks after the walkout began, management pitched in to help run the presses and the packaging and the ancillary equipment to keep the *Tribune* on schedule.

Source: Frame, R.M., Neilsen, W.R., & Pate, L.E. (2000). Creating excellence out of crisis. In C.H. Bell, W.L. French, & R.A. Zawacki, (Eds.), *Organisation development and transformation: Managing effective change* (pp. 411–423). Boston: Irwin McGraw-Hill.

investigations in the workplace. What do employers want from employees? What do employees want from employers? How have these needs and interests changed?

The traditional employment relationship has been an important and successful centrepiece of industry since the dawn of the Industrial Revolution, yet the relationship has been under strain lately because the marketplace has changed dramatically in the last 25 years. The 1980s signalled widespread and extensive downsizing and outsourcing to decrease the number of permanent employees in the workforce (Leans & Feldman, 1992). Prior to this upheaval, the marketplace was characterised by a relatively stable and predictable work environment for 200 years. This ideally suited the traditional management/labour relationship. Since the 1980s, the relatively secure and consistent marketplace has been replaced by rapid change, uncertainty, and global competition (see case study on p. 5). The consequences of the rapidly evolving global economy have placed considerable pressure and tension on the traditional employment relationship.

Since the 1980s upheaval, the needs and interests of organisations and workers and their expectations of each other have changed profoundly. This workplace revolution has put considerable stress on the psychological contract between workers and organisations. The changing paradigm in the relationship between individual and organisation has been called many things: 'new worker-organisation co-dependency' (Noer, 1997); 'person–organisation relationship' (Coulson-Thomas, 1998; Herriot, 1992; Hosking & Andersen, 1992); 'workplace community' (Fairholm, 1997); 'corporate citizenship' (Grint, 1997); 'new psychological contract' (Boswell, Moynihan, Roehling, & Cavanaugh, 2001; De Meuse, Bergmann, & Lester, 2001; Morrison & Robinson, 1997; Noe, 1999; Robinson, 1996; Schein, 1965); 'new employment relationship' (Adamson, 1997; Albrow, 1997; Baker, 2000; Boswell et al., 2001; Bridges, 1994; Drucker, 1992; Eldridge, Cressey, & MacInnes, 1991; Gee, Hull, & Lankshear, 1996; Grint, 1997; Handy, 1989; Noer, 1997; Roehling, Cavanaugh, Moynihan, & Boswell, 2000); or 'development culture' (Simonsen, 1997). All of these terms emphasise different aspects of the shifting relationship between the individual and the organisation. The terms 'psychological contract' and 'employment relationship' are used interchangeably throughout the book as they are the most commonly used terms to describe the changing paradigm between workers and organisations. Specifically, the term 'psychological contract' is used to describe the field of study. Alternatively, the term 'employment relationship' is used to portray the relationship between employer and employee in an organisational context.

The Futility of Popular HRD Strategies

It is timely to develop and apply models of a new employment relationship to reflect new mindsets about the management/labour relationship. It is increasingly likely that until this new employment relationship is practised in organisational settings, the majority of HRD techniques, based as they are on assumptions underpinning traditional employment relationships, will fail. Superficial and unsustainable attempts at addressing the perennial challenges of how to treat people at work will therefore continue. In particular, HRD programs will be unsuccessful in motivating employees for higher performance. What we need are fresh approaches based on the new reality of the employer/employee relationship.

Much of the popular management literature enthusiastically advocates the need for a new employment relationship without providing us with the necessary tools to change the mindsets of employers and employees. Managers want practical change — management approaches that are grounded in the new mindsets about the employment relationship. The primary purpose of these tools should be to align the changing organisational and individual requirements. This will assist both the employer and employee. Approaches like this are ground breaking. Most current HRD practices either do not address the issue of conflict between management and labour, or assume there is a commonality of interests between the two parties.

The big challenge now is: How do we change people's thinking after 200 years of 'them and us' thinking borne of the Industrial Revolution? Then again, the futility of previously popular HRD strategies will become more evident. In an increasingly competitive environment, the old employment conventions are being challenged more than ever as they appear increasingly irrelevant in a climate of accelerated economic change and uncertainty.

Despite the need for a new approach to the employment relationship, there has not been a credible framework for applying these changing individual and organisational values in the workplace. There is often a gap between the reality and rhetoric of the 'high performance workplace' (OECD, 1996; Gee et al., 1996). Superficial accounts of how companies have revolutionised themselves overnight are everywhere. These exaggerated accounts of high-performing workplaces and the inadequacy of the tools with which to implement workplace culture change have been a source of frustration to many managers trying to change their companies. Most HRD approaches are 'top down' models, driven by organisational leaders without regard for the strategic involvement of employees at all levels of the organisational structure.

The 8 Values of Highly Productive Companies intends to fill this gap. It provides a rigorous framework for change based on research and the author's experience over a decade as an international HRD consultant. The framework detailed in this book is a genuinely collaborative approach involving employers and employees, and is based on a model comprising eight values. These core values have the capacity to bring into line the new requirements of employers and employees in a time of rapid change and ambiguity. In a nutshell, it provides managers and management researchers with the tools to create and monitor a sustainably productive workplace culture.

Defining the Traditional 'Them and Us' Relationship

Before defining a new working model, it would be helpful to define the traditional employment relationship in order to highlight its shortcomings.

The traditional employment relationship is a result of a form of work organisation commonly referred to as 'Fordism' (Fuchs, 2002). Basically, Fordism has four features:

1. a rationalisation and mechanisation of production
2. it is highly centralised
3. there is minimal opportunity to advance from the shop floor
4. designated tasks are expected to be performed at an acceptable rate.

Fordism breaks the total company into small parts or tasks. People are then employed to do these tasks. These tasks are to be performed in specific, pre-scribed ways. Fordism results in clearly defined roles and responsibilities between management and labour.

This results in an exchange process between employer and employee. The exchange in the traditional employment relationship consists of the manager specifying the work requirements and, in return for a willingness to comply, the worker receives a wage. This has been the conventional lynchpin of the relationship between manager and worker since the birth of industry. Any failure to heed a work instruction, or to pay the agreed wage, means that the contract collapses.

This basic understanding evolved between employees and employers. It was expected that employees would work hard, cause few problems, and generally do whatever the boss wanted. In return, it was expected that employers would provide 'good jobs' with 'good pay', offer plenty of advance-ment opportunities, and virtually guarantee lifetime employment. It was a stable, predictable world, the employee would be loyal to the employer and, in return, the employer would provide job security for the employee. This unwritten agreement between the two parties came to be referred to as the 'psychological contract'.

The traditional manager/worker relationship is easy to follow despite its shortcomings. Generally speaking, Fordism as a model has proven to be par-ticularly successful for most of the previous two centuries. However, now traditional organisations are increasingly regarded as being incapable of adapting to the challenges of a globalised and increasingly interactive world; they are generally too inflexible in their deployment of employees. As Fuchs (2002) points out:

> ... the traditional organisation has proved to be largely incapable of defining, exploiting and operationalising such knowledge-incentive assets, but has nev-ertheless been able to retain these assets within the firm boundaries. (p. 155)

The essence of the problem is this: while the traditional model is simple, people are more complicated. Managers are given responsibility and workers are given tasks. But this creates a dilemma: employees who are not given responsibility tend to shirk responsibilities and therefore never become responsible. The fewer the people who take on responsibilities, the greater the burden of responsibility that falls on the shoulders of the manager. In reality, managers can disappoint and workers can surprise others by their initiative and enterprise.

Against a backdrop of a far less predictable and stable marketplace, the answer to this dilemma would seem to be fairly obvious. Surely a less formal employment relationship, where managers provide workers with the freedom to be flexible and innovative in their approach to problem-solving is the way forward. This is the approach advocated by most popular management authors.

However, these new approaches open the door for workers to manipulate the system. The overlapping areas of freedom open the way for political operators to seize the opportunity and exercise their unwelcome skills. These areas of freedom are absent in the traditional manager/worker relationship. Under this more flexible relationship, managers may, and undoubtedly do, feel threatened. The likely outcome is to revert to the simple demarcation of responsibilities explicit in the traditional relationship. This is despite the need for a fresh perspective on the relationship between individual and organisation.

The challenge is to create a new mode of working relationship with the same degree of straightforwardness, but without the pitfalls, of the traditional system. Under the old paradigm, there is a considerable price to pay for developing a new model for the manager, worker and organisation. Under a new employment relationship, managers will not be able to give and supervise tasks to the same extent. Employees, on the other hand, are expected to take greater responsibility and be more accountable for their output. In the context of the uncertainty of a new system it is likely to result in disagreement, frustration and confusion.

Nevertheless, there are enormous advantages (and little choice) in breaking the bonds of this traditional mindset in the 21st century. There are many rewards for employees. They can choose to invest themselves in satisfying, meaningful work, engage in continuous learning, and reclaim their self-esteem, which was probably lost under the traditional employer/employee relationship. The company payoff is equally positive: a workforce filled with free, independent employees working on tasks they find fulfilling. The result for the company under those circumstances is likely to be a long-term competitive advantage in the global marketplace. Some authors refer to this new association as 'corporate citizenship' (see Grint, 1997; Fairholm, 1997). Employees have rights that employers must honour. Conversely, employees also have responsibilities to the company to be involved, committed, and supportive. Obligation, consent and participation are elements of organisational citizenship. In other words, values become the glue of citizenship in the company. This new approach is still based on an exchange process between employer and employee. The difference is that it does away with the 'them and us' concept of the old industrial model.

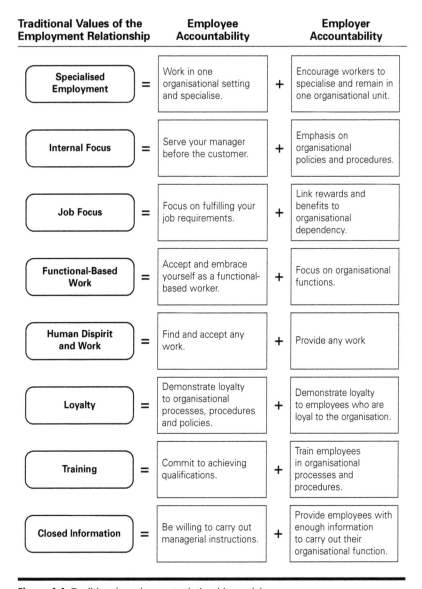

Traditional Values of the Employment Relationship		Employee Accountability		Employer Accountability
Specialised Employment	=	Work in one organisational setting and specialise.	+	Encourage workers to specialise and remain in one organisational unit.
Internal Focus	=	Serve your manager before the customer.	+	Emphasis on organisational policies and procedures.
Job Focus	=	Focus on fulfilling your job requirements.	+	Link rewards and benefits to organisational dependency.
Functional-Based Work	=	Accept and embrace yourself as a functional-based worker.	+	Focus on organisational functions.
Human Dispirit and Work	=	Find and accept any work.	+	Provide any work
Loyalty	=	Demonstrate loyalty to organisational processes, procedures and policies.	+	Demonstrate loyalty to employees who are loyal to the organisation.
Training	=	Commit to achieving qualifications.	+	Train employees in organisational processes and procedures.
Closed Information	=	Be willing to carry out managerial instructions.	+	Provide employees with enough information to carry out their organisational function.

Figure 1.1 Traditional employment relationship model.

Achieving this is not an easy process. It requires new ways of thinking for both individuals and organisational leaders. The employee must choose to break free and claim the new freedom, and the organisation must accommodate and facilitate that choice. It is increasingly evident that the traditional employment relationship is no longer adequate in today's business environment.

To summarise, Figure 1.1 illustrates the traditional employment relationship. The left-hand column signifies eight core values of the traditional employment relationship. In the middle column, the eight descriptors characterise the appropriate response or accountability to each value by the employee. This response is the employee's fulfilment of the traditional psychological contract. The right-hand side represents the appropriate response from the employer's perspective for each value. This response is the employer's fulfilment of the traditional psychological contract. The psychological contract is about the workers meeting the needs of their employers and about the employers meeting the needs of their workers. Should any of these responses to the traditional values be violated by the employee or employer, the psychological contract would be broken. This could be a temporary or permanent breakdown, depending on the severity of the violation.

The Case for a New Employment Relationship

Many writers have argued that shifting economic trends, competitive pressures, and organisational structures have led to a changing employment relationship in the workplace (e.g., Burack, 1993; Capelli, Bassi, Katz, Knoke, Osterman, & Useem, 1997; Kissler, 1994). At the same time, some researchers have a view that the fundamental transformation of employment relations has not yet occurred (e.g., Fuchs, 2002). There is general agreement, however, that relatively recent work practices such as downsizing, reengineering, restructuring, flexible contracts, and outsourcing have increased mistrust in the workplace. Furthermore, increased global competition has spurred organisations to develop new strategies focused on being more responsive. The requirement to be more responsive is due to rapidly changing market conditions and innovation. Technological advancement has further sped up the pace of change in business. All of these changes in the economy and business environment have led to changes in what companies and employees expect from each other in the employment relationship.

As mentioned earlier, there is plenty of advice in the popular management literature to counter the impact of these changes. These recommendations usually come in the form of techniques and strategies to get workers to give of their best and to make companies more manoeuvrable in the marketplace. However, a new employment relationship model cannot be implemented and sustained with a traditional mindset. Heightened competition fuelled by the move to a global economy has bought into sharper focus the need to abandon traditional thinking about the employment relationship.

The HRD industry has responded to these changes extensively. For the past 25 years in particular, we have witnessed unprecedented HRD interventions. These strategies have changed the way organisations have conducted business, as companies have embraced new concepts, undertaken new initiatives for improvement, and in so doing have changed the way work is performed. As Neusch and Siebenaler (1998) put it, companies have

> ... done TQM and JIT. They've been Kaizened and QFDed, activity-base costed, reengineered, flattened and right-sized, moved from low gear to third gear in speed-to-market, and have focused mightily on customer satisfaction. They have asked employees to work in teams and to become involved, empowered, committed, and productive. (p. xv)

These HRD initiatives have generally been an inadequate response to the demands on companies to become more manoeuvrable in the marketplace. And the results have largely failed to gain sustainable commitment from employees.

So what have these shifts in thinking from the individual and organisation been over the past 25 years?

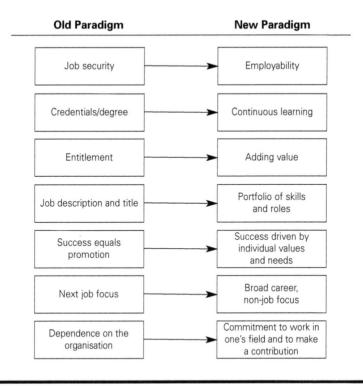

Figure 1.2 The changing individual paradigm.
Source: Simonsen, P. (1997). *Promoting a development culture in your organization*. Newbury Park, CA: Davies-Black, p. 22.

The Changing Individual and Organisational Paradigm

From the perspective of the individual worker, the ever-changing economic circumstances have dramatically altered their vocational, learning and development needs. Qualities such as employability, continuous learning, flexibility and independence have replaced job security, qualifications, predictability and organisational dependence as important employee success, or even survival, traits.

Figure 1.2 illustrates the changing individual paradigm. The traditional workplace is unlikely to suit the needs of the worker with a new career mindset listed in the right-hand column. Just as it is in the interests of employees to change their mindset about careers, development, and organisational involvement, so too is it advantageous for the people who lead them to alter their own attitudes. Employer/employee partnerships will inevitably need to replace the boss/worker mindset of the traditional workplace.

From the employer's perspective, Figure 1.3 illustrates the changing organisational mindset.

The Challenges of Changing Paradigms

If individuals and organisational leaders genuinely embrace these new paradigms outlined in Figures 1.2 and 1.3 it is a good start. They are then

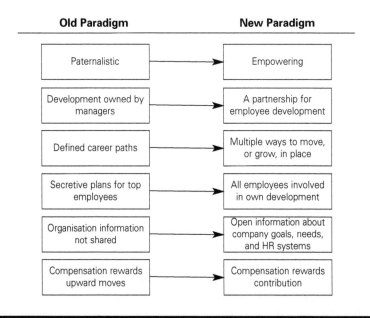

Figure 1.3 The changing organisational paradigm.
Source: Simonsen, P. (1997). *Promoting a development culture in your organization*. Newbury Park, CA: Davies-Black, p. 22.

well positioned to meet the challenges of the rapidly changing global marketplace. However, many companies are in limbo between the old, paternalistic culture that worked in a stable, hierarchical environment and the new developmentally focused culture needed to meet the challenges of the new economy shown in Figure 1.3. On the other hand, behaviours in employees suggest that they too are not always fully embracing the new paradigm as shown in Figure 1.2. For instance, organisational leaders may expect workers to change, yet their management practices and systems are more often than not based on the traditional 'command and control' mindset. Likewise, workers may expect managers to exhibit modern management practices, yet they may continue to exhibit an organisation–dependency mindset. There are many obstacles to changing these old paradigms and many challenges to shifting to new mindsets — for both the individual and organisation.

Organisations are generally not viewed by workers as cooperative enterprises where 'sharing of the cake' is negotiated on any principled basis. Worker/management conflict has been the dominant historical model. It is therefore not surprising that this dichotomy has led to a self-fulfilling prophecy: management beliefs about workers needing tight control mechanisms and specific roles have encouraged workers to adopt a narrow and detached view of their organisational role. There may be some evidence that this psychological contract is changing. However, it is unlikely that this move towards a new psychological contract is keeping pace with the changing commercial environment.

Conclusion

More than anything else, the corporate restructuring and downsizing strategies of the 1980s and 1990s have bought into question the traditional employer/employee relationship. Today's workplace is one of increased workload and stress and decreased job security and commitment. Furthermore, the current work environment sends confusing signals that have lead to employee uncertainty, cynicism, fear and anger. On the one hand, HRD initiatives convey to employees that employers value them and that they are an integral corporate asset. Strategies such as total quality management, employee-empowerment programs, and self-directed work teams (SDWTs) have contributed to this. On the other hand, employees are being exposed to strategies such as downsizing and re-engineering that seem to run contrary to the notion of the critical role that people play in organisational success. Overall, this has led to a great deal of scepticism from employees about the motives of management. Despite this, there is a strong case for a new working relationship based on new paradigms about the psychological contract. This shift from the 'them and us' relationship to a new employment relationship is critical for both organisations and individual.

■ **Reflective Questions for Managers**

In relation to the case study on page 5, management saw this as an opportunity to change the psychological contract between employer and employee by changing the mindsets of employer and employee in order to transform the workplace culture. Consider the following question.

1. Workplace culture was characterised by the traditional employment relationship exhibited in Figure 1.1. If you had to advise *Chicago Tribune*, what strategies would you consider to assist in changing each of the individual and organisational paradigms shown in Figures 1.2 and 1.3? How would you go about implementing these approaches to facilitate a new psychological contract based on the new individual and organisation paradigms?

Consider how the following questions can be addressed in your own organisation:

2. How closely aligned is your organisation to the traditional employment relationship model shown in Figure 1.1?

3. One of the drivers for a new employment relationship is the need to be more responsive in the marketplace. In your industry, how has the need to be more responsive and manoeuvrable affected your business?

4. In your career, what exposure have you had to traditional HRD interventions? How effective or ineffective have they been?

5. Where are the majority of your employees in terms of The Changing Individual Paradigm shown in Figure 1.2? Do they embrace the Old Paradigm, New Paradigm, or are they in transition between the Old and New?

6. Where is your organisation's mindset in terms of The Changing Organisational Paradigm shown in Figure 1.3? Do managers generally embrace the Old Paradigm, New Paradigm, or are they in transition between the Old and New?

■ **Top 10 Key Points from Chapter 1**

1. The traditional employment relationship has been an important and successful centrepiece of industry since the Industrial Revolution.

2. The employment relationship has radically changed since the 1980s.

3. Since the 1980s, the needs and interests of organisations and workers and their expectations of each other have changed profoundly.

4. Much of the popular management literature enthusiastically advocates the need for a new employment relationship, without providing the necessary tools to change the mindsets of employers and employees.

5. The traditional employment relationship is a result of a form of work organisation commonly referred to as 'Fordism'.

6. The challenge is to create a new mode of working relationship with the same degree of straightforwardness, but without the pitfalls, of the traditional system.

7. Shifting economic trends, competitive pressures, and organisational structures have led to a changing employment relationship in the workplace.

8. For the past 25 years in particular, we have witnessed unprecedented HRD interventions.

9. The ever-changing economic circumstances have dramatically altered the vocational, learning and development needs of individual employees.

10. Globalisation has put pressure on organisations to be more responsive and flexible in the rapidly changing and competitive marketplace.

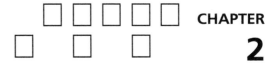

The Psychological Contract

Ironically, most human resource development approaches fail to take into consideration the needs and interests of employees.

The dramatically changing individual and organisational paradigms over the past 25 years outlined in Chapter 1 are the catalyst for a profoundly different psychological contract between employer and employee. Consequently, the new employment relationship is based on a completely different set of values from the traditional relationship. There is a need for new models of the relationship that are based on credible research. It is only relatively recently that researchers have looked at this phenomenon in detail. Most of the studies in the literature have researched the views and perspectives of employees. There is a need to address this imbalance and view the new employment relationship from the dual perspective of the employer and employee. In spite of the growing interest in this new psychological contract, managers require practical change management tools to assist organisations to facilitate a move from a 'them and us' employment mentality. Popular management books suggest that the presence of this new psychological contract is more prevalent than it really is. One of the core challenges for management researchers is to create fresh insights about the person–organisation relationship. This test should not be underrated.

Understanding the Psychological Contract

The psychological contract was briefly defined in Chapter 1. A more detailed understanding of the psychological contract is necessary. As pointed out in the previous chapter, underpinning the changing individual and organisation mindset since the later part of the 20th century is a profoundly different psychological contract. Over the past decade or so, there has been a plethora of writing on the subject of the psychological contract, particularly in the past 6 years (e.g., Beaumont & Harris, 2002; Grimmer & Oddy, 2007; Guest & Conway, 2002; Maguire, 2002; Nelson & Tonks, 2007). Pate and Malone (2000) define the psychological contract as an individual's perceptions of the employment relationship. More specifically, Noe (1999) states that 'a psychological contract is the expectation that employers and employees have about each other' (p. 290). Therefore, a breach of the psychological contract takes place when an employee believes that the organisation has failed to deliver its promises or obligations. On the other hand, an infringement can result when a manager perceives that an employee is not living up to his or her responsibility. Guest (1998) argues that the psychological contract was originally devised as a heuristic device and not as a serious analytical construct. Nonetheless, it can be interpreted that the burgeoning interest in the concept is an endorsement of its high face validity (Marks, 2000).

There are two dimensions to the psychological contract: transactional and relational (Morrison & Robinson, 1997). These two components emphasise different aspects of the exchange relationship. The transactional exchange is associated with providing specific, monetary remuneration for certain services performed by the employee. These promises can be explicit and/or implicit. A transactional exchange results in a short-term, almost contract-like agreement between the two parties.

In contrast, the relational component emphasises a socioemotive interaction between the employee and employer. Relational elements revolve around trust, respect, and the development of loyalty. The relational component of the psychological contract is becoming a more complex issue for organisations. This is because some companies are forced to downsize, while others face a tight labour market, making it difficult to find and retain qualified employees. In this currently competitive environment, an understanding of how to attract and retain critical talent is increasingly important. People's relational values are a critical component of the psychological contract that needs addressing.

Values drive behaviour. In other words, the values managers and employees have of their employment relationship will determine the way they interact. For instance, the traditional psychological contract is largely based on the value of Loyalty: employees would be loyal to the boss and, in return, the boss would provide job security for the employee. So, this traditional relational value of Loyalty is likely to manifest into loyalty behaviour in a traditional workplace. However, a new employment relationship is based on a completely different set of values. As a consequence, the relational aspects of the contract need reviewing and updating.

CASE STUDY
SEMCO

For more than 25 years, Ricardo Semler, CEO of Brazil-based SEMCO, has let his employees set their own hours, wages, even choose their own IT. The result: increased productivity, long-term loyalty and phenomenal growth.

Semler determined to balance his work and personal life more carefully and to do the same for his employees — all while improving SEMCO's fortunes. To his great relief, he discovered he didn't have to reconcile these two goals: the more freedom he gave his staff to set their own schedules, the more versatile, productive and loyal they became, and the better SEMCO performed.

Nor did he stop with flexi-time. He did away with dedicated receptionists, organisational charts, even the central office; it now resembles an airlines' VIP lounge, with people working in different areas each day. He encouraged employees to suggest what they should be paid, to evaluate their bosses, to learn each other's jobs, and to tolerate dissent — even when divisive. He set up a profit-sharing system and insisted that the company's financials be published internally, so that everyone could see how the company was doing.

SEMCO's revenues have jumped from $35 million to $212 million in the last 6 years, and the firm grew from several hundred employees to 3000, with an employee turnover of about 1%.

Semler, relishes the role of provocateur:

> The desire for uniformity is a major problem with IT. But it is a subproduct of the same problems that plague management, which is the need to feel in control, that we're all on the same page, and everyone is being treated equally. But what I want to ask is, Why do we all need to be on the same page? And you realise, of course, that no two people are equal in any respect.
>
> The first anxiety executives have about workers setting their own hours is that people are going to suggest that they come in as late as possible, leave as early as possible, make as much as possible — end of story. And in 25 years we've never heard that. I don't think [that sort of behaviour] comes to people as naturally as the anxiety about it comes to the [manager] who's thinking about it. [At SEMCO] we always assume that we're dealing with responsible adults, which we are. And when you start treating employees like adolescents by saying that you can't come late, you can't use this bathroom — that's when you start to bring out the adolescent in people.
>
> Last week CNN spent 4 days with a bunch of our guys probing in all directions, and they concluded that our people balance their lives much better, and that there are an unusually high number of people who take their kids to school, etc. But a recent statistic of ours shows that 27% of our people are online on Sunday at 8 p.m. — 27%. So they probably do work hard.

Research Studies of the New Psychological Contract

Despite the need for a new conceptualisation of the employment relationship, until recently there has been a lack of credible research in applying new models in the workplace. Underpinning the difference between the changing individual and organisation mindset is a different psychological contract. Figures 1.2 and 1.3 in Chapter 1 illustrate these changing paradigms. Despite the lack of workable research-based models, over the past decade or so there has been a excess of writing on the subject of the psychological contract (e.g., Beaumont & Harris, 2002; Grimmer & Oddy, 2007; Guest & Conway, 2002; Maguire, 2002; Nelson & Tonks, 2007).

Studies of the psychological contract have focused mostly on contract violations (e.g., Beaumont & Harris, 2002; Grimmer & Oddy, 2007; Llewellyn, 2001; Nelson & Tonks, 2007; Pate, Martin, Beaumont, & McGoldrick, 2000). Other studies have examined the relationship between job security, career development and the psychological contract (Atkinson, 2000; Lankhuijzen, Stavenga de Jong, & Thijssen, 2006). Some studies have tested theoretical models of the psychological contract (Schalk & Roe, 2007); others have looked at marketplace changes and their impact on the psychological contract (Cassar, 2001; Pavlou & Gefen, 2005). Most of the recent studies have focused on employee attitudes to the psychological contract (Jordan, Schraeder, Field, & Armenakis, 2007; Nelson & Tonks, 2007; Pate, Martin, & McGoldrick, 2003; Schalk & Freese, 2007). However, a few researchers have studied managers' perspectives about the psychological contract and have redressed the imbalance (e.g., Shore, Bommer, & Shore, 2008; Tekleab & Taylor, 2003).

Research has predominantly focused on employees' views and has largely neglected the organisational perspective and the management of the psychological contract (Guest & Conway, 2002). This disproportionate emphasis on surveying employees' attitudes in the employment relationship has been remedied to some extent. For example, Guest and Conway's research, based on a survey of 1306 senior human resource (HR) managers, explored the management of the psychological contract, and in particular the role of organisational communication. Three distinct and relevant aspects of organisational communication were identified, concerned with initial entry, day-to-day work and more future-oriented top-down communication.

Lack of Applied New Employment Relationship Models

Despite the growing number of advocates for a new psychological contract in the research literature, there is a shortage of practical change management tools. It is true that the business environment in the early part of the 21st century is too chaotic and organisational change too complex to establish firm objectives, fixed plans, and concrete programs of change. Even so, without the guidelines and directions models bring, it is more difficult to emphasise the appropriate HRD measures consistently. Models founded on sound research can assist organisational leaders to benchmark their organisation on a regular basis.

Change management is a relatively new area of study. The test for this subject area — like all HRD fields — is to be both theoretically rigorous and practically relevant. This dual challenge should not be underestimated. For instance, Kahn (1974) made this observation over 30 years ago about the change management literature:

> A few theoretical propositions repeated without additional data or development; a few bits of homely advice reiterated without proof or disproof; and a few sturdy empirical observations quoted with reverence but without refinement or explication. (p. 487)

More recent change scholars such as Denis, Lamothe and Langley (2001) consider that Kahn's observation remains dismayingly accurate a quarter of a century later.

The shortage of valid and reliable change tools is further compounded by a lack of new models of the employment relationship. Generalisations about change are also difficult to make across international, institutional, and cultural borders. Nevertheless, managers would benefit from understanding the core issues associated with changing the psychological contract. Empirical studies validating new employment relationship models will assist both employers and employees evolve their partnership.

Ironically, most HRD approaches fail to take into consideration the needs and interests of employees. Many HRD approaches emphasise the actions of organisational leaders and correspondingly de-emphasise the strategic involvement of the rest of the organisation. While it is acknowledged that the formal catalyst for organisational change usually begins at the top management level, the strategic involvement of organisational members needs to be considered and sought in most large scale change processes. A considerable amount of change management literature tends to highlight strategies for overcoming employee resistance to change. Instead, a better approach would be to focus on strategies that involve all employees in the change process.

To illustrate, popular management books give inordinate attention to chief executive officers (CEOs) and their senior management teams, and their role in the change process. However, researchers have recently stressed that strategic leadership requires the contributions of all organisational members. As an example, Denis et al's. (2001) research validates the worth of collective leadership, emphasising the need for involvement in the change process beyond the top management level. In other words, they view strategic leadership as a collective phenomenon. In particular, any attempt to develop new thinking about the employment relationship must consider the dual involvement and impact of workers and organisational leaders.

Most models of the new psychological contract illustrate the characteristics of the new relationship and how these features are formed from a sociocultural perspective. For instance, Guest's (1998) model emphasises some of the organisational factors required to create a new psychological contract. Kissler's (1994) model makes the distinction between the characteristics of the 'old' and 'new' contracts. Sparrow's (1996) model illustrates the relationship between culture and the formation of the psychological contract. While useful for understanding the cause and effect of this phenomenon, these models do not emphasise change from the twofold perspective of employee and employer.

Popular Management Literature

In addition to the research literature, what do the popular management books say about the new employment relationship?

Popular management literature typically reflects an assumption that the new employment relationship is found across several 'high performance' workplaces. These workplaces are often written up as examples of ideal employer/employee relationships. The reality is, however, that these anecdotes are usually superficial accounts without any credible basis of evidence. So, we are led to believe that the new employment relationship is prevalent across a number of corporations.

Without sustained research in organisational settings, the popular management literature has a tendency to paint a simplistic and overly optimistic picture of the 'new' workplace. As Gee et al. (1996) rightly points out, 'the reality 'on the ground' is often much more complex than the theories in the books might imply' (p. 4). Often the substitute for sound workplace research in the popular management literature is arguments bolstered by stories and uncritical accounts of particular corporations that have been transformed. For instance, Gee et al. (1996) make the following observation after viewing a team meeting in a company implementing SDWT:

> On the one hand, self-directed work teams were supposed to be empowered to solve their own problems. However, on the other hand, managers and engineers appeared so compelled to measure and document quality and productivity, workers were left very little room in which to manoeuvre. (pp. 122–123)

Observations like this caution managers and management researchers to look closely at popular management accounts of successful workplace practices. There is more often than not a gap between the rhetoric of the new management literature and the reality in the workplace.

To address these rapid and constantly changing needs in today's world, managers everywhere are using a variety of strategies to involve and 'empower' employees. These strategies are espoused by most popular management authors. Studies from different countries confirm a rise in the proportion of companies implementing approaches to involve their staff in decision-making. Other studies indicate an explosion in the variety of empowerment practices (see Hyman & Mason, 1995; Pickard, 1993). Most of these involve communication, such as team briefings, suggestions and approaches to problem-solving schemes and staff appraisals. While empowerment strategies are growing, research reveals that a lot of these approaches are applied in an ad hoc manner and their impact is fairly shallow (Hyman & Mason, 1995). In most cases, these empowerment strategies do not challenge the core conventions of the traditional employment relationship. They are therefore likely to be unsustainable attempts at enhancing workplace productivity.

The use of empowerment is written about extensively in the popular management literature. Its main feature is to involve employees in the ownership of their job so that they can take personal interest in improving the performance of the organisation. The concept sounds great in principle. Nevertheless, the indications are that empowerment tends to be introduced in companies that have removed layers of supervisory management. So, it is used to cover existing tasks with fewer staff. There are often no corresponding rewards for the added responsibilities associated with the 'empowered' jobs. This makes individual employees vulnerable on two fronts. First, added responsibility without adequate training invariably increases stress levels. Second, empowered employees are held accountable for their new responsibilities. But the boundaries around that accountability are fuzzy and fluctuate. Any performance failures can then be easily attributed to the empowered employees. In these circumstances, a lack of organisational support and managerial incompetence can be 'swept under the carpet'. Empowerment — used in this way — is a euphemism for work intensification.

The deployment of empowerment strategies is not a straightforward matter. It can be paradoxical and confusing. On the one hand, modern employees are expected to be less dependent on the company and more self-reliant in terms of their career. On the other hand, employees are encouraged to be more reliant on group decision-making processes and increasingly being expected to work as a team member within the company. Empowerment means that companies are promoting self-reliance in their employees. However, people who are already self-reliant do not need empowering by the organisation. Then again, people who are too dependent on the company need empowering. As a result of this, the empowerment strategy can be confusing and send employees conflicting messages. On the surface, empowerment strategies appear to be an appropriate solution to raising company productivity in a more competitive and uncertain marketplace. However, in practice, the complexity of issues, paradoxical nature, and the true intent of these popular HRD strategies, can present a different picture.

Furthermore, the popular management literature conveys the clear impression that specific HRD strategies are responsible for creating high performing workplaces. However, these one-off HRD events fail to address the core challenge of evolving the employment relationship beyond the 'them and us' relationship. The failure of these popular HRD techniques and strategies to gain sustainable commitment from workers is occurring when the need for performance improvement is greater now than at any time in history. Corporations of all sizes and in all fields must now face up to issues of heightened dynamic competition, ever-accelerating technological demands, and the shortages of key technical and management skills, all in a pervading climate of economic uncertainty. The global economy is creating new market standards in productivity, quality, variety, customisation, convenience, and timeliness. Meeting these standards requires great changes in organisational structures, skill needs and jobs. Social and economic changes of this magnitude are putting renewed tension on the nature of the relationship between employer and employee.

The assumed new employment relationship described in popular management writing is not as commonplace as espoused. Managers should therefore not simply take for granted that individuals hold similar expectations or that those expectations are consistent with that of the company. Equally, employees should not presume that managers hold assumptions that are consistent with characteristics of the new employment relationship.

New Management Challenges

Because of these factors, one of the core challenges for managers and management researchers is to generate new perspectives of the person–organisation relationship. Most managers separate the person and the organisation. So they more or less neglect the relationship between the two entities. Instead, they are conceptualised as detached bodies. The focus is usually on structures, processes, workplace culture, change management and so on. However, in all these cases, they are created by people. So, to separate people from organisational outcomes does not make sense. Managers need to change their focus from company outcomes alone to understanding and appreciating the transforming relationship with staff. This involves new management thinking. Managers can no longer afford to ignore the psychological contract. No longer can they assume a coincidence of interests between workers and the company.

The challenge is that this change in perspective requires a completely new way of thinking. Values that underpin the traditional and new employment relationships contradict each other. Because of the magnitude of the mind shifts, it is hardly surprising that these old beliefs are being maintained in modern organisations by traditional managers. Traditional managers use habitual punishment and reward strategies they have learned from their parents. Thompson (1995, p. 89) points out that 'managers treat their direct reports and co-workers in ways similar to how their mothers and fathers treated them. It is a family system'. Modern management literature would have us believe that these outdated attitudes are changing. But if they are deeply entrenched patterns of thinking, can they really be changed effortlessly? It is very difficult for people who have patterns of thinking and habits of work that have been deeply ingrained for a lifetime to learn and change their approach.

Popular management books fail to take into account (or at least underrate) the magnitude of changing managers' patterns of thinking. The popular literature often prescribes adopting and applying a new set of management skills, without considering the thought processes underpinning new management practices. So, changing management mindsets is a critically important and challenging aspect of replacing the traditional psychological contract.

Conclusion

Within the rapidly growing field of the psychological contract, several factors should be considered. First, the changing individual and organisational paradigms over the last 25 years bring into sharper focus the concept of the psychological contract. Since the downsizing movement in the 1980s, the needs and interests of organisations and workers and their expectations of each other have changed significantly. This has put considerable stress on the psychological contract between workers and organisations. As a result, there has been an explosion of interest in the changing psychological contract. Second, since most of the research in the past has been in the area of contract violations and the emphasis has been on the employee, there is a need for more focus on examining both the employee and employer perspectives. A dual perspective promises to shed light on issues of aligning the changing needs and interests of employer and employee. Third, from the perspective of leadership and organisational development, a model that assists in providing a conceptual framework of this new employment relationship promises to be useful for both managers and management researchers. Fourth, as discussed in this chapter, the popular management literature often exaggerates the existence of the high performing workplace. It is for these four reasons that the research-based model presented in this book promises to contribute to the literature on the psychological contract for the benefit of both practitioners and researchers.

■ Reflective Questions for Managers

In relation to the case study on page 19 consider the following questions:

1. SEMCO has managed to break the shackles of the traditional employment relationship. What sort of leadership traits are needed to create this new psychological contract?

2. Do you agree with Semler that managers letting go of their power and control is one of the greatest inhibiters of creating a workplace like SEMCO?

3. Semler assumes that employees are reliable and trustworthy. Is this realistic from an employment perspective?

Consider how the following questions can be addressed in your own organisation:

4. What issues are you currently facing regarding the employment relationship? Are they transactional issues or relational issues?

5. Do you think loyalty in organisations is a thing of the past? Are employees loyal to the organisation? Are managers loyal to staff?

6. Can you think of an instance when a psychological contract violation took place in your workplace? What was it? Was the violation an employee or employer violation? Was the violation based on the traditional or new psychological contract?

7. Why do you think the focus of research has been on the employee rather than the employer in the employment relationship?

8. Why have most change management approaches been focused on what managers need to do and not on employees?

9. Do you think empowerment is a genuine attempt at getting employees engaged in the organisation or a strategy to replace middle management and save costs and shift responsibility?

■ Top 10 Key Points from Chapter 2

1. The individual and organisational paradigms underpin a profoundly different psychological contract between employer and employee.

2. The psychological contract is the expectation that employers and employees have about each other.

3. The conceptualisation of the psychological contract is only a relatively recent area of research.

4. The existing literature distinguishes between two components of the psychological contract: transactional and relational.

5. There is a shortage of empirically based research on the psychological contract that can be applied in organisational setting.

6. Most of the studies on the psychological contract have focused on employees and their perception of contract violations.

7. There is a need for more practical change management tools for managers to change the psychological contract in their organisations.

8. Most HRD approaches focus on what managers need to do rather than emphasising the strategic involvement of the rest of the organisation.

9. Popular management books create the impression that there are more high performing workplaces that espouse the characteristics of the new employment relationship than is necessarily the case.

10. Management researchers need to continue to create new perspectives on the person/organisation interface.

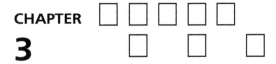

The New World of Work

> Enlightened workplaces are likely to attract the critical
> self-led workers needed for success. The self-motivated
> employee, particularly with a modern mindset about
> the employment relationship, is increasingly in demand.

Before presenting the New Employment Relationship Model in the next chapter, we need to put the model in perspective by understanding the radically changing workplace. An understanding of the challenges associated with the evolution of work will put the model into context. The challenges include the continual reliance on outdated HRD models that are predicated on stable and predictable work environments. In particular, the need for speed and the ambiguous and unpredictable nature of work renders many of these models redundant for effective skills acquisition. Work specialisation and role segmentation has now been largely replaced by flexible deployment of skills and interdependence of roles and functions. Short-term cross-functional work teams are a more important organising unit than the traditional functional hierarchies. Project teams are more likely to be able to create, share and distribute knowledge across and throughout the organisation. Conflicting expectations between managers and workers are likely to increase in the short term during the current transition between the traditional and new psychological contracts. This presents challenges for employees and employers. At the same time, competitive advantage is likely to increasingly come from adequate deployment and management of workers. Learning is more likely to become a critical factor for speed and flexibility in response to a rapidly changing marketplace. These issues place a strain on the traditional employment relationship and need to be understood as a context for the model.

Outdated Human Resource Development Models

The evolution of work creates its own challenges for employees. Workers are often asked to apply outdated models and processes to develop new workplace skills. For instance, most of the training and development models available presume a predictable, certain, and straightforward working environment. Modern work environments are characterised by increasing speed and greater ambiguity arising from multiple factors. This adds to the likelihood that workers are increasingly likely to face new and unusual work problems. Obsolete HRD models have little application under these circumstances. Progressively, more work activity is contingent and hard to predict. This places new demands on employees. These burdens are difficult to identify and plan for. Adding to this uncertainty, the expertise for work is increasingly shared across members of teams. Even work environments are becoming fluid. Technology enables productive work from almost anywhere. Organisations are evolving into new, 'boundaryless' forms. All of these developments lead to the conclusion that the design and implementation of new workplace learning models are required.

Developing the expertise needed for skilled performance in this environment has become a seamless and ongoing process. For employees to maintain their skill base, they need to be flexible. Workers are continuously adding, replacing, enhancing, and retrofitting their expertise. This learning agility has come as a result of changes in the marketplace, technology, and new ways of doing things. The new world of work eliminates the need for old skills and necessitates the development of new ones. And the pace of this turnover of skills has quickened considerably. Efforts to develop and define HRD models to accommodate this new way of learning are overdue. Learning and development interventions that go beyond traditional training are needed.

Present models for developing work skills originated in the military. They have evolved into the widely used training instructional systems. Modern skill development approaches are perhaps more comprehensive and systematic than in the past. However, they reflect a view of developing work expertise that is prescriptive and determinant. Present models are useful for some types of employee development, although it is questionable how effective they are for developing the type of skilled performance needed in a contingent and dynamic work environment.

The Challenges of Work Segmentation

Another challenge facing employees is to break free from the Fordism concept of role specialisation and work segregation discussed in Chapter 1. The contemporary workplace requires the opposite approach to Fordism.

METAPHOR

Change in Organisations

Here is a metaphor that illustrates many of the ways most organisations struggle with the changing world of work. Take a minute or two to reflect on what you think the illustration means to you and answer the questions below.

1. Who might the person at the front represent in an organisational context? What challenges do they face in the modern organisation?

2. Who are the people at the rear and who might they represent? What challenges do they face in the modern organisation?

3. What does the body of the wagon represent in the modern organisation?

4. What do the square wheels represent in the modern organisation?

5. What do the round wheels represent?

Note: Square Wheels image © Performance Management Company, 1993. Square Wheels® is a registered service-mark of PMC. Reproduced with permission. More information at www.PerformanceManagementCompany.com

It entails an approach based on flexibility and interdependence. How do people break free from the traditional emphasis on specialisation and clearly defined job roles? The key is to continually redesign organisational roles to reflect this change. These new work roles need to be reshaped to encourage a set of attitudes recognising, emphasising, and reinforcing the importance of interdependence of the whole workforce of a company. At the same time, these new roles should reflect the significance of each individual for the whole. For this to occur there is a need for a new way of distinguishing work from jobs.

The concept of the job as we know it has run its course. Over a decade ago, Bridges (1996) advanced a compelling argument for the 'de-jobbed organisation' that is even more relevant today. Jobs with clearly defined tasks, according to Bridges, are ill-equipped to respond to rapid change due to their inherent inflexibility. Also, the 'knowledge worker' of today spends more time manipulating information than undertaking specific tasks. This handling of information often transcends the job task itself. For example, a medical professional these days has a variety of sophisticated machinery that can assist him or her to make a diagnosis. It follows from this that their role now is more likely to be about interpreting data through these instruments, rather than carrying out the full task of diagnosis from start to finish. In a similar way, a production worker now spends more time managing large scale machinery than doing the production task itself. This emphasis on working with and through technology means that the boundaries around the specific task are blurred. The diagnosis from technology used for the medical analysis may, for instance, reveal symptoms beyond the scope of the medical professional. So, he or she may need to refer the patient to other medical professionals. Similarly, technology used by a production worker is likely to be interrelated with other processes beyond the scope of his or her job description. Job boundaries are now largely obsolete.

To add to the futility of having clearly defined job tasks, production and support activities are more likely to be short-term project-based rather than long-term functionally-based. So, the new way of thinking is to forget the concept of jobs as we know them and move toward the work that needs doing.

Work itself is changing so fast that job descriptions are outdated almost as quickly as they are written. It is not only job descriptions, but also the nature of jobs themselves that are becoming outdated. As Bridges (1996) points out, work is not going away but jobs are. The possibility that an individual can be employed to do a specific job and nothing else is long gone. Apart from a move from specific job roles to flexible work roles, a shift from dependent to interdependent work relations provides another steep learning curve for the 21st Century employee.

Cross-Functional Teams

Functional boundaries are declining and organisations are increasingly accomplishing their work through cross-functional teams. The rise of teamwork and the decline of functional boundaries is occurring for three reasons:

1. There is a greater need to create new knowledge within an organisation.
2. Information — more than ever — needs to be shared across departmental boundaries.

3. Rapid changes in the marketplace require the sharing and distribution of information across the entire organisation.

It is therefore not surprising that SDWTs are now the basic organisational work unit. As a result, the individual worker no longer receives specific tasks to accomplish, but the team receives a task 'bundle' that is to be accomplished by the team in a holistic fashion. Put simply, the work team is responsible for the completion of these tasks as an entity. Individuals working together, doing whatever needs to be done to make the business a success represents the new entrepreneurial model.

On the surface at least, the evolving workplace signals losses for the organisation and the individual. On the one hand, employees have lost job security and the sense of long-term organisational identity. On the other hand, companies have lost the predictability of managing a dependent and internally-orientated workforce. What alternatives are available to traditional ways of dividing up work? According to Noer (1997):

> Organisations that will thrive in the new reality are those that will be filled with employees who have the option to leave, but choose to stay because of the work. Those that fail will be populated by employees who are only there because they are afraid to go elsewhere. (p. 218)

For this to become reality, new paradigms about the worker/organisation interface are essential. These new ways of thinking are a dramatic departure from the paradigms underpinning the traditional employment relationship.

Conflicting Expectations

As mentioned in Chapter 2, much of the unrest in workplaces today is the result of conflicting expectations workers and managers have of each other. Conflicting employment relationship mindsets can even be found in the one company. For instance, managers want, and need, employees to take more responsibility for their work. But at the same time, managers have traditionally focused almost exclusively on organisational output, which is what they have been measured against. This is often at the expense of nurturing personal growth in employees. From the employees' perspective, they generally want managers to provide them with more say in the day-to-day decision-making process. But others may come with a traditional mindset that managers are paid to make decisions and workers are paid to follow instructions. These conflicting viewpoints create misunderstanding and confusion between managers and staff. Today's workplaces are filled with these paradoxes. These are indicators of a transition in the employment relationship paradigm.

The manager who understands and encourages this shift in thinking about the expectations managers and workers have of each other has a huge advantage in recruiting talent to a preferred workplace. Enlightened companies are likely to attract the critical self-led workers needed for success. The self-motivated employee, with a modern mindset about the employment relationship, is increasingly in demand. At least 33% of individuals in the current workforce in the United States are contingent and self-employed. (Cummings & Kreiss, 2008). As this percentage continues to inevitably increase, so too will the requirement for independent-thinking workers. The implications of managing an increasingly itinerant workforce on the one hand, and learning to be an itinerant worker on the other, go beyond the bounds of the traditional boss/worker way of thinking. A new employment paradigm is the cornerstone for managers to help workers develop and master the portable career skills needed in the 21st century. In return, workers need to commit to, and embrace, a spirit of competitive urgency and performance learning.

Shift from Technical to Human Capabilities

Another important feature of the modern workplace is the shift from technical to human capabilities. The strategic potential to achieve competitive advantage for companies is more and more shifting away from the traditional factors such as production and process technology, economies of scale, financial resources or protected and regulated markets. The focus is increasingly likely to be in the direction of adequate deployment and management of people. More than ever, managers are compelled to view their employees as an investment needing careful attention, rather than a cost factor that needs reducing. Individuals in this context are being seen as 'entrepreneurs within the enterprise' (Wigand, Picot, & Reichwald, 1997) and consequently find themselves as central to business success. Increasingly, qualifications, capacities, experiences, and the creative potential of the worker are primary success factors in the current competitive marketplace.

The idea that 'the most important resource in this business is its people' may well be a cliché, but it is increasingly the case in the highly productive company. Businesses are depending more and more on fewer people. Consequently, the traditional concept of loyalty of workers can no longer be assumed. These factors are clear indicators that companies must be conscious and concerned with how human beings are used, developed, resourced, and motivated. Such factors compel organisational leaders to find new ways for a more effective use of 'human capital'.

Furthermore, what constitutes productivity has changed. The goals of corporate action have changed from profit alone to profit and individual employee development. Commercially successful companies are those that seek to achieve competitive advantage, not in terms of cost, but in the form of product quality and range, or reliability of service. Companies are becoming 'boundaryless' and there is an increasing need to move away from treating organisations and their elements as fragmented objects towards an approach that values integration. Jobs are increasingly being shaped more by the qualities of those performing them. Status and compensation is increasingly attached to people, not positions. This, in turn, requires a workforce that is highly skilled, motivated, and adaptive. Also, this call for a workforce that is not only allowed to give of its full creativity and talent, but also enabled, encouraged, and rewarded for doing so. Productivity is increasingly becoming a function more of the intellectual processes of knowledge workers than their physical capacities.

Accordingly, the dominant competitive force now is the company's capacity derived from people. Making huge profits is an inadequate definition of productivity if, for instance, the company is embroiled in litigation. Similarly, a view that focuses only on extracting more performance from workers is also misguided. The interests of all stakeholders in the modern marketplace need to be considered. Kanter (1995) sums up this change in the following way:

> Study after study around the world shows that employees today are less loyal, less committed and more mobile than ever before. In industry after industry power is systematically shifting away from those who produce goods and services towards those who buy or consume goods and services. The customer, like the employee, is less loyal, more fickle and therefore demands a different kind of response from organisations: more flexibility, greater innovation, more attention to where the customer's needs are heading in the future, rather than expecting them to take today's goods and services. (p. 72)

A broader definition of company productivity needs to incorporate these changing requirements of customer and worker.

Learning, Speed and Flexibility

Learning over the past 20 years has progressively being recognised as a critical factor in the company's ability to create ongoing economic value for its shareholders. Thompson (1995, p. 85) points out that 'the purpose of organisational learning and the acquisition of organisational knowledge is to provide the foundation for rapid, dramatic organisational change; increasingly the fundamental requirement for organisational success'.

However, instead of seeing knowledge as an 'acquisition' of objective known truth, managers would be better off viewing knowledge as a process founded on the capacity and potential of workers.

The company's ability to learn and innovate is increasingly linked to the firm's capability to increase revenues, profits, and economic value. To launch new and superior products, to continually improve operating efficiencies, and to create more value for customers, requires the ability to learn. Szablowski (2000, p. 11) claims that, 'true business success will be measured by that nebulous asset called 'quality customer service', also known as customer loyalty or customer value'. On a larger scale, the penetration of new markets and the achievement of sustained market leadership increasingly depend on applied learning.

Applied learning enhances speed, which is increasingly linked to productivity. Kanter (1995) emphasises speed as a fundamental measure of organisational efficiency. There are three kinds of speed that companies need today in order to be productive.

Innovative Speed

Innovative speed refers to being in the marketplace first with the goods and services that customers want; to be constantly innovating and experimenting with new features that give the customer what the customer desires, before a company runs the risk of loosing the customer. Product life cycles are shortening and, therefore, first-mover advantages will become ever more important. Agility means taking advantage of opportunities as they arise.

Processing Speed

Processing speed means processing everything through the organisation as quickly as possible. For instance, this could mean shorter cycle times for designing training programs, restructuring companies, and implementing new products or services.

Recovery Speed

Recovery speed refers to the time it takes to respond to and fix problems. Speed is therefore a fundamental yardstick by which a modern company's productivity can be measured.

Speed is dependent on a high degree of organisational flexibility. Organisations that are faster moving are also more flexible in how they use their workforce. Employees are much more likely to have broader rather than narrower definitions of their job. In many occupations, versatility in dealing with varying demands and situations is more highly valued than work volume in some given activity. For instance, dealing thoughtfully and effectively with a customer complaint rather than chasing new business requires adaptability. It could be considered a better investment of time and consequently more profitable in the long term. Effective managers tend to treat every employee as a professional who knows and understands their work. So, organisational leaders wanting to foster flexible work practices see their role as primarily one of providing workers with adequate tools and systems to solve problems and get results.

Cross-functional work teams are another HRD process for creating quick decision-making in the workplace. Modern managers, in their quest for organisational flexibility, encourage, promote and build project teams that bridge functions and departments. Companies that move faster, innovate quickly, progress things through the organisation quicker, and solve problems quicker, are much more likely to be organised around cross-functional teams than they are to be structured in old fashioned hierarchical departments. Today's organisational structures are more likely to emphasise the horizontal dimension of the company. The horizontal dimension brings people together across departments to tackle something new or to solve a problem. In contrast, an emphasis on the vertical dimension up and down the hierarchy is likely to slow the pace of decision-making.

The concepts of learning, speed, and flexibility support a new definition of productivity. Productivity is broader and more pervasive than the old concept of profitability. The concept of productivity is based on changing from a mindset of accuracy and precision to one of innovation and risk taking. The traditional manager/worker relationship is ill-equipped to accommodate this new notion of productivity.

In summary, the changing individual and organisational paradigms, the evolution of work, and the shift from technical to human capacities has brought into question the relevance of the traditional employment relationship. Although it is clear and timely for new models of the employment relationship to be implemented in the workplace, the management literature is surprisingly short of applied research in this area as discussed in Chapter 2. More concerning, is an absence of sustained research in actual workplaces until recently. This limits managers' capacity to anticipate some potentially disastrous problems and to envisage an array of alternative future possibilities.

Conclusion

There are many challenges confronting organisational leaders in changing mindsets needed for the 21st century. Alternatively, the costs of continuing to embrace the traditional employment relationship are too high for both employer and employee. The imperative for changing the psychological contract is the rapidly changing economic environment that has arisen over the past quarter of a century. This dramatically altered marketplace has profoundly changed the needs employers and employees have of each other in their relationship. Contemporary organisations need to be more flexible and adaptable rather than stable and hierarchical. Therefore, increased employee participation and involvement in decision-making is now paramount. Without the promise of job security, modern workers need to be continually employable. Therefore, enlightened employees want companies to provide them with opportunities to maintain and develop their skills set. These external market forces have put unprecedented pressure on the established employment relationship.

■ Reflective Questions for Managers

1. How would you assess the majority of training and development programs you are exposed to? Do they help or hinder skill development in a time of accelerated change and uncertainty?

2. From your observations, do younger employees have different expectations than older workers? And if so, what are the differences?

3. Do position descriptions help or hinder in dealing with the challenges facing work?

4. What, if any, relationships exist in your workplace between applied learning and enhancement of the three forms of speed necessary for growth: innovation, processing, and recovery?

5. How are cross-functional teams assisting with knowledge sharing? Can you give examples from your own experiences?

6. From your own experience, how prevalent is the psychological contract and do popular management books paint an overly optimistic picture of its commonness?

■ Top 10 Key Points from Chapter 3

1. There is a continuing reliance on outdated human resource development models in a climate that increasingly requires speed and ambiguity.

2. The majority of HRD models are based on the assumption that work skills are prescriptive and predetermined.

3. The Fordism concept of role specialisation and work segregation is counter to the need to recognise, emphasise, and reinforce the importance of the interdependence of the whole workforce of a company.

4. To maintain their skills base, employees need to be flexible and multi-skilled.

5. Cross-functional work teams are replacing functional departments as the dominant organisational unit.

6. Project teams are more capable of creating, sharing and distributing knowledge across and throughout the organisation.

7. Conflicting expectations between managers and workers are a result of the evolving changes in work and the challenges they bring.

8. The strategic potential to achieve competitive advantage for companies is shifting away from the traditional factors (such as production and process technology, economies of scale, financial resources or protected and regulated markets) to human capabilities.

9. Learning is increasingly being recognised as a critical factor in the organisation's ability to create ongoing economic value for its shareholders.

10. There are three kinds of speed that companies need today in order to be productive: innovation, processing, and recovery.

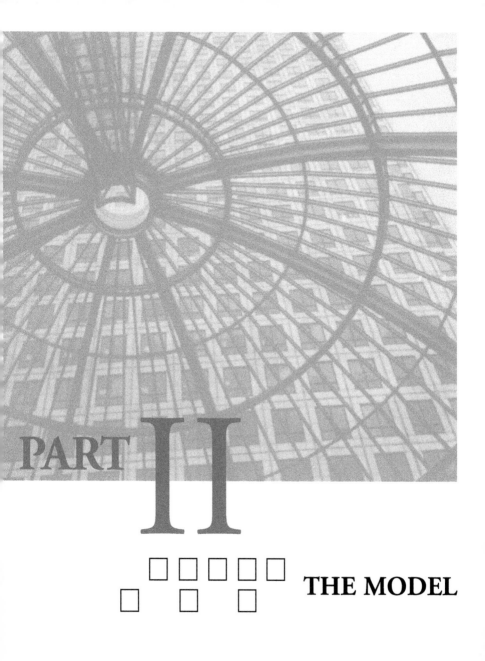

PART II

THE MODEL

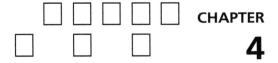

The New Employment Relationship Model

The successful and sustainable application of the New Employment Relationship Model is about changing the culture of an organisation.

This chapter introduces the New Employment Relationship Model. The model is the basis for creating a productive workplace culture with a backdrop of increasing market instability and uncertainty. It consists of eight values: Flexible Deployment, Customer Focus, Performance Focus, Project-Based Work, Human Spirit and Work, Commitment, Learning and Development, and Open Information. There are several features that make this model distinctive. One of the distinguishing features of the model is that it illustrates the appropriate responses to each value from the individual and organisational perspective in a balanced way. The eight values underpinning the model are diametrically opposite to those of the traditional employment relationship. There are significant benefits for both the employee and employer in embracing these new values in their workplace. The successful implementation of each value can be benchmarked. Established HRD strategies fail to tackle the employment relationship and are more concerned with changing people's behaviour than their thinking. These are shortcomings that this model addresses. There are significant overlaps between the eight values and their associated elements. Corporate culture change ought to take into account the interdependence of the eight values.

What is Organisational Culture?

The successful application of the New Employment Relationship Model is about changing the culture of a company in a sustainable way. Changing corporate culture is based on transforming the psychological contract between employee and employer. A modern productive culture can be founded on the eight values in the model. The eight values meet the requirements of the current worker and organisation by addressing the issues and challenges raised in Part 1.

Workplace culture has a direct and indirect relationship with productivity. Most managers are aware that a suitable workplace culture is likely to lead to higher levels of productivity and, equally, an inappropriate culture tends to result in lower levels of productivity. Most managers understand and appreciate this connection, but are not too sure where and how to start this process. Consequently, they have, and may possibly continue, to employ ad hoc HRD approaches that sidestep the employer/employee relationship. Changing workplace culture is not just about changing the thinking of workers. There must be a commitment to change the thinking of management as well. Organisational culture is a by-product of the interaction between employer and employee. Transforming the culture of a company from a traditional employment mindset to the new employment relationship will provide the basis for an increase in sustainable productivity.

Organisational culture has of late attracted considerable attention from researchers (Carmeli, Sternberg, & Elizur, 2008). Nonetheless, it is difficult to find a universally accepted definition of organisational culture. McNamara (2008) broadly defines organisational culture as the personality of the organisation. Culture is one of those terms that are difficult to express distinctly, but everyone knows it when they sense it. In layman's terms, organisational culture is the 'way we do things around here'. The way things are done in an organisational setting is a reflection of the relationship between employer and employee. As defined in Chapter 2, the psychological contract is based on the expectations the two parties have of each other in the employment relationship. Generally speaking, the new employment relationship is a collaborative association, as distinct from the 'them and us' mindset underpinning the traditional employment relationship.

As we have discussed in Chapter 1, the past 25 years have seen dramatic changes in the requirements of employees and employers. Accelerated change and uncertainty in the marketplace has meant that company structures have had to transform from stable and predictable to manoeuvrable and responsive. At the same time, the requirements of employees have altered from job security to expanding their portfolio of skills so that they can be more employable. These fundamental shifts in priorities have not necessarily translated into accommodating workplace cultures. The model provides a roadmap for navigating the change process to produce an organisational culture that is more receptive to the demands of employee and employer.

Where would you like to work?

The following **Corporate Culture Preference Scale** will help you to understand the kind of organisational culture you would prefer to work in. Simply select (a) or (b) for each of the 12 statements. See scoring key on following page for how to score this scale.

I would prefer to work in an organisation:

No.	(a)	or	(b)
1.	Where employees work well together in teams.		That produces highly respected products or services.
2.	Where top management maintains a sense of order in the workplace.		Where the organisation listens to customers and responds quickly to their needs.
3.	Where employees are treated fairly.		Where employees continuously search for ways to work more effectively.
4.	Where employees adapt quickly to new work requirements.		Where corporate leaders work hard to keep employees happy.
5.	Where senior executives receive special benefits not available to other employees.		Where employees are proud when the organisation achieves its performance goals.
6.	Where employees who perform the best get paid the most.		Where senior executives are respected.
7.	Where everyone gets their job done like clockwork.		That is on top of new innovations in the industry.
8.	Where employees receive assistance to overcome any personal problems.		Where employees abide by company rules.
9.	That are always experimenting with new ideas in the marketplace.		That expects everyone to put in 110% for peak performance.
10.	That quickly benefits from market opportunities.		Where employees are always kept informed of what is happening in the organisation.
11.	That can quickly respond to competitive threats.		Where most decisions are made by the top executives.
12.	Where management keeps everything under control.		Where employees care for each other.

SCORING KEY

Corporate Culture Preference Scale

In each space below, write in a '1' if you circled the item and '0' if you did not. Then add up the scores for each subscale. The maximum score for each subscale is 6 and the minimum score is 0. The higher your score, the more likely you would feel comfortable in that type of culture.

Control culture   ___ + ___ + ___ + ___ + ___ + ___ = ___
                    (2a) (5a) (6b) (8b) (11b) (12a)

Performance culture ___ + ___ + ___ + ___ + ___ + ___ = ___
                    (2a) (5a) (6b) (8b) (11b) (12a)

Relationship culture ___ + ___ + ___ + ___ + ___ + ___ = ___
                    (2a) (5a) (6b) (8b) (11b) (12a)

Responsive culture ___ + ___ + ___ + ___ + ___ + ___ = ___
                    (2a) (5a) (6b) (8b) (11b) (12a)

Explanation of Subscales

These subscales can be found in many organisations, but they represent only four of the many possible organisation culture values. Also, keep in mind that none of these subscales is inherently good or bad. Each is effective in different situations.

Control Culture: This culture values the role of senior executives to lead the organisation. Its goal is to keep everyone aligned and in control.

Performance Culture: This culture values individual and organisational performance and strives for effectiveness and efficiency.

Relationship Culture: This culture values nurturing and wellbeing. It considers open communication, fairness, teamwork, and sharing as a vital part of organisational life.

Responsive Culture: This culture values its ability to keep in tune with the external environment, including being competitive and realising new opportunities.

Source: McShane, S., & Travaglione, T. (2005). *Organisational Behaviour on the Pacific Rim*. Sydney, Australia: McGraw-Hill. Reproduced with permission.

New Employment Relationship Model

There are four characteristics that distinguish this model from other models found in the management literature.

1. This model is one of the few empirically researched models, which means that it has a degree of academic rigor.

2. The model looks at the employment relationship from the dual perspective of the individual and the organisation. Most models look at the psychological contract from the perspective of the employee and how he or she needs

to change. Few models consider how the employer and employee relate to each other based on a set of specific values.

3. The model is based on eight values that can be used to align the shifting individual and organisation paradigms.

4. An in-depth description of each value is provided, in terms of why it is important and what the appropriate individual and organisational response needs to be to implant the value as a feature of the company's culture.

Indeed, this chapter gives a comprehensive overview of the model and its uniqueness. The subsequent eight chapters in Part 2 will take a deeper look at each of the eight values.

Figure 4.1 illustrates the model with the eight values and the appropriate responses from the perspectives of the individual and the organisation.
In summary, the eight values are defined as follows:

1. **Flexible Deployment** is the provision of a functionally flexible workforce.
2. **Customer Focus** is breaking the organisational barriers to focus on the requirements of the customer.
3. **Performance Focus** is linking rewards and benefits with performance rather than organisational dependency.
4. **Project-Based Work** is boundary managing the shift from functional to cross-functional organisational structures.
5. **Human Spirit and Work** is increasing the likelihood that workers will find their organisational work meaningful.
6. **Learning and Development** is shifting from a training culture to a broader learning and development culture.
7. **Commitment** is a more pragmatic substitute for loyalty.
8. **Open Information** is moving from a closed to an open information environment.

The application of these eight values in a company culture is a dual responsibility of the individual and the organisation.

The model is in direct contrast to the traditional employment relationship, as illustrated in Chapter 1, Figure 1.1.

By comparing Figures 1.1 and 4.1, it is easy to see the completely opposing values and the individual and organisation responses.

The Changing Employment Relationship Values

For convenience, Figure 4.2 illustrates the changing employment relationship values. Figure 4.2 illustrates the polarised shift in mindsets from the traditional to new psychological contract between employer and employee.

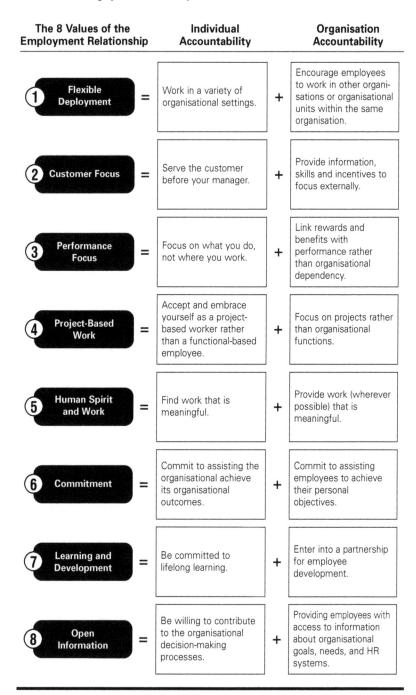

The 8 Values of the Employment Relationship	Individual Accountability	Organisation Accountability
(1) Flexible Deployment =	Work in a variety of organisational settings. +	Encourage employees to work in other organisations or organisational units within the same organisation.
(2) Customer Focus =	Serve the customer before your manager. +	Provide information, skills and incentives to focus externally.
(3) Performance Focus =	Focus on what you do, not where you work. +	Link rewards and benefits with performance rather than organisational dependency.
(4) Project-Based Work =	Accept and embrace yourself as a project-based worker rather than a functional-based employee. +	Focus on projects rather than organisational functions.
(5) Human Spirit and Work =	Find work that is meaningful. +	Provide work (wherever possible) that is meaningful.
(6) Commitment =	Commit to assisting the organisational achieve its organisational outcomes. +	Commit to assisting employees to achieve their personal objectives.
(7) Learning and Development =	Be committed to lifelong learning. +	Enter into a partnership for employee development.
(8) Open Information =	Be willing to contribute to the organisational decision-making processes. +	Providing employees with access to information about organisational goals, needs, and HR systems.

Figure 4.1 New employment relationship model.

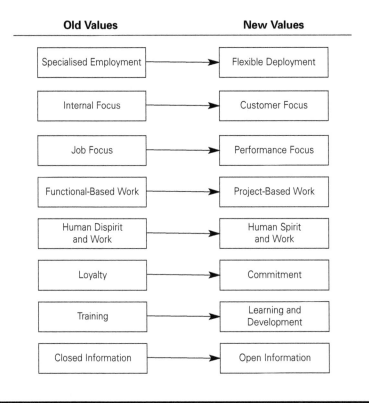

Figure 4.2 The changing employment relationship values.

To fully appreciate these paradigm shifts, a brief summary of Figure 4.2 is given here. Specialisation in the workplace, once highly valued, has now been replaced by flexible deployment of skills. The focus was once on internal processes and procedures as the basis of providing consistency to the customer. Although this is still important, the shift in companies must be to a customer focus. A performance focus is now more important than focusing on carrying out the duties of a clearly defined job. Project-based work is now more important than functional-based work. It is increasingly significant and in the interests of employees and employers that work is meaningful and nurtures the human spirit, hence the emphasis on human spirit and work. Organisational commitment has now replaced a sense of loyalty between organisation and individual. Learning and development with its broader emphasis is now more important than a narrower focus on technical training. Open information systems are likely to assist employees to make quality decisions in their day-to-day work than closed information channels. These shifting positions will be discussed in more detail in the following chapters.

The juxtaposition of the 'old' and 'new' employment relationship models underpins the speedy transformation from a stable and constant marketplace to a turbulent and uncertain environment. In particular, the changing employment relationship values illustrated in Figure 4.2 shows the dramatic shift in focus in a relatively short timeframe.

The Model as an Exchange Process

The model functions as a typical exchange process. In other words, the new employment relationship is formed jointly by fulfilling the requirements of both parties. To satisfy the wants of both parties in the employment relationship, there needs to be a shared understanding of what these shifting priorities are, and how they can be met in the modern day workplace. If managers do not appreciate the requirements of modern employees, they are unlikely to be in a position to fulfil their requirements. Alternatively, if traditional workers are unfamiliar with the needs of a modern company, they will not be able to fulfil their obligations. In summary, to apply the model in an organisational setting, both entities have responsibilities that need to be fulfilled.

This conceptualisation of the individual/organisation interface can be likened to the 'yin and yang' freedom dance. In a yin/yang relationship, both halves are incomplete and need each other to achieve the unified whole. In a similar way, the model specifies eight values of an employer/employee relationship. In this model, the individual and organisation are co-dependent on each other. Co-dependency is defined in relational terms as the individual and organisation being reliant on each other. The worker and organisation were also co-dependent in the traditional employment relationship. In essence, the difference is the needs of the employee and employer were diametrically opposite to those in the new model and therefore the values and responses from both parties were fundamentally different.

Managers and workers operating out of a conflicting mindset will be confused about the signals they are receiving from each other. For instance, an organisationally dependent worker is less likely to be flexible with customer requests, particularly if they interfere with company policy. The traditional worker, confusing the act with a gesture of organisational loyalty, is likely to disappoint a customer-focused boss. Likewise, a modern thinking worker will find proactive behaviour may be detrimental to his or her career in a traditional bureaucratically run organisation. These misunderstandings, covered in Chapter 2, occur on a daily basis in most companies and generate a lack of trust and elevate stress levels. Nevertheless, these paradigm shifts, and the inevitable tension they bring, provide companies with an opportunity to develop of a new form of collaboration based on appreciating the changing individual and organisation requirements.

Benefits of the Model

Figure 4.3 illustrates the benefits of each of the eight values from the perspective of the employee and employer.

As Figure 4.3 illustrates, the individual benefits are linked to employability, development of new skills, greater job satisfaction, and more autonomy to make decisions. These advantages are consistent with the changing individual paradigm (see Figure 1.2). Therefore, employees who have these mindsets are likely to want to work in an organisation that fosters these values. From the organisational perspective, Figure 4.3 illustrates the organisational benefits as having greater flexibility, responsiveness and manoeuvrability in the marketplace. These advantages are consistent with the changing organisational paradigm (see Figure 1.3). Consequently, employers who foster these values are likely to attract and retain employees that have similar mindsets. So these eight values can be conceptualised as the glue that binds the changing paradigms.

Applying the Model

Figure 4.4 is a summary of how to apply the eight values in a company. This table illustrates the necessary interventions, Key Performance Indicators (KPIs) and targets for developing a productive company culture based on the model.

As Figure 4.4 illustrates, the interventions necessary to facilitate the model are a combination of implementing programs, processes, engagements and strategies, learning and development initiatives, and agreements. These interventions will provide the basis for instilling eight values in the workplace. The KPIs indicate how these interventions will be monitored. As Figure 4.4 shows, these KPIs include internal and external annual surveys, performance appraisals, training program take-up, staff involvement in cross-functional activities and skill development, budgets, enterprise agreements, and up-to-date role descriptions. The targets are quantitative and qualitative benchmarks to determine the success or otherwise of the KPIs. These yardsticks will put into action the values of the model.

Flaws in Traditional HRD Approaches

There is no shortage of HRD approaches designed to make organisations more flexible, customer-focused, performance-based, less functionally structured, capture the 'hearts and minds' of employees, obtain employee commitment, develop skills and competencies, and open information channels. Part 1 has been critical of established HRD approaches. Within the context of the model,

8 Values	Benefits to Individual	Benefits to Organisation
① Flexible Deployment =	A variety of skills to be more employable within and outside the organisation. +	More manoeuvrability to respond faster to changing market forces.
② Customer Focus =	Improvement of customer service skills enhances employability. +	Retain and increase market share.
③ Performance Focus =	Potential to increase value to the organisation and be rewarded for this. +	Focusing on performance is likely to increase productivity.
④ Project-Based Work =	Opportunity to develop team building skills, add variety and interest beyond their functional role. +	Ability to respond quickly to challenges and opportunities in the marketplace.
⑤ Human Spirit and Work =	Opportunity to gain greater satisfaction and meaning from work. +	Retention of staff and knowledge.
⑥ Commitment =	Opportunity to build career capabilities. +	Instilling greater commitment from individuals to achieve organisational outcomes.
⑦ Learning and Development =	Opportunity to learn and develop skills beyond the scope of the current job. +	Organisational growth and development.
⑧ Open Information =	Greater capacity to make decisions within the organisational setting. +	More responsive to customers through quicker decision-making processes.

Figure 4.3 Benefits of the model.

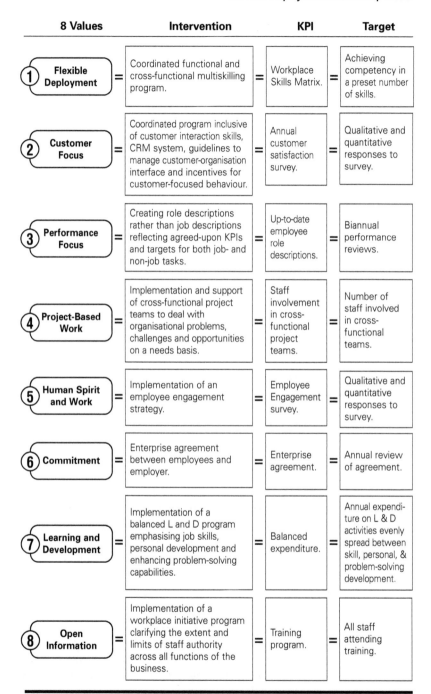

8 Values	Intervention	KPI	Target
① **Flexible Deployment** =	Coordinated functional and cross-functional multiskilling program. =	Workplace Skills Matrix. =	Achieving competency in a preset number of skills.
② **Customer Focus** =	Coordinated program inclusive of customer interaction skills, CRM system, guidelines to manage customer-organisation interface and incentives for customer-focused behaviour. =	Annual customer satisfaction survey. =	Qualitative and quantitative responses to survey.
③ **Performance Focus** =	Creating role descriptions rather than job descriptions reflecting agreed-upon KPIs and targets for both job- and non-job tasks. =	Up-to-date employee role descriptions. =	Biannual performance reviews.
④ **Project-Based Work** =	Implementation and support of cross-functional project teams to deal with organisational problems, challenges and opportunities on a needs basis. =	Staff involvement in cross-functional project teams. =	Number of staff involved in cross-functional teams.
⑤ **Human Spirit and Work** =	Implementation of an employee engagement strategy. =	Employee Engagement survey. =	Qualitative and quantitative responses to survey.
⑥ **Commitment** =	Enterprise agreement between employees and employer. =	Enterprise agreement. =	Annual review of agreement.
⑦ **Learning and Development** =	Implementation of a balanced L and D program emphasising job skills, personal development and enhancing problem-solving capabilities. =	Balanced expenditure. =	Annual expenditure on L & D activities evenly spread between skill, personal, & problem-solving development.
⑧ **Open Information** =	Implementation of a workplace initiative program clarifying the extent and limits of staff authority across all functions of the business. =	Training program. =	All staff attending training.

Figure 4.4 Applying the new employment relationship model.

these archetypal HRD approaches have two flaws. First, they usually deal with a single issue, failing to take into account the interdependency of workplace dilemmas. At the same time, traditional HRD approaches often handle these issues with a linear start and finish stage. In other words, they fail to take a broad viewpoint incorporating a multidimensional insight. By not taking a more eclectic outlook, these typical HRD methods are more often techniques that fail to deal with the employer/employee relationship. Many of these established HRD approaches are therefore ill-equipped to deal strategically with the changing individual and organisational paradigms. Organisational change should be viewed as continuous processes rather than just detached episodes.

The second defect of most HRD programs (from the point of view of the model) is that they are intent on changing people's behaviour more than their thinking. For instance, most training programs are designed to assist participants to develop or acquire new skills or competencies. There is often an assumption supporting these programs that participants understand why and how these new skills will benefit them and those they come in contact with. So, little or no time is spent on changing the participants' perspective. Sustainable behaviour change arguably comes from changing people's thinking. Most HRD programs either assume that people's perspectives will change as an outcome of the training, or that performing these newly acquired skills is more important than thinking about why and how they can and should be used. Prolonged behaviour change comes from fresh thinking and new insights about the issues at hand. In contrast, the model is about changing the mindsets of employees and employers as a precondition for changing behaviour.

In the following chapters in Part 2, the eight values of the model are discussed in depth. Each value is treated as a separate entity. This is done to convey a clear understanding of the essential elements characteristic of each value, and how they may be applied in a company. Understanding the elements associated with each value gives a clear pathway for applying them in a workplace setting. So, apart from a clear description of each value, the subsequent chapters provide some practical approaches to applying these values to create a sustainable new organisational culture. It is, however, acknowledged that there are overlapping characteristics in the model.

For instance, the presence of the value of Flexible Deployment in a company's culture is dependent on secondary elements of the related values of Customer Focus, Performance Focus, Human Spirit and Work, Commitment, Learning and Development, and Open Information. As an example, customer service training — an element of Customer Focus — broadens and consequently enhances the skills of employees as a basis for greater flexibility (Flexible Deployment). These interdependences between the eight values in the model are discussed in depth in Part 3.

Conclusion

The New Employment Relationship Model gives companies a framework for changing their workplace culture. The model illustrates the appropriate individual and organisation responses to this changing value system. In a broader context, the model serves as a useful starting point to explore some of the relational and transactional issues associated with the changing requirements of employees and employers. Further, the model provides managers and management researchers with a conceptual framework for benchmarking an organisation's transition from the traditional to new organisational culture with regard to the psychological contract (see Part 3). The eight values conceptualise and operationalise a framework for a new employment relationship. There may well be (and probably are) other values that could be included in the model. Nonetheless, by understanding and applying these eight paradigm shifts, managers and management researchers have a potentially useful tool to consciously align the changing needs and interests of individuals and organisations for the benefit of all stakeholders (employees, employers, and customers).

■ Reflective Questions for Managers

1. If you had to describe your organisation as a colour, animal, and motor vehicle, what would they be and why? What would others say? Do they agree?

2. Think about your own workplace. How closely aligned are employees and the organisation to the New Employment Relationship Model?

3. In contrast, how closely aligned are employees and the organisation to the Traditional Employment Relationship Model?

4. Refer to Figure 4.3. What practical methods can you as a manager use to sell the benefits of the eight values to employees?

5. Refer to Figure 4.4. Which of the eight interventions have you seen implemented in your workplace? How successful have these interventions been in promoting the corresponding new employment relationship values?

■ Top 10 Key Points from Chapter 4

1. In plain English, workplace culture is 'the way we do things around here'.

2. The value of Flexible Deployment is associated with the provision of a functionally flexible workforce.

3. The value of Customer Focus is associated with breaking the organisational barriers to focussing on the needs and interests of the customer.

4. The value of Performance Focus is associated with linking rewards and benefits with performance rather than organisational dependency.

5. The value of Project-Based Work is associated with boundary managing the shift from function to project-based structures.

6. The value of Human Spirit and Work is associated with increasing the likelihood that workers will find their organisational work meaningful.

7. The value of Learning and Development is associated with shifting from a training culture to a learning and development culture.

8. The value of Commitment is associated with replacing loyalty with organisational commitment.

9. The value of Open Information is associated with moving from a closed to open information environment.

10. Each of the eight values can be implemented in a workplace through a particular intervention that has associated KPIs and targets.

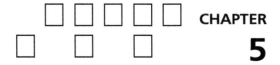

CHAPTER

5

Learning and Earning
From Specialist Employment to Flexible Deployment

> Contemporary organisations need to be strategically
> adept, adaptable and responsive, which minimises
> hierarchy, and encourages its highly skilled workforce
> to engage in lifelong learning, problem-solving and
> creative thinking.

The value of Flexible Deployment is defined as the ability to transfer labour between organisational tasks. This is commonly referred to as multiskilling. Flexible deployment comprises a number of elements and broadly includes retraining, multiskilling and the provision of a motivation and incentive scheme for staff who are willing to learn new job skills. A flexible deployment program is often used in traditional organisations as a cost-cutting strategy by management. This is counter to the aim of the value. Used correctly, there are benefits for the individual and organisation. Individuals become more self-sufficient and employable and organisations become more elastic and malleable in a rapidly changing global marketplace. A skills matrix can be a useful and effective means for coordinating and monitoring a functionally flexible workforce. This tool can be used within departments and cross-functionally.

Defining Flexible Deployment

There are four ways to define flexible deployment. Flexibility in an organisational context can be functional, financial, temporal or numerical (Casey, Keep, & Mayhew, 1999). Of the four forms of flexibility, functional deployment has the greatest capacity to serve the changing mutual needs of the modern worker and organisation. Functional flexibility can be defined as the ability to transfer labour between tasks (Cook, 1998). An organisation that values functional flexibility has the capacity to break down job demarcations, or the ability to place boundaries around clearly defined functions within the business. The following management strategies assist to create and encourage functional flexibility in the workplace:

- retraining staff in areas beyond their normal job function
- multiskilling programs across the organisation
- providing motivation and incentives schemes for staff who are willing to learn new job skills (Greene, 2000).

Used together, these approaches have the capacity to assist the organisation to develop a flexibly deployed workplace.

Elements of Flexible Deployment

Like all the values in the model, the value of Flexible Deployment is a complex interplay between employer and employee. Figure 5.1 illustrates the interaction of the primary elements associated with the value of Flexible Deployment in an organisation.

Figure 5.1 displays the three primary elements of shifting from a value of Specialist Employment to one of Flexible Deployment. The three core elements are an increase and preparedness to increase task responsibilities, an openness to incentives for skills development, and the implementation and preparedness to multiskill.

In contrast, in most traditional organisations there is usually a weak link between flexible employment practices and training and development of staff. Workers employed in organisations operating from a traditional mindset are generally inclined to be severely disadvantaged in terms of their skill development. The traditional mindset associated with implementing flexible work

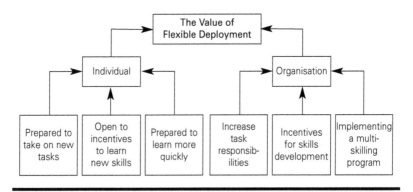

Figure 5.1 Elements of flexible deployment.

CASE STUDY

A Major Change

Chan has been thinking long and hard. As part of the latest workplace agreement, the organisation is about to embark on a course of job redesign for all non-salaried employees. Multiskilling will be the major emphasis of this job redesign. The goal is to enhance flexibility, efficiency and job satisfaction.

In keeping with employee wishes and with the national trend towards industrial democracy, this job redesign will be undertaken 'participatively'. Managers will be responsible for leading the job redesign in their own departments. They are to ensure that all employees have a fair input into the process, that Equal Employment Opportunity (EEO), health, safety and welfare issues take top priority, and that a net 3% gain in output results. Measures of each department's success will include attendance rates, number of grievances registered, output, production costs and other benchmark measures of efficiency and quality.

As Chan rolled this around in his mind, he can see some obvious benefits to the employees. They will have greater variety of tasks to do and therefore will learn more skills and derive more job satisfaction; they will have a greater say in how their department operates (he tries to give them that anyway); they will have better career opportunities; and, hopefully, they will have safer jobs. Depending on how the redesign takes shape, they will probably even have the opportunity to undertake complete projects and have more responsibility and decision-making in their jobs.

And he can see plenty of benefits to the organisation, apart from those stated in the workplace agreement. Multiskilled staff, improved occupational health and safety, improved and easier recruitment and retention due to increased levels of job satisfaction, more effective use of technology, improved staff morale … it sounds too good to be true!

What is the downside of all this, then, he wonders?

Source: Cole, K. (2005). *Management theory and practice* (3rd ed.). French's Forest, Sydney: Pearson Education Australia.

practices is to cut costs. If the principal motive of managers in implementing flexible labour strategies is to minimise operating costs, then one of the costs that is usually minimised is training. Therefore, in these traditional organisational settings, the responsibility for upskilling usually comes to rest with the individual worker. Managers with a traditional attitude have sought to employ flexible workers precisely to minimise the organisation's training obligations and commitments towards that worker. Although commonplace, the traditional cost minimisation approach is not the right motive for implementing the value of Flexible Deployment.

The implementation of any given form of flexibility within a particular company is dependent largely on particular managerial policies and approaches to its use. Flexible forms of employment do not have to be used primarily as a cost cutting device, despite research suggesting that in many organisations, flexibility is synonymous with deregulation and the opportunity to cut labour costs (NACAB, 1997). Consequently, functional flexibility or 'enterprise flexibility' as Casey et al. (1999) refers to it, does not necessarily mean deregulating the workforce. It can (and should) be used as an important tool in fulfilling the changing requirements of workers and organisations.

Benefits of Flexible Deployment

Various forms of flexible deployment offer managers a range of options for structuring and deploying the workforce to meet changing circumstances in the marketplace. An organisation's commitment to the value of functional deployment can be measured by the degree to which there is evidence of the commitment and application of the three management initiatives outlined earlier in the chapter. From the individual's perspective, flexible deployment means learning a variety of skills and competencies beyond the scope of their current position description. Apart from the variety and challenge, functional flexibility assists the individual to become more skilled and, as a result, more employable.

From the organisation's perspective, there is an important relationship between the significance of flexible work practices and the type of modern manoeuvrable organisation mentioned in Part 1. Contemporary organisations need to be strategically adept, adaptable and responsive, which minimises hierarchy, and encourages its highly skilled workforce to engage in lifelong learning, problem-solving and creative thinking. Investment in people development is therefore critical to marketplace success. Learning and development thus becomes the foundation for creating a flexibly deployed workforce. To create a learning organisation, managers need to place a high degree of trust in staff, and have a strong adherence to the value of Flexible Deployment. Furthermore, flexible deployment must be backed up by sound systems of communication and participation and involvement. Investment in time and money needs to be high for an unrelenting period of time. The preferred model of the flexible company stresses the need for flexible forms of organising work in ways that fulfil both the wishes of employees and the requirements of external competition. This focus needs long-term commitment from both entities in the employment relationship. Flexible deployment work practices go a long way to meeting the criteria for the high performance workplace. At the same time, it provides workers with a greater degree of self-sufficiency.

In particular, functional flexibility enables the capacity for an organisation to be more responsive to market changes. When rapid change occurs in the marketplace, a company needs to respond with speed and agility. The most innovative organisations are those that are likely to have workforces that are flexible and multiskilled. Undoubtedly, the best firms are those that create a culture of learning that encourages the exchange of information (Carnoy, 1998). It is knowledge and information that creates flexibility in the way work can be carried out. For instance, flexible deployment practices have the potential for improved product lines, production processes and marketing strategies, all with the same workforce. To do this, employees need to be encouraged to learn new work processes, to shift jobs several times in the course of a working life, to move geographically and, if necessary, to learn entirely new vocations.

At the same time, functional flexibility is also a value that is in keeping with the requirements of the modern employee. The information economy places a premium on the worker's ability to move from a job in one workplace to another. This requires the capacity to learn new jobs in the same company, to do several different types of tasks in the same day, or to adjust quickly to several different kinds of employment cultures and different group situations. So, there is motivation for progressive employees to move beyond the old functional model that promotes specialisation, to develop and broaden their skill base. Companies that promote and reward functional flexibility tend to be more successful in a fast-moving marketplace. The old concept of 'knowing more to get promoted' needs to give way to the idea of rewarding employees for working outside their functional specialisation (Atkinson, 2000). The adaptable employee is a catalyst and product of the new age economy.

There is a strong link between adaptable workers and learning and development strategies. Although employers cannot predict which employees will be more flexible, flexibility has consistently been associated with higher levels of general education and general job training (Carnoy, 1998). Individual workers with more education are more able to adjust to new situations, learn new tasks and adopt new methods of performing old tasks. Companies that provide relatively large amounts of general training tied to workers taking on multiple tasks, are more likely to show larger gains in productivity than companies that follow traditional, more inflexible production methods. This is particularly the case when the training is coupled with wage incentives.

Applying Flexible Deployment

The first practical step to implant the value of Flexible Deployment in an organisation's culture is to implement a coordinated multiskilling and retraining program for all staff. This program should initially start within each team, department or function. Once implemented in each business unit, a cross-departmental or cross-functional program should follow. In other words, before looking at cross-functional flexible deployment, all employees within their functional areas should be exposed to a variety of skills within their departmental area. After demonstrating their mastery of several skills, tasks or competencies within their functional area, employees can then embark on acquiring skills in other departments. Not all roles within and outside an organisational function need necessarily to be open to flexible deployment. That would, in the case of large companies, be impractical. However, wherever possible, an attempt should be made to ensure that more than one (and possibly several employees) can perform each organisational role or task to a minimum required standard. The more multiskilled employees are, the more flexible the organisation is in terms of staff deployment, and the more skilled the workforce. This is what is commonly referred to as a 'win–win' situation. Or, if you consider the consumer as well, you might refer to this circumstance as a 'win–win–win' situation.

Skills Matrix

To coordinate and monitor this process, each department within the company should develop and adopt a skills matrix. A skills matrix can be defined as the breakdown and recording of all the tasks necessary for the department to function effectively and achieve its objective. All employees are then assessed against these tasks in terms of their degree of competency. So, the first step in this process is to identify the range of tasks, roles or competencies required within that particular department or section of the business.

Once this has been defined and established, the second step is to assess the level of skill each employee has in carrying out each of those tasks. The third step is to coordinate a learning and development program for all staff so they can become multiskilled beyond their immediate role. To supplement this process, and to encourage a flexible learning environment, each employee ought to receive some form of incentive to learn a predetermined number of skills, beyond the scope of their current role.

Figure 5.2 is an illustration of what the Skills Matrix could look like. Six employees are shown in Figure 5.2 within a specific function of a business. For instance, this could be the marketing, accounts, or human resources departments. Numbers 1 to 9 illustrate that there are nine core tasks, roles or competencies required within that particular department or section of the business. White spaces on the matrix, signifying 'Not Yet Trained', represent competencies that require training for that particular staff member. For instance, Joe requires training in competencies 5, 6, 7, 8 and 9. In other

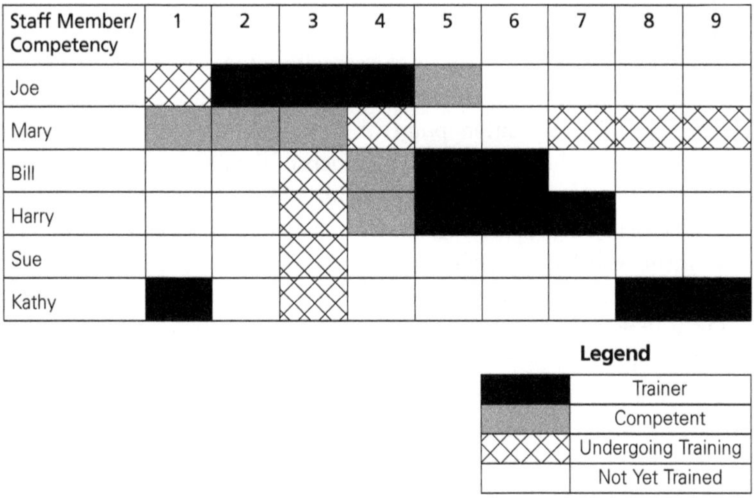

Staff Member/ Competency	1	2	3	4	5	6	7	8	9
Joe	Undergoing Training	Trainer	Trainer	Trainer	Competent				
Mary	Competent	Competent	Competent	Undergoing Training			Undergoing Training	Undergoing Training	Undergoing Training
Bill			Undergoing Training	Competent	Trainer	Trainer			
Harry			Undergoing Training	Competent	Trainer	Trainer			
Sue			Undergoing Training						
Kathy	Trainer		Undergoing Training					Trainer	Trainer

Legend

▓ (black)	Trainer
▒ (dark grey)	Competent
⨯⨯⨯ (cross-hatched)	Undergoing Training
(white)	Not Yet Trained

Figure 5.2 Skills matrix.

words, this skills matrix indicates that Joe has had no exposure in the form of training or coaching in these organisational tasks.

Cross-hatched spaces on the matrix — 'Undergoing Training' — represent competencies where the individual has commenced some training or coaching, but has not yet achieved a consistent minimum acceptable standard of performance without close supervision, coaching or training. For example, Joe has commenced training in competency 1 in Figure 5.2, but has not achieved proficiency. Consequently, Joe needs more training on competency 1 before he is considered competent.

Dark grey spaces ('Competent') represent tasks where the individual has achieved competency. For example, Joe has achieved mastery in competency 5 shown in the above table. Competency in this case can be defined as having achieved a consistent minimum acceptable standard of performance on the job and so is able to complete that task in an unsupervised capacity.

Black spaces — 'Trainer'— identify individuals who have achieved competency and have been delegated the task to train or coach their fellow employees in that skill area. For example, Joe is qualified to train or coach his fellow workers in competencies 2, 3 and 4. To qualify as a workplace trainer, that individual must have certain qualifications and attributes. They must have reasonably good communication skills, have achieved and demonstrated competency in that skill area, and completed a foundation 'train-the-trainer' program.

A rewards and incentives program should be linked to this skills matrix. For example, Harry and Joe, according to the skills matrix in Figure 5.2, are the most multiskilled of the six employees within the department. They have achieved a minimum acceptable standard of performance in four task areas. So, from a skills acquisition point of view, they are currently the most valuable, and arguably, most crucial members of the department. They therefore qualify for some form of reward or incentive for learning and applying these new skills. Also, apart from Kathy, they are the only employees in that department who have qualified to train or coach their colleagues in three tasks. Harry and Joe should be rewarded for this level of proficiency also.

Once all the departments or functional areas within an organisation have a flexibly deployed workforce, the next step is to create a skills matrix that is cross-functional. A new skills matrix can then be developed and adopted across functional boundaries and include cross-functional competencies. The objective in the first instance is to generate multiskilling within each functional area of the business.

Benefits of the Skills Matrix

The benefit for the employee by accumulating a broad range of competencies is becoming more employable within and beyond the company. For the business, the benefit is a more flexible and manoeuvrable organisation that is able to respond to the ever changing demands of the marketplace. Specifically, the skills matrix serves four important purposes:

1. It provides an up-to-date visual representation of the status of skill development for a group of employees.

2. The matrix assists both the manager and staff to plan skills development for the future. For instance, on competency 1 in Figure 5.2, it is clear that Kathy could plan to commence training with Sue, Harry and Bill. She could also complete Joe's training. On the other hand, Harry, being qualified to train in competencies 5, 6 and 7, can plan with Bill, who is qualified to train and/or coach in competencies 5 and 6, who will commence training with Sue, Kathy, Joe and Mary.

3. With the linkage between incentives and skills development, the matrix can add some degree of objectivity to the decision as to who is rewarded for acquiring new skills.

4. The matrix can be used to strategically plan training for new and existing staff. New competencies can be added to the matrix as the business grows or changes direction. This maintains the currency of the matrix and is an up-to-date reflection of the functional skills required and the status of skill levels within that part of the company.

In the interests of consistency, it is important that one person (usually the manager) assess the skill level and be the only one charged with the responsibility of changing the status of the skills matrix. For example, if the manager has observed a staff member on several occasions carry out a task or competency to a minimum standard of performance they can indicate this on the matrix. In this way, it encourages the manager to specify their standards of performance and communicate this to staff members. It also requires the manager to be objective in his or her assessment of staff. In terms of targets, the ideal would be for all staff to be assessed as competent in all areas of the business by a set date. This date can be negotiated between the manager and his or her staff.

Conclusion

In broad terms, and referring back to the model in Chapter 4, the individual appropriate response to the value of Flexible Deployment is to work in a variety of organisational settings. To display this mindset, the individual needs to be willing to be prepared to take on new tasks, be open to incentives to learn new skills, and be prepared to learn more quickly. The appropriate organisational response is to encourage employees to work in other organisations or organisational units within the same organisation. To be able to do this, the organisation needs to increase the task responsibilities of employees, put in place incentives for skills' acquisition, and implementing a multiskilling program. These elements and the right responses from both entities in the employment relationship will go a long way towards shifting from a value of Specialist Employment to Flexible Deployment.

■ Reflective Questions for Managers

The following questions relate to the case study on page 57.

1. Analyse and describe how this change might affect individuals in Chan's department and what their concerns are likely to be. How might it affect the work team as a whole? What should Chan do to deal with their concerns?

2. What do you predict will be the major resistance points or obstacles to this change? How would Chan handle them?

3. If you were to coach Chan on how to plan, introduce and manage this important organisational change in his department, what steps would you recommend he follow and why?

Consider how the following questions can be addressed in your own organisation:

4. What, if any, management approaches have you, or can you, apply in your workplace to encourage functional flexibility?

5. Do your staff have a preparedness to take on new tasks and learn more quickly? If so, in what ways can you demonstrate this? If not, why is this so?

6. Referring to Figure 5.1, which of the organisational elements associated with flexible deployment are present in your workplace? Can you provide examples?

7. How and where could you apply the skills matrix illustrated in Figure 5.2 in your workplace?

8. Considering your industry, what are the benefits of the value of Flexible Deployment for the individual and how would you communicate these to your employees?

■ Top 10 Key Points from Chapter 5

1. Flexible deployment can be defined in four ways. Flexibility can be functional, financial, temporal or numerical.

2. Functional deployment has the greatest capacity to serve the changing mutual interests of the worker and organisation.

3. Functional flexibility can be defined as the ability to transfer labour between tasks.

4. Management approaches to create and encourage functional flexibility include strategies such as retraining staff in areas beyond their normal job function, multiskilling programs across the organisation, and providing motivation and incentive schemes for staff that are wiling to learn new job skills.

5. An organisation's commitment to the value of functional deployment can be measured by the degree to which there is evidence of the commitment and application of these three management initiatives.

6. From the individual's perspective, commitment to the value of Flexible Deployment can be measured by their willingness to learn a variety of skills beyond the scope of their position description.

7. Modern organisations need to be strategically adept, adaptable and responsive, which minimises hierarchy, and encourages its highly skilled workforce to engage in lifelong learning, problem-solving and creative thinking.

8. The information economy places a premium on the worker's ability to move from a job in one workplace to another. This requires the capacity to learn new jobs in the same company, to do several different types of tasks in the same day or to adjust quickly to several different kinds of employment cultures and different group situations.

9. A skills matrix is one practical way of coordinating and monitoring progress towards multiskilling.

10. A skills matrix can be used for intra- and interdepartmental multiskilling.

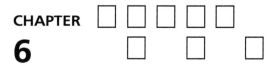

Customer Culture
From Internal to Customer Focus

> Being clear about who your customer is, and spending time providing value-added service is a much less energy draining and more personally affirming use of an employee's time than wallowing in the internal ambiguity of a dying bureaucracy.

Despite the fact that the value of Customer Focus has been around since the beginning of industry, organisational leaders are still challenged putting into practice strategies that will assist in increasing and maintaining the spotlight on the needs and interests of the customer. In particular, three key challenges are still requiring the attention of managers: valid and reliable reward systems for exemplary customer-focused behaviour, the development of new skills to deal with the customer interface, and restrictive career paths for customer workers. Several elements have a significant bearing on enhancing the customer focus system. A clear and understood role for customer workers helps the customer worker develop confidence and avoid the inevitable conflict between the often competing demands of the customer and the company. In concert with this is a requirement for a consistent, fair, and valid incentive's system for desirable customer-focused behaviour. A comprehensive, well-implemented and used customer focus system balances technical and human customer service conditions. All staff are likely to benefit from tailored, timely and relevant customer service training and development opportunities. Three additional elements are implicit in developing a customer-focused culture within an organisation. These are an effective internal customer service climate, adequate resources for customer workers, and committed leadership from management to implement these elements. These elements combine to facilitate a customer-focused company culture and require the energy and input from both the individual and organisation.

Defining Customer Focus

In its most common usage, customer focus captures the relationship between an employee of a company and the customer of an organisation after a sale has been made or a service has been rendered. Put another way, customer workers are brokers between the organisation and its customers (Troyer, Mueller, & Osinsky, 2000). Adams (1976) refers to this function as a 'boundary-spanning' role. In this way, customer workers are the agents who negotiate between organisational needs and customer expectations.

The range of employees involved in customer work is broadening. For instance, companies have increasingly recognised that sales work involves a component of customer work. Salespersons are brokers between the company and the customer. Promoting a firm's products or services increasingly involves sales people meeting customers' needs long after the sale has been completed.

One definition of a customer-focused company is that it uses groups of customers related by industry, application, usage situation, or some non-geographic similarity as the primary basis for structuring the organisation (Homburg, Workman, & Jensen, 2000, p. 471). The perennial challenges of implementing customer-focused organisational structures, processes, and systems are more confronting now than ever before in a climate of intense competition and heightened customer expectations (Bathie & Sarkar, 2002; Sebastianelli & Nabil Tamimi, 2003; Wright, 2002). The interface between the customer and organisation continues to pose special challenges for organisations and employees.

The shift from product-focused to customer-focused organisational structures is motivated by the need to come closer to the problems the customer is trying to solve. Implementing organisational structures, processes, and systems that facilitate a focus on customers is still problematic in most industries (Homburg et al., 2000). This is probably attributable to the relatively little discussion in the popular management literature of strategic organisational changes required to achieve a customer-focus objective, and little empirical research on the challenges of implementing these changes. Most of the attention has been on interactional issues between the customer worker and the customer.

CASE STUDY
When Customer Focus is King

Christopher Milliken has seen the future — and it's not about selling paper, pens and waste baskets at rock-bottom prices. In 1998, the CEO of Itasca (Illinois-based Boise Office Solutions) recognised that the only way to escape the bruising price competition and razor-thin margins of office supply superstores such as Staples and Office Depot was to provide greater value and superior customer service.

Three years and $20 million later, the $3.5 billion subsidiary of Boise Cascade switched on a CRM system that was revolutionary in the office supplies industry.

The company can share customer data across five business units, 47 distribution centres and three customer-service centres. That has helped Boise cross-market, cross-sell and service accounts more effectively. It also has enabled integration of CRM with Web collaboration tools so customer service representatives can co-browse and chat with customers while making recommendations.

Milliken sees it as a way to crumple the inefficiencies of paper and manual processes. The 23-year veteran of Boise Office Solutions learned technology on the job. 'In the '80s, we were doing cost centre billing and sophisticated usage reports', he recalls, 'In the '90s we were among the first to sell on the Web'.

Today, Milliken is taking an active role in Boise's tech projects, and the CRM initiative is a good example. He began by sitting down with two other Boise executives (CIO Gary Massel and David Goudge, Senior Vice President of Marketing) to map out how sales and support staff could tap into data to do their jobs more effectively. He then established a steering committee for the CRM project and promptly joined it. He attended meetings, reviewed memos and monitored spending and development schedules. After installing CRM applications from Epiphany and Amdocs (formerly Clarify), Boise went live with the system in September 2001.

It appears to be a winner. The company is saving about $3.5 million annually and expects to achieve ROI on the project within 3 years. Customer retention is up and profit margins are expanding. 'We are now in a position to outperform our competitors', Milliken says.

And despite the recent controversy over whether CRM projects pay off, Milliken remains optimistic, as he has been from the start. After the project had already begun, one of his top executives stumbled across market research indicating that 70% of CRM projects ultimately fail. Milliken's response? 'That meant that 30% of projects succeed. I was intent on making sure we were in the latter group.'

Source: Greenguard, S. (2002). *When customer-focus is king*. Retrieved June 8, 2008, from http://www.allbusiness.com/business-planning/business-structures-incorporation/203272-1.html

Challenges for Employer and Employee

Three of the main challenges in implementing customer-focused organisation strategies are:

1. The provision of valid and reliable reward systems for exemplary customer-focused behaviour. This whole area of recognition becomes problematic even knowing where to begin. Should employees be rewarded for following customer service processes or for accomplishing outcomes, or inputs to the business? It is easy to suggest both ways, but then how do companies ensure that the value of the rewards is commensurate with the deed? Then you have the implementation issues of where and when to start in the business and how often and how much? Still, the challenge is well worth resolving.

2. The development of new skills to deal with the customer interface. Anyone managing long-term relationships with major customer accounts would know that it requires skills well beyond personal selling and negotiating skills. The qualities needed for an orientation towards customer focus are many and varied. Some qualities include an emphasis on teamwork, a breadth of experience, greater empathy for the goals and constraints on people in other functional areas of the organisation, and more flexibility in being able to respond to changing business conditions. The test is often to source challenging, comprehensive and up-to-date training programs. There needs to be, more than anywhere else in the business, relevant and continual people-skills programs.

3. Typically, there are restrictive career paths for employees working in the customer service area of the business. In terms of career paths, vertical career progression for staff in the sales and marketing departments is often limited. Additionally, there still seems to be a general belief that to advance to general management, people need experience in a variety of functional areas.

These three issues create a number of challenges for managers. Strategically, the organisational response to these three challenges involves structural changes to facilitate a focus on the customer. Operationally, organisational accounting, information and reward systems must be changed to assist and support a focus on customer interaction. Apart from the technical considerations, there are a number of human relations issues required to support the transition to a customer-focused structure. These changes include new staff recruitment practices, re-evaluating training programs that are tailored to the specific needs of a company, and a need to rethinking career paths for employees. And finally, managers need to confront the issue that some workers may have skills that are no longer relevant when firms move towards a greater customer focus. Nonetheless, tackling these matters provides the necessary framework for greater customer responsiveness.

From the employee perspective, these structural changes are just as demanding. For instance, one of the fundamental difficulties of implementing customer-focused strategies is an acceptance by those working with customers of a new way of working (see Homburg et al., 2000). Customer service employees often resist these new changes in work practices because of the threat of social isolation information technology systems can bring. Also, there can be significant resistance in internally sharing customer-based information (Atkinson, 2000). Apart from this (as mentioned) employees in customer service areas often have less scope for moving up the organisation than their colleagues. While it is easy and well accepted to say modern companies should be more customer focused, there are often very different interpretations of what it means to be customer focused and little understanding and appreciation of the magnitude of the challenges ahead.

As challenging as it is for employees and organisational leaders, the paradigm shift from a value of Internal to Customer Focus has never been more important than now. In some cases, a dramatic change of thinking is required. This can mean a shift from a process-driven, quality-controlled internal business environment to one that sees itself as a business entity existing and revolving around the customers' orbit. Failure to make this shift from Internal to Customer Focus, is likely to result in those companies being left behind their competitors.

Elements of Customer Focus

Like all eight values in the model, promoting the value of Customer Focus is a successful interchange between employer and employee. Figure 6.1 shows the interaction of core elements necessary to instil the value of Customer Focus in a workplace.

It follows from Figure 6.1 that customer-focused organisations take a multidimensional approach to implant this value as part of their workplace culture. This multifaceted approach transforms the value from Internal to Customer Focus. There are four important elements: clear and understood customer workers' roles, responsibilities and priorities; consistent, fair and valid incentives for customer-focused behaviour; a comprehensive, well-implemented and utilised CRM system, and tailored, timely and relevant customer service training opportunities.

Even with the obvious overlap, we will look at each element separately and consider some practical advice in their successful implementation and adoption.

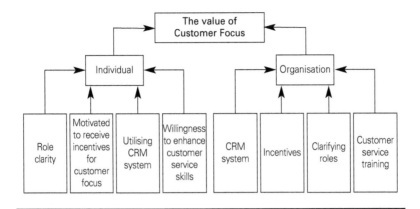

Figure 6.1 Elements of customer focus.

Role Clarity

The boundary spanning nature of the customer workers' role does provide unique challenges. Because of this distinct position in a brokerage role between the organisation and customer, customer workers are open to experiencing conflict in their role. This is because customer workers have to confront the competing demands from the organisation and the customer on a regular basis (Troyer et al., 2000). In other words, any work associated with the interaction between a company and its customers can potentially generate some role conflict. This possible role conflict can negatively affect the customer worker, their customer and the associated company.

Customer work places employees in the unique position of answering to two bosses: the organisation and the customer. Although not formally designated as a boss, the customer nonetheless represents an additional set of interests and demands to which the customer worker has to respond.

In practice, this role conflict can be played out in a variety of ways. For example, consider the situation in which a customer worker is asked by a customer to provide technical support for a product that is not covered by the customer's purchase contract with the company. In many cases such a demand by the customer could be met by resistance on the part of the firm because it would be considered an inappropriate diversion of the organisation's resources. As an agent of the organisation, the customer worker might be required to turn down the customer's request. In doing so, the worker fails to meet the requirements of the customer. Conversely, the customer worker may have 'cut a few corners' to satisfy the customer to the displeasure of their boss. If success is defined in terms of meeting both the company's and the customer's expectations, then both employees in this example have failed. The first employee is internally focused; that is, one who has a preference for pleasing his or her manager over meeting the needs of the customer. The second employee is customer focused; that is, one who favours the customer's needs over pleasing his or her boss. Managing this role conflict can be quite complex and demanding.

In general terms, customer service and sales roles require different approaches to reduce the potential for role conflict. On the one hand, it is crucial for employees in the customer service interface to have authority to make certain decisions for providing and maintaining good service. This is largely because customer service employees have an important role to play in creating a positive impression in the eye of the customer. Therefore, having the freedom to make certain decisions in the interests of serving the customer will most likely create a good impression. On the other hand, people in sales need to have adequate resources and a clear understanding of their role. They are primarily in the business of influencing the customer's decision to purchase their firm's product or service. In the sales role, meeting demands of both the customers and the company is likely to be about negotiating on quality and price. It is important for the salesperson to understand his or her responsibility to each. These two distinctive approaches are an important starting point for understanding and applying strategies to overcome role conflict in customer-focused roles.

Another issue for employees is in understanding their customer service role priorities. This understanding can come from several sources. For instance, role clarity can come from observing an experienced mentor, clear lines of communication with their manager, or formal customer service training. Irrespective of how an employee learns the company's expectations, the greater their sense of role clarity, the more confident they will be in avoiding role conflict. Of course, all positions in companies will from time to time have conflicting expectations. Nevertheless, where clear priorities are established and effectively communicated, the employee has little difficulty in deciding on the appropriate course of action. This reduces the likelihood of role conflict for customer workers. However, completely eliminating conflict in carrying out a customer role is almost impossible.

Customer workers' uncertainty in carrying out their role can depend on a variety of factors. For instance, two of the most common are a lack of managerial support and the confusing design of their job. Although it may be difficult to completely eliminate ambiguity in customer roles, it can be significantly reduced by designing jobs to help customer workers cope with uncertainty in their role. For example, communicating the extent and limits of their authority in certain situations will assist the employee to carry out their role with a degree of self-assurance. This involves consideration and empathy and regular feedback on the manager's part. Managers will find it less frustrating and more rewarding to put their efforts behind strategies that reduce and/or help customer workers cope with ambiguity in specific facets of their role. Staff too, will gain from role clarity. Customers, of course, are likely to suffer less from poor service encounters.

In practice, this means that customer workers need to meet with their managers on a regular basis to maintain role clarity. These meetings should be about discussing potential and real-life scenarios that place the customer worker in a difficult position. From these examples, policies and practices should be agreed upon to provide the customer worker with some guidelines to work with when faced with a similar dilemma. These sessions are not supposed to be about managers communicating their organisational needs to their customer workers. To be effective, they should involve two-way communication and be based on developing ideas and strategies to overcome these dilemmas. In other words, the manager's responsibility in these sessions is to facilitate a problem-solving process with customer workers in order to develop some practical guidelines for resolving these conflicts. If, after developing appropriate guidelines, these issues cannot be resolved in the field, the customer service representative can refer the matter to their manager. The most convenient and practical way to operationalise this process of reducing role conflict is to make this an item of discussion at the weekly sales and customer service meetings, using real-life examples and cases.

Rewards and Incentives

There is a link between role clarity and reward structures. A lack of role clarity for customer employees will most likely occur when there is non-alignment between company incentives and the particular requirements of the customer. For example, if management rewards customer workers on the basis of how many customers they process (all things being equal) this is likely to lead to greater processing of orders. However, if the role also requires spending time and attention on each particular customer's needs, this aspect of their role is likely to be neglected. A properly thought-out approach to rewards and incentives that is understood, consistent and fair by all staff will maximise appropriate customer behaviour and minimise role incongruity.

As the cliché goes, 'this is easier said than done'. As a common illustration, how do you measure and reward the 'people factor' (Berry, Parasuraman, & Zeithaml, 1988)? A customer worker's skill in the service sector may be reflected in knowledge, courtesy, competence, and communication abilities. These are all undeniable traits of quality service. These people-factor dimensions of customer service (albeit critical skills) are difficult to measure objectively.

To reward desirable customer service behaviour fairly and equitably, the following questions need to be asked and answered thoroughly:

• What behaviours define an appropriate customer-focused mindset?

- How is the company going to reward such behaviour?
- When is the company going to reward such behaviour?
- What should the reward be?
- How frequently should a reward be made?
- Who is going to decide whether it is going to be appropriate behaviour?

The answers to these questions will depend on the kind of industry and the nature of the company. A small cross-functional project team, representative of the overall business structure, could be set up to answer these questions. In this way, the rewards process is not being imposed on the company by management.

Customer Relationship Management

CRM as a business strategy helps a company integrate itself and forge a tight connection with the customer. In their haste to implement CRM systems, many companies have discovered that something with such a simple basis can be extremely difficult and expensive to implement successfully (Brighton, 2000; Nancarrow, Rees, & Stone, 2003). Success requires more than simply buying new software and installing it in the sales centres. As a business strategy intended to gain market share and competitive advantage through improving customer loyalty, CRM has been discredited because of overreliance on technology (Rogers, 2003), and a reciprocal under-reliance on interpersonal communication. The successful implementation of a CRM strategy involves a holistic approach that scrutinises the company's customer focus, its operations, systems, and culture. CRM therefore requires a mix of technical and human capabilities, and requires internal and external organisational attention.

Internally, CRM requires companies to quickly integrate all the internal information that they have on a particular customer. Externally, businesses need to recognise and treat customers consistently and knowledgeably across channels, whether they reach you via a call centre, web site, catalogue or retail outlet. This critical enterprise-wide single view of the customer has been an expensive stumbling block for most businesses trying to manage their information in a multichannel environment.

Technically, CRM merges information with employees. Creating focused customer connections comes from several factors that include:

- databases that identify and track customer's preferences
- dedicated account teams that build long-term relationships with targeted accounts
- involving customers in staffing, training, compensation, and communication practices.

To maximise customer knowledge, a company needs to have the capacity to link all customer information to be available to managers and customer workers. Globalisation will continue to put pressure on an organisation's technical, human and administrative resources. Organisations that succeed over the next decade are likely to be leaner, with a crystal-clear focus on service delivery. At the same time, these successful companies will be required to have more to do with less resources and time. On top of this, the 'Internet economy' (Brocklebank, 2000) promises even more challenges than are currently present in creating and managing focused customer connections in an ever-expanding scope of information to be managed and analysed.

A CRM system is the important technological facet associated with creating a better connection with the customer. The CRM system needs to be implemented with a number of important considerations in mind. It must be:

- user-friendly
- adaptable to the needs of the organisation
- cost-effective
- implemented as a strategy rather than a piece of software.

CRM software is one of the tools that help the company carry out this strategy. Depending on its implementation, it can help the business identify who their customers are, what they need, and anticipate what they may need in the future. It allows businesses to tailor offers to their current customers, and build closer relationships that make them feel valuable. It can help eliminate contact and data overlap between departments and improve consumer service. Overall, CRM can be an important facet for a company to be more efficient and customer-friendly to capture greater market share, increase customer loyalty, and attract more customers.

The implementation of a CRM system requires careful planning. The project should be split into four phases:

- Phase 1: Scoping and Business Needs Assessment
- Phase 2: CRM Installation
- Phase 3: Concept Pilot
- Phase 4: Training and Skills Transfer.

Let's briefly look at these four phases.

Phase 1: Scoping and Business Needs Assessment

Scoping and business needs assessment entails clarifying project roles and responsibilities with the service provider, the implementation of a proactive risk management strategy, milestone-driven processes and resilience to change in project requirements. In terms of assessing business requirements, the service provider will need access to a selection of users and business managers to assess their needs. Documentation will then be produced listing the desired features and functionalities and business drivers for project success.

Phase 2: CRM Installation

Once the scoping phase has been completed, costing for the project can be confirmed and the installation phase will begin. This phase will require the service provider to liaise with technical staff before installation to ensure there is a key understanding of the technical requirements and implications. Once installation is complete, configuration and development will be applied with the service provider working on- or off-site, depending on the needs and desires of the business. During this phase, the service provider should work closely with managers and usability teams to ensure that the product is developed with rich consistent functionality and minimal training requirements.

Phase 3: Concept Pilot

Depending on timescales, a pilot will then be installed for a number of users and initial training will be given for this group. The feedback from this phase will be managed and some system updates and changes may be required before a complete 'roll-out' to all customer workers.

Phase 4: Training and Skills Transfer

Skills transfer is essential for the success of the project. Hands-on business-relevant training will be required either through a 'train the trainer' approach or through specifically designed training programs for the end users.

After the CRM project has completed its first life cycle, the service provider should host a follow-up workshop for all parties to review the project, voice opinions and questions, identify lessons learned, assess any skills gaps and agree on the next steps.

Customer Service Training

Apart from CRM training, employees should embark on a quality customer service training program. This program ought not to be an 'off-the-shelf' training package. It should be completely tailored to the requirements of a particular business. This involves someone either inside the organisation or an external consultant to write the program. Although many of the customer service concepts can be applied to any organisational-setting, the examples, illustrations, application tools and case studies need to be unique to the business. It should also emphasise the importance and relevance of internal customer service as a basis for creating a customer-focused workplace culture. For this to occur, it is advisable for all employees to participate in this training program. It may even be useful for some external service providers to the business to undertake the program too, so that they are more aware and appreciative of their role in servicing the requirements of the customer.

Attendance at these training programs ought to be structured cross-functionally. In other words, participants in each training program should represent a slice of the organisation, that is, one individual from the marketing department, one from production, one from finance and so on. This will greatly contribute to cross-functional communication that elevates the relevance of internal customer service as a prelude to providing quality external service. Also, all new staff to the business, as part of their induction training with the company, should undertake this program. This training program needs to be more than a 'one-off'. It is advisable that the program be conducted on an annual basis, and all staff be exposed to aspects the program once a year as reinforcement.

Three addition elements are implicit in developing a customer-focused culture. These include internal customer service, adequate resources, and committed leadership. An important and often neglected dimension of the value of Customer Focus is internal customers. Managers need to be mindful of clarifying the roles of workers who do not have an external interface with customers. In particular, managers ought to clarify the role of support staff in their relationship with customer workers.

A lack of adequate resources can negatively affect the relationship between the customer and the company. Resources could mean things such as having available time to service customer requirements, having the right products and services available and the support materials, product knowledge and the authority to make certain decisions when dealing with the customer. Any customer role requires these resources to be effective. This can be referred to as 'role overload' (Heiss, 1990).

Managers who have a genuine customer-focus mindset are in huge demand worldwide to deliver and implement these fundamental changes in thinking in businesses. Unfortunately there is a shortage of people with these capabilities and experience at a senior level in the Western world. These managers are more often than not the catalysts for successfully driving the value of Customer Focus throughout the company. Organisations, more than ever before, need what is commonly referred to as the 'transformational leader'. These people with the right mindset and vision will continue to gain high premium (and will be increasingly valued) over those who can only offer technical expertise.

In spite of all these technical and human challenges, given support, incentives, skills and growth opportunities by managers, modern employees are helping themselves (as well as the company) by serving and fulfilling customer's needs. The alternative behaviour by employees is to please their boss and playing organisational politics in the interests of their career; in other words, to make the choice of satisfying the manager instead of the customer. This is exhibiting the outdated value of Internal Focus, an artefact of the traditional employment relationship. Being clear about who your customer is, and spending time providing value-added service, is a much less energy draining and more personally affirming use of an employee's time than wallowing in the internal ambiguity of a dying bureaucracy.

From the organisation's perspective, it is better served by insisting on workers identifying and measuring their own value by servicing the needs and interests of their customers. To create this attitude, managers ought to provide the necessary means by which their workers can focus and assess their contribution to satisfying the customer's needs. Time and effort spent focusing internally by the manager or the staff member will ultimately detract from a customer-focus mindset.

Conclusion

With reference to the New Employment Relationship Model in Chapter 4, the appropriate individual reaction to the value of Customer Focus is to serve the customer before your manager. From an individual point of view, evidence of customer focus may include:

- a clear understanding and execution of their customer service role, particularly when they face inevitable conflict between the interests of the organisation and the customer
- a respect for, and willingness to be motivated by, rewards and incentives for exceptional customer service behaviour
- confidence and skill in using the CRM system
- a willingness to attend and participate in customer skills' development programs.

From the organisation's perspective, the proper response is to provide information, skills and incentives to focus externally. Evidence includes a commitment to clarify potential conflicting situations for customer workers in their dealings with customers, the implementation of a fair and equitable rewards and incentives program, the implementation of a well thought through CRM system, and relevant and timely customer service training opportunities. These individual and organisation responses are likely to be characteristic of an organisation culture that has moved from a value of Internal Focus to Customer Focus.

■ **Reflective Questions for Managers**

Reading through the case study on page 68 consider the following questions:

1. What do you think where the main reasons that this CRM implementation was successful for Boise when 70% are unsuccessful implementations?

2. Why do so many businesses fail to successfully implement CRM systems?

3. As a manager what sort of resistance are staff likely to have with the introduction of CRM in their business? How would you manage this anticipated resistance?

4. In setting up a steering committee, who should its membership comprise?

Consider how the following questions can be addressed in your own organisation:

5. How do you assess your level of customer responsiveness in your organisation? Is it a valid and reliable measure? What do you do with the information?

6. What has been your experience with customer service training programs? Have they been effective in changing attitudes and behaviours?

7. Have restrictive career paths for employees working in the customer service area been an issue in your industry?

8. What strategies do you use with customer service representatives to clarify their role? Is it effective?

9. Rewards and incentives for customer workers is an issue. How do you reward exceptional service in your organisation? Are these incentives successful in reinforcing exceptional service?

10. What has been your experience with CRM systems? Has it been a positive or negative experience? Please explain.

■ **Top 10 Key Points from Chapter 6**

1. Customer workers are brokers between the organisation and its customers.

2. The transfer from product-focused to customer-focused organisational formations is motivated by the need to come closer to the problems the customer is trying to solve.

3. Three of the main challenges in implementing customer-focused organisation strategies are: the provision of valid and reliable reward systems

for exemplary customer-focused behaviour; the development of new skills to deal with the customer interface; and restrictive career paths for employees working in the customer service area of the business.

4. Four important issues for creating a customer-focused culture are (1) clear and understood customer workers' roles, responsibilities and priorities; (2) consistent, fair and valid incentives for customer-focused behaviour; (3) a comprehensive, well implemented and used CRM system; and (4) tailored, timely and relevant customer service training opportunities.

5. Managers need to meet with customer service representatives on a regular basis to maintain their role clarity.

6. To reward desirable customer service behaviour, the following six questions need to be answered: What behaviours define an appropriate customer-focused mindset? How is the organisation going to reward such behaviour? When is the organisation going to reward such behaviour? What should the reward be? How frequently should a reward be made? Who is going to decide whether it is going to be appropriate behaviour?

7. The CRM system needs to be implemented with four considerations in mind: it must be user-friendly, adaptable to the needs of the organisation, cost-effective, and CRM should be implemented as a strategy rather than a piece of software.

8. The implementation of a CRM system should be split into four phases: Phase 1: Scoping and Business Needs Assessment; Phase 2: CRM Installation; Phase 3: Concept Pilot; and Phase 4: Training and Skills Transfer.

9. The customer service training program needs to be completely tailored to the needs of a particular business.

10. Three additional elements are implicit in developing a customer-focus culture: internal customer service, adequate resources, and committed leadership.

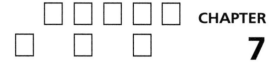

Roles Replacing Jobs
From Job to Performance Focus

> The modern employee, embracing a new mindset about
> their work performance, should acknowledge that who
> they are is not where they work, but what they do.

A value of Performance Focus benefits the organisation and individual. Although there has been a plethora of writing on the subject of organisational performance over the past few decades, there is still a shortage of models that emphasise performance beyond the confines of the job. The overreliance on job descriptions and the need to create a legally defensible performance appraisal system have contributed to this traditional way of thinking. Simultaneously, it is widely acknowledged that non-job dimensions such as teamwork, skill acquisition and entrepreneurial behaviour do contribute positively to company performance. A multidimensional approach provides the individual and organisation with a broader and more realistic frame of reference on organisational performance. Apart from the job and organisational functions employees perform, team, career, and innovator roles should also be taken into account in an up-to-date performance model. These three additional roles can be generalised to most industries and occupations. The first important practical step in moving towards a performance-focused culture is to change job descriptions to role descriptions for all employees in the company. Role profiles ought to incorporate team, career and innovation responsibilities. An analysis of a role can be done in a variety of collaborate ways.

Performance-Based Organisational Culture

It is in the best interests of progressive individuals and organisations for systems of remuneration to favour performance over job-related behaviours (Sturman, Trevor, Boudreau, & Gerhart, 2003). As 'The Changing Individual Paradigm' (Chapter 1) illustrates, one of the drivers of individual success in the modern workplace is a paradigm shift from one of Entitlement to one of Adding Value. In other words, employees who constructively contribute beyond the narrow confines of their job description are likely to be more valued by companies. From the organisation's perspective, establishing criteria to identify and reward value-added behaviours in the workplace can more closely align desirable performance with appropriate rewards.

Surprisingly, it is only relatively recently that researchers in organisational performance have changed their view of what constitutes individual performance in organisational settings. This is despite significant and sustained competitive pressures to do so (Welbourne, Johnson, & Erez, 1998). In fact, for the last 20 years, job performance has been one of the most widely studied criterion variable in the organisational behaviour and HR management literature (Bommer, Johnson, Rich, Podsakoff, & MacKenzie, 1995). Not withstanding this interest, most performance measurement systems are limited in that they ignore dimensions of work behaviour that lie beyond what has been traditionally included in the scope of a specific job itself. For instance, job descriptions have traditionally ignored non-job related behaviours such as suggestion making, organisational citizenship, or even extraordinary customer service (Welbourne, et al., 1998). A broader interpretation of performance is needed that goes beyond job-specific behaviours as the basis for understanding and reinforcing desirable workplace accomplishment. Companies are slowly coming around to linking pay more strongly to performance (Sturman, Trevor, Boudreau, & Gerhart, 2003).

Job descriptions have traditionally focused only on the attributes of the job. This is still pretty much the case in most companies. Although there is a trend towards competency models that focus on the skills people need to be effective in their current and future jobs, job descriptions continue to be defined by the explicit features of the job. A competency model is a detailed, behaviourally specific description of the skills and traits that employees need to be effective in a job. This continual emphasis on job orientation in performance is likely to be the result of a need to create a legally defensible performance appraisal system based on a formal job analysis (Welbourne et al., 1998).

These apparent legal constraints do not stress the value and importance of non-job components in workplace performance. However, work performance is two-dimensional, composed both of work required by a company and by discretionary employee work behaviours. Work required by a company is

COMPANY-IN-FOCUS

Apple Computer

This example refers to the Boston Consulting Group's annual global survey of senior executives on innovation. A total of 1070 executives, representing 63 countries and all major industries responded to the survey. Apple Computer, for the third year running was the clear answer to the question: Which company do you consider most innovative?

Specifically, respondents raved foremost about the company's deep understanding of its customers, its seeming ability to, in the words of one executive, 'know what customers want before the customers themselves know it'. Said another executive, 'Apple is telling its customers what's next. It's not following the classic 'market-led' innovation path that inevitably leads to incrementalism and 'me-too' innovation ... Customers trust Apple and view it as a lighthouse guiding them on what to adopt next. If Apple has it, it must be useful'.

Executives were nearly as complimentary about Apple's ability to marry technology and design. 'Steve Jobs' vision for seamless integration between hardware and software, and knack for understanding user interfaces, drives that company', said one respondent. Another said, 'Apple is very focused on the user experience and how design impacts that experience. It's tough to delight typically jaded customers in this day and age, but Apple pulls it off'. A third respondent praised the company's ability to deliver 'high quality, user-friendly technology products that tie platforms, channels, and user patterns together in new ways'. A fourth noted 'the superior physical and user-interaction design of its products'.

Apple drew high praise as well for its marketing, which 'creates a must-have mentality that appeals to the mass consumer'. Respondents also cited the company's resilience, its 'track record for having the courage to challenge what it does as a company and reinvent itself'. Finally, they praised its culture, which one executive identified as 'perhaps its biggest innovation success: every single person in the company contributes to Apple's innovation success every day'.

Source: Andrew, J.P. (2006). *Senior executive innovation survey.* Retrieved June 9, 2008. from http://www.bcg.com/publications/files/2006_Innovation_Survey_report.pdf. Reproduced with permission from the Boston Consulting Group.

usually covered in the job description. But optional employee work activities such as continuous improvement of systems and processes, exhibiting team behaviour, and the capacity and willingness to grow and develop on the job are valuable parts of performing in the workplace that are usually not formally considered in the job description. Consequently, developing a two-dimensional model that recognises the importance of non-task performance is critical in valuing overall performance. This has been refered to as 'contextual performance' (Borman & Motowidlo, 1997; Motowidlo, Borman, & Schmit, 1997). Contextual performance covers multiple subdimensions of work such as teamwork, commitment, and the capacity to grow and develop.

Two-Dimensional Model of Performance

Although multidimensional models of performance that include job and non-job dimensions have been introduced in some companies, they lack a unifying structure. Without a universal framework, there is little guidance for managers to choose which dimensions of job or non-job performance to include (or exclude) from an assessment of performance. As a result of this deficiency, managers tend to use customised performance measures. This practice results in using measures that do not typically allow for comparison among jobs or across companies. This lack of generalisability of the performance criterion hinders the capacity to link rewards specifically to a broader range of performance indicators.

A combination of role theory and identity theory can be used to develop a generalisable measure of performance (Welbourne et al., 1998). Role theory provides an explanation for why work performance should be multidimensional, and identity theory suggests how to determine which dimensions to include in a model of work performance. The combination of both approaches assists to broaden the concept of performance to incorporate several additional work roles other than job-holder.

According to role theory, individuals' role expectations are influenced by both their personal attributes and the context in which they exist. A job role consists of core or central features and peripheral features. In other words, role theory combines an individual's contribution (psychological) perspective with an organisational framework (sociological) perspective. The greater the role identification that incorporates both of these perspectives, the more likely it is that an employee will value job and non-job dimensions in their work.

Traditionally, measuring performance has neglected the value of non-job indicators, notwithstanding the recognition that these intangible aspects of work do contribute to overall performance on the job. As a result, the emphasis has been on developing performance measures for the job-holder role only. Performance systems that rely on evaluating only those work behaviours defined by a company as related to a specific job are deficient. Role theory, recognising this shortfall, has attempted to take into account the need for multiple roles at work.

Role theory only suggests roles as a way of considering that there are multiple behaviours at work; it does not provide a way to define which dimensions of performance (or roles) should be included or excluded in a multidimensional measure of performance. The number of potential roles employees may take on at work is limitless. Identity theory, on the other hand, can assist in understanding which of these roles should be considered in the context of the workplace.

According to identity theory, it is not the existence of roles, but their relevance, that affects behaviour (Burke, 1991; Thoits, 1992). Identity theory suggests a process by which people use an internal control system to filter information. Put simply, the roles that are most prominent to people provide the strongest meaning or purpose. In turn, the more meaning that is derived from the role, the greater the likelihood of them performing behaviours associated with that role. Companies influence work-related role relevance in a variety of ways, including rewarding particular behaviours, such as making a sale. Other ways to influence a work-related role include formally recognising behaviours such as issuing a certificate of completion for undertaking technical training. Influencing specific behaviours informally may include, for instance, a manager thanking a staff member for staying back late to finish a report. Work-related behaviour can be influenced even by punishing employees when certain behaviours are not carried out, such as non-attendance at a meeting. The importance and relevance of roles will vary depending on the company. Because organisations differ in the roles considered important for individual success, it has been difficult to create a standard performance measure applicable to all firms.

Five Common Work Roles

Despite the variations in roles performed and valued in the workplace, research has determined that there are five prominent roles applicable in all organisations (Welbourne et al., 1998). These roles include:

- job role
- organisation role
- team role
- career role
- innovator role.

These roles were identified by reviewing several compensation systems in different organisations and the roles that they rewarded. The roles were then compared with roles that had been emphasised in the management literature as important for organisational success. This multidimensional definition of performance suggests that employees enact multiple roles beyond that of job-holder (role theory). By considering roles that are thought to be universally important from an organisational perspective (identity theory), four additional roles have been identified. Team, career, and innovation roles are briefly defined below.

Team Role

Apart from job and organisation roles, the team role (as discussed in Chapter 3) played by employees is becoming increasingly important. Teamwork has, and will continue to be, a critical component of organisational performance. Gain sharing plans and team-based incentives encourage team-based behaviours associated with being a team member, such as multiskilling (see Chapter 5). Consequently, many of the new performance models adopted across a wide range of industries emphasise the importance and relevance of teamwork. Nonetheless, the predominant basis for pay-for-performance still continues to be individual performance.

Career Role

The career role should be considered in any comprehensive performance model. Evidence in companies of career role performance systems is individuals being rewarded for career accomplishment (Noe, Hollenbeck, Gerhart, & Wright, 1994). Employers can emphasise the importance of career roles either directly through compensation plans, or indirectly by providing career development opportunities for employees. This may take the form of rewards and incentives linked to training. For instance, another pay system that emphasises the career role is skill-based pay. These pay programs provide employees with increases in their base pay when they participate in training and acquire new skills. Organisations can no longer offer job security and promotional opportunities the way they could in the 20th century under the traditional employment relationship. In the new employment relationship a broad based performance model that emphasises learning and career development, replaces a narrow work performance model stressing job security and an organisationally based career path. The importance of the career role has been covered as part of the value of Flexible Deployment in Chapter 5.

Innovation Role

Innovation is another important dimension in work performance. Almost 30 years ago, the prominent organisational theorist Edgar Schein (1980) predicted that if firms intend to remain competitive in a complex and changing environment, they must have employees who are creative on behalf of an entire organisation, not just creative in their job. Including innovation in a work performance model implies that employees need to behave in original ways, not just applying their creative skills to their specific jobs, but also contributing to the effectiveness and adaptability of their organisation as a whole. An increasing number of companies are providing compensation incentives, such as gain sharing and cash rewards for suggestions, for original and entrepreneurial contributions. The only thing that has changed in 30 years since Schein acknowledged employee innovation as a vital part of work performance, is a greater relevance and appreciation of the innovator role in work performance.

Benefits of the Multidimensional Model of Performance

Undoubtedly there are other relevant roles that should be considered in the realm of work performance. Nonetheless, these three additional dimensions of performance provide a useful starting point in viewing performance as a multidimensional concept. These roles are distinct from each other and identify components of performance that cannot necessarily be measured via a firm's traditional approach to performance appraisal systems.

This work performance model addresses several weaknesses in traditional methods. The company benefits of using this multidimensional approach to performance are many:

1. This model is multidimensional rather than one-dimensional, accounting for multiple roles employees may take on in the workplace.
2. Because this model accounts for multiple roles, it reduces some of the deficiency error associated with typical performance measures that only focus on the job role.
3. This multidimensional representation of performance has a theoretical underpinning that adds credibility and rigor to the process.
4. The model has a broader, more general application than traditional techniques, which have been (and still are in most cases) job- or organisation-specific.
5. The five dimensions can be applied to a broad range of industries and occupations.

The modern employee, embracing a new mindset about their work performance, should acknowledge that who they are is not where they work, but what they do (Baker, 2005). In other words, a worker's sense of identity, self-esteem, and purpose should not necessarily be contingent on their organisational connection. When an individual allows their identity to reside in their workplace, they become organisationally dependent. This places workers in a permanent 'victim relationship' (Noer, 1997), perpetually subservient to the company. Instead, contemporary employees are better served by viewing their skills and self-esteem as portable and not dependent on a particular organisational setting. It is also in the interests of organisations now to foster independent relationships with their workforce. Benefits, status symbols, and policies that favour tenure over performance and internal pleasing over customer service are characteristics of the traditional employment relationship. If the organisation's Performance Focus is dependent on anything other than doing quality work in the service of customers, the system is toxic to long-term organisational survival. Reinforced in the previous chapter, independent and task-focused employees who look outward toward their customers will increasingly be in greater demand by companies and undoubtedly one of the continual keys to a robust commercial future.

Elements of Performance Focus

As with the other seven values in the model, advancing the value of Performance Focus is a result of a successful exchange between employer and employee. Figure 7.1 illustrates the interaction of core elements necessary to implant the value of Performance Focus in a workplace.

It follows from Figure 7.1 that performance-based companies take a multidimensional approach to instil this value in their workplace culture. Three important issues are evident in Figure 7.1: willingness on the part of the individual and incentives on the part of the organisation to acknowledge the relevance and importance of team-based behaviour, skill enhancement, and innovation and entrepreneurial contributions.

Performance-based work starts with changing the focus from remunerating employees on the basis of time spent on the job to remuneration based on the achievement of KPIs. These KPIs should cover both job and non-job roles. The old saying: 'A fair day's work for a fair day's pay' is no longer applicable in the new reality.

So, what can be done to fundamentally change the value of Job Focus to Performance Focus?

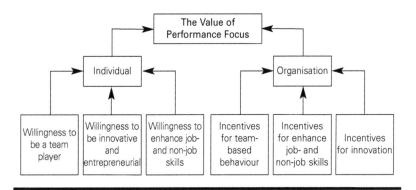

Figure 7.1 Elements of performance focus.

Role Descriptions

The first important step in moving towards a performance-focused culture is to change job descriptions to role descriptions for all employees in the organisation. Job descriptions usually define a set of specific tasks and responsibilities that are performed by a particular job-holder. Specific tasks are usually expressed in terms of outputs; for example, 'to maintain filing and record systems'. They tend to specify a narrow set of behaviours defined as a job. It typically includes employee characteristics required for competent performance of the job. However, a job description usually describes and focuses on the job itself and not on any specific individual who might undertake that particular job.

A role description, on the other hand, is concerned with elements such as which groups or areas the position serves, the end accountabilities of the role, and the overall skills and abilities required for the specific type of work. When viewed from this perspective, a number of jobs can usually be grouped into a role because, while tasks and specific goals may differ, the overall purpose, elements, and skills or competencies required are very similar.

Role descriptions define the organisational role of the individual and link these with KPIs. A role is a more generalised description of what is required in a job for effective performance; that is, what the individual needs to bring in terms of skills, knowledge and behaviour, the focus is therefore on inputs. They are less likely to define the activities of the job and more likely to define the performance criteria of the role in the context of the organisation. The same role description can be applicable to a number of different jobs where even though the tasks are different, the inputs required are essentially the same.

For example, consider a production engineer with a designated work site and structure. Apart from the specifics of the work site and structure, this job plays a similar role to other production engineers stationed at other sites. Therefore, it may make sense to develop one production engineer role document rather than have a job description for each particular site. By doing this, it streamlines the documentation and fewer documents are required. The role document consequently focuses on role similarities, rather than job differences, and provides more flexibility for both the individual and the organisation. Employees then have the scope to take on new assignments and tasks within the same role, or move into similar roles in different areas of the company. Organisations, on the other hand, have the capacity of being more flexible and responsive to changing market trends.

As a starting point in changing from job descriptions to role descriptions, a questionnaire can be designed to collect meaningful information about role content, performance requirements and the employee's required skills.

Each section of the questionnaire can deal with a different aspect of the role being described and can include:

- general identifying information
- role summary
- primary responsibilities and
- performance expectations.

Team, Career and Innovation Responsibilities

Open-ended and multiple choice questions are designed to collect information about competencies that are critical to the success of the company. As well, data collection needs to be broadened to include the following characteristics of the employee's non-job role that cover team, career and innovation responsibilities.

Leadership

Leadership includes the ability to influence others within the organisation in a positive way. For instance, this may cover the impact the employee has on improving processes, outcomes and efficiencies. It should also comprise the degree of involvement the employee has in team meetings and their capacity to be solution focused.

Accountability/Responsibility

Accountability/Responsibility includes the degree to which employees accept responsible for their own work and the work of others they work with. It ought to take into account the impact of a position's end results on the work unit, function or organisation as a whole and those it serves, the degree of autonomy in decision-making required for success, and the level of review generally given to work process and results.

Collaboration

Collaboration is concerned with the ability to produce successful outcomes by working cooperatively with others. For instance, an important aspect of collaboration is sharing relevant information and soliciting input and assistance from others. Other components include the capacity to integrate input and seek consensus to reach organisational goals. To collaborate effectively, an employee needs to understand team process and apply problem-solving techniques.

Communication

Communication in this context refers to the ability to effectively interact and exchange information with other members of the organisation and external constituencies. More specifically, effective communication includes developing factual and logical presentations of ideas and opinions using written and verbal skills and demonstrating effective listening skills.

Development of Self

Development of self is associated with a commitment to personal and professional development. To do this, employees actively seek out appropriate opportunities to expand work-related knowledge, skills and experiences and personal development.

Innovation, Problem-Solving and Critical Thinking

These traits are associated with continuously seeking to identify, define, critically analyse and resolve work problems through research and testing alternative ideas and approaches. In other words, this involves thinking outside traditional parameters, using innovative and creative ideas and actions to improve work processes and service to constituents. The appropriate mindset is one of seldom settling for a service or process that is 'good enough'. To do this, employees add value and take measured risks to enhance the achievement of the company's mission.

Service to Customers

Service to customers involves the ability to identify, understand, build relationships with and respond to the requirements of external and internal customers in an appropriate manner, reflecting the goals and values of the company and demonstrating fiscal responsibility. Employees need to be knowledgeable of, and responsive to, the expectations of customers, focusing particularly on the quality and timeliness of service. The important and relevance of this core value was covered in the previous chapter related to the value of Customer Focus.

These non-job responsibilities are supplementary to the core functional competencies associated with organisational and job roles. They cover aspects of the employee's team, career and innovation roles. A complete and accurate role document is very important for classification, performance planning and performance management.

Collaborative Approaches for Formulating Role Descriptions

The process for completing a role description is directly connected to its quality and accuracy. The key to successfully writing a role description is collaboration between manager and employee, among fellow employees, and across hierarchical levels. Several collaborative approaches are outlined below for compiling the information necessary for the development of an accurate role description.

Dynamic Duo Method

With this approach, the manager or supervisor chooses two individuals who perform the same role to complete the questionnaire together. For example, two accounts receivable clerks could share similar tasks. Following this method, the document is written reflecting more than one perspective of the role. The manager or supervisor discusses and modifies the role document in partnership with the two employees, providing a third perspective.

Team Method

In this approach, the manager or supervisor chooses three or four individuals, all of whom perform the same role, to complete the document. This method is particularly useful when a role has many incumbents, or when the role can be found in several departments, calling for multiple viewpoints. Teams should be kept small, as groups larger than three or four employees can have difficulty reaching consensus and are much slower to complete the task of defining the core role. The manager or supervisor reviews and discusses the document with the whole team.

Supervisor–Incumbent Method

In this case, the supervisor or manager works with a single employee to complete role documentation. This method is particularly effective when an employee is new to a role within the company, in cases where there are concerns about performance or understanding of the role's components, or where the role is undergoing major content changes. This method involves a similar review and approval process to the Team Method.

Single Employee Method

The Single Employee Method allows for the employee or the manager of the role to complete the questionnaire. For roles with only one employee, or for a vacant/new position, this may be the only method available, but it is the least collaborative, and therefore, the least preferred. A review with the employee (if applicable) by the manager and by the senior staff person for the area is particularly critical when using this method, in order to provide a broader perspective.

Role Analysis

The process just described, using any of the methods outlined above, is referred to as a Role Analysis. Role Analysis is defined as the process of collecting, analysing and recording information about the requirements of roles in order to provide the basis for a role profile. Role analyses focus on the demands made on role holders in terms of what they need to know and be able to do to deliver the expected level of performance.

From an individual perspective, the key purpose in conducting a role analysis is to describe a job as it is actually performed and understand the job well enough to reliably and accurately define worker requirements. Done well, a role analysis provides the most relevant position-specific information, which may then be used in a variety of HR functions, including recruitment and selection, performance management, and assessment.

On the other hand, from an organisational perspective, a role analysis helps to create a shared view of a job, fostering greater acceptance among interested parties as to the job's actual portrayal. It also provides documentation that allows the employer to record and defend processes and decisions, should they be challenged.

Several guidelines for completing role analyses are helpful. These include:

- training to all those involved in analysing and evaluating jobs and roles in terms of the skills involved and the operation of the analysis and evaluation process
- an agreed format on how role descriptions are to be written to enable jobs to be assessed to a common standard
- a comprehensive list of the elements made available to role analysts covered in the jobs being analysed
- a representative sample of people from the spread of jobs to be covered by the role
- selecting the facilitators of job evaluation panels for their knowledge of job evaluation, their impartiality, and their concern that decisions of the panel are not discriminatory
- not overly relying on generic job descriptions, especially when there are significant clear variations in job duties
- the removal of gender, race and individual identification from role profiles.

Once these job descriptions have been converted to role descriptions, KPIs and Targets can be established for each Key Performance Area (KPA).

Performance Management Framework

Figure 7.2 illustrates the relationship between role descriptions and the performance management structure of a company.

Figure 7.2 shows the links between the key elements essential for managing performance. The Vision is a broad statement related to the direction the company is headed and the Mission is how the company intends to fulfil that vision. Core Values are the guiding attitudes underpinning performance. Role Descriptions are reflective of the vision, mission, and core values and also incorporate KPAs, KPIs, and Targets. This framework puts the focus on performance into context.

Once KPAs, KPIs and Targets have been identified and include job and non-job behaviours, valid and reliable reward structures can be put in place to rein-

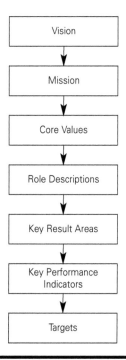

Figure 7.2 Performance management framework.

force a focus on performance. This rewards and incentives system can be either monetary or nonmonetary or a combination of the two. Chapter 8 details some of the reward systems available for recognising team performance.

Conclusion

Referring to the New Employment Relationship Model discussed in Chapter 4, the suitable individual response to the value of Performance Focus is to focus on what you do, not where you work. Evidence of this may include a willingness on the part of the individual to acknowledge the relevance and importance of team-based behaviour, skill enhancement, and innovation and entrepreneurial contributions. From an organisational perspective, the reciprocal reaction is to link rewards and benefits with performance rather than organisational dependency. Evidence includes the provision and administration of a valid and reliable reward and incentive system to encourage teamwork, skill acquisition, and innovation. The next chapter looks specifically at appropriate team-based behaviour. These individual and organisation responses are likely to be characteristic of an organisation culture that has moved from a value of Job Focus to Performance Focus.

■ Reflective Questions for Managers

The following questions relate to the company in focus on page 83.

1. If you were sceptical about these accounts, what could you do to investigate these claims further?

2. What are the key factors in the article that seem to contribute to Apple's innovation performance?

3. How can a company be so in touch with the needs of their customers that they 'know what customers want before the customers themselves know it'? Discuss.

4. What role do you think Steve Jobs plays in creating a corporate culture where 'every single person in the company contributes to Apple's innovation success every day'?

5. How much of this innovation success is attributable to clever marketing, not only of their products, but also their performance-focused culture? Discuss.

Consider how the following questions can be addressed in your own organisation:

6. 'The traditional job description is an outdated characteristic of the traditional employment relationship.' Do you agree with this statement? Justify your response.

7. Why is it that some companies can be highly innovative like Apple Computer and others have great difficulty being innovative?

8. How would you implement a fair incentives program for suggestion-making that leads to improvements in efficiency or effectiveness within an organisation?

9. The traditional employment relationship has been more concerned with individual rather than team performance. Under the new employment relationship, it is the opposite: team performance is more important than individual performance. Do you agree or disagree with this statement?

10. Apart from team, career and innovator roles, what other roles do you think are critical to modern-day organisational performance?

■ Top 10 Key Points from Chapter 7

1. A performance focus benefits both the organisation and individual.

2. Job descriptions have traditionally focused only on the attributes of the job, rather than non-job attributes.

3. A combination of role theory and identity theory can be used to develop a multidimensional model of performance that can be generalised to most industries and occupations.

4. Five common role roles include job, organisation, team, career, and innovator.

5. The team role emphasises the relevance and importance of teamwork as a critical component of organisational performance.

6. The career role emphasises the acquisition of new skills.

7. The innovator role is associated with innovative and entrepreneurial behaviour.

8. The modern employee should acknowledge that who they are is not where they work, but what they do.

9. Performance-based work is based on remunerating employees for the achievement of KPIs, and not based on time spent on the job.

10. Moving from job descriptions to role descriptions is the starting point for moving to a performance focus.

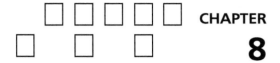

Managing Tribalism
From Functional- to Project-Based Work

People are by nature tribal; that is, they naturally build alliances and associations with others.

The transfer from functional-based to project-based work is beneficial for both the individual and organisation in a rapidly changing global environment. Teams founded on temporary and ongoing project work are an important feature of the postbureacratic organisational structure. Specifically, accelerated change and uncertainty, globalisation and the information economy, and a move towards a customer focus are the drivers for a move away from the constraints and limitations of the old bureaucratic model to more receptive and flexible cross-functional structures. Employees are increasingly likely to find their work identity tied to the cross-functional work team. Research indicates that the move towards project-based work is reshaping psychological boundaries in the workplace. Changes in organisational structures are likely to see these boundaries between functions migrate to the cross-functional team level. Managers are encouraged to therefore acknowledge and facilitate this repositioning of boundary activity in a constructive way. Cross-functional teamwork is rapidly becoming the dominant organising structure and, as such, should be reinforced with appropriate rewards and recognition.

Defining Project-Based Work

Inflexible, hierarchical organisational structures are no longer suitable in the 21st century marketplace. Being responsive and adaptable to an increasingly global and competitive environment is more important than ever (Zhang & Cao, 2002). To be quick to respond, the emphasis needs to shift from an organisational structure based on function to one based on a cross-functional arrangement. This requires a greater emphasis on project-based teamwork.

Project-based teamwork can be classified as either:

- ad hoc project teams or
- ongoing project teams (Devine, Clayton, Philips, Dunford, & Melner, 1999).

Ad hoc project teams exist for a finite period of time and ongoing project teams are standing teams with relatively stable membership. The use of project teams (both short- and long-term) wherever possible, as distinct from functional work groups, provides organisations with adaptable and flexible structures.

A project-based team is a group of employees from various functional areas of the organisation; for example, research, engineering, marketing, finance, human resources, and operations, who are all focused on a specific cross-functional project. As a team, they are responsible for working together to improve coordination and innovation across traditional divisions or departments and to resolve mutual problems between company functions.

The Shift from Functional to Project-Based Work

Cross-functional teams, and, in particular, project teams, are characteristic of the postbureaucratic form of organisation referred to as the 'network organisation' (Baker, 1992). A network organisation is more flexible and manoeuvrable than a bureaucracy. Unlike a bureaucracy, which is a fixed set of relationships for processing all problems, the network organisation moulds itself to each problem. This kind of organisational arrangement adapts itself by the interactions of problems, people and resources within the broad confines of corporate strategy rather than by top management directives. As Baker (1992, p. 398) defines it, the postbureaucratic organisation, 'is a social network that is integrated across formal boundaries. Interpersonal ties of any type are formed without respect to formal groups or categories'.

The structure of a network organisation changes from a hierarchical to a flat form and management goals change from being functional to global. From the individual worker's perspective, work changes from being fragmented to team-oriented.

Despite the superficial nature of some anecdotal and case study accounts about the so-called 'postbureaucratic organisation' and the abundance of titles and labels used to describe organisational transformation, the network organisation is generally seen to be a response to the same drivers for change. These drivers include: globalisation, the move to an information economy, rapid environmental change, and a service orientation. As Sheridan (1996, p. 17) points out:

CASE STUDY

Poor Performing Project Team at Xerox

Consider Customer Service Teams (CSTs) at Xerox. When a photocopier stops working, the customer wants it fixed instantly. The task of the CSTs is to do just that: to do it efficiently (spend no more time with a machine than actually is needed), inexpensively (keep parts costs low), and well (fixing the machines so it stays fixed). Each team has a set of machines for which members are collectively responsible, usually associated with a geographical area or a single large customer such as a university or a corporation. Consider CSTs at Xerox generally perform quite well. But imagine, for a moment, the pattern of interaction that might have characterised one of the worst teams in the company.

As is common for CSTs, members of this hypothetical, poorly performing team meet at a coffee shop before launching the day's work. Members dawdle over breakfast, talking about anything but their work. The rest of the day is also leisurely, with technicians spending nearly as much time idly chatting to customers as working on machines. Individual technicians go through their paces, responding to the dispatcher's directives about where to go next, and calling a headquarters' technical specialist if they encounter an unfamiliar machine malfunction. Any lessons learned in the course of the day are kept to oneself, and individuals rarely ask their team mates for help when a machine insists on staying broken. For this team, collective effort is low, members have no shared strategy about how they will approach their team's work, and they neither share their expertise with one another nor draw on their team mates' special skills. The customers of teams with these work processes would not enthuse about the service they receive, and company managers probably would have reason for concern about the team's speed of response and parts expenses. Nor is it likely that the team would spontaneously become stronger as a performing unit over time, or that members would get much learning or fulfilment from their work experiences.

Source: Hackman, J.R. (2002). *Leading teams: Setting the stage for great performances*. Boston, MA: Harvard Business School Publication. Reproduced with permission.

Today's business environment is notable because companies are doing more with less: revenues are increasing as sizes of organisations are decreasing. Leading companies are developing organisations that are improving quality and adding greater value while reducing cycle time. One of the key elements of these corporate transformations has been the manner in which people who work in organisations are used.

In particular, one of the tasks of the new organisation is to make use of the 'intellectual capital' (Stewart, 1994) of individuals effectively to achieve some advantage over competitors. A combination of valuing the individual input of workers with that of increased cross-functional communication is the integration of valued aspects of both individualism and connectivity (Symon, 2000). However, this shift from functional to project-based organisational communication presents challenges for employees, as well as organisations.

Team Identity

The development of a cross-functional team identity can replace functional identity. This team identity is referred to as 'superordinate identity' (Ashforth & Mael, 1989). In the context of cross-functional teams, superordinate identity refers to the extent to which members identify with the team (rather than merely with their functional areas). In other words, a superordinate identity reflects a greater degree of loyalty to the team over the organisation. Moreover, in this situation, individuals perceive a greater stake in the success of the cross-functional team than their functional department. This is different from social cohesion (Ashforth & Mael, 1989). The adverse effect of these functional identities can be replaced in a team of individuals from diverse functional areas by creating a new team-based identity or superordinate identity (Cross, Yang, & Louis, 2000).

People are by nature tribal; that is, they naturally build alliances and associations with others. So, in an organisational context, it is common for people to form groupings with other employees. The formal groupings in organisations are traditionally organised around departments. When groups are formed formally or informally, they differentiate themselves from others by creating physical and/or psychological boundaries. This is to protect their superordinate identity. Physical boundaries can be doorways, buildings or passageways. Psychological boundaries are not necessarily visible or tangible.

Psychological boundaries are created through particular boundary activities. According to Cross et al. (2000, p. 842), 'boundary activities are those in which the focal organisational entity engages to create and maintain its boundaries and to manage interactions across those boundaries'.

Until recently, studies of work units have generally ignored researching evidence of intraorganisational boundaries. As the first to conceptualise boundary activities at the work unit level, Yang and Louis's (1999) empirical research investigated and validated the presence of three types of boundary activities in a large organisation undergoing transformation from a functionally dominant firm to a cross-functional structure. The three generic boundary activities they confirmed are referred to as:

- buffering
- spanning
- bring up boundaries.

From Cross et al.'s (2000) findings, they claim that boundary activities transfer downward from the formal organisational structure to the work unit level when organisations are undergoing transformation. Organisational transformation may result from redesigning core work processes, increasing the diversification of the workforce, the adoption of team-based structures, or the employment of sophisticated information technologies. How in practice do these boundary activities manifest themselves to protect the new identity of the team? Briefly, each of the three boundary activities are defined below.

Buffering

Buffering is a conscious or unconscious strategy used by team members to build and protect the team's unique identity. This strategy emphasises the need to protect the team from the exposure of anticipatory or real uncertainties and disturbances from outside the team's boundaries (Cross et al., 2000). By doing this, the team is able to function effectively. Practical team-based strategies include such activities as:

- forecasting and preparing for the future
- deflecting work to other teams or organisational units that may disrupt the team's core activities
- stockpiling resources
- the development of systems for processing the work of the team.

Managers who encourage and support these activities are assisting to transfer boundaries from functional units to cross-functional units. Such corresponding management initiatives would include:

- encouraging and supporting team planning and forecasting
- coordinating workflow throughout the organisation
- encouraging teams to be self-sufficient in their resourcing
- supporting teams to develop their own systems and processes.

In summary, by abiding by, and promoting these activities, managers are not allowing outside pressures, demands and interference to adversely effect the team's output.

Boundary Spanning

While buffering is an internal defence mechanism to protect the team, boundary spanning entails reaching out to critical people and resources outside the team. Boundary spanning activities are designed to maintain and build on interdependent relationships within and outside the organisation to guarantee the team's relevance, or reason for existence (Scott, 1992).

Team member activities that can be classified as boundary spanning include:

- bargaining and negotiation between teams
- contracting outside assistance and seeking external support
- building alliances within and outside the organisation with influential stakeholders.

Managers who consciously or unconsciously discourage these activities reinforce functional silos at the expense of cross-functional teamwork.

Positive corresponding management initiatives to encourage and support boundary spanning include:

- encouraging teams to bargain and negotiate with each other
- assisting teams to seek out assistance and external support
- supporting teams to build constructive alliances with influential stakeholders within and outside the business.

In summary, by abiding by and promoting these activities, managers are assisting project teams to create constructive external links with important constituencies.

Bringing Up Boundaries

Bringing up boundaries involves two primary functions: creating and maintaining a common vision for tasks performed by the team and building and sustaining a shared team culture. In contrast to buffering, in which energy largely goes into keeping out external forces that might interrupt and distract the work unit, bringing up boundaries is focused on attracting the energies of team members to the unit's task by utilising and containing resources available within the work unit (Cross et al., 2000). In contrast to spanning, where the effort is to import the critical resources from the external environment, bringing up boundaries entails shaping and applying internal resources to the task at hand. For example, team-based activities would include:

- multiskilling team members so that they can perform several tasks within the confines of the team
- creating a team values charter
- team celebrations.

Managers should encourage these activities to assist the team develop a superordinate identity. For instance, they could:

- facilitate an organisation-wide commitment to a multiskilling program
- encourage teams to articulate their own identity and values
- promote team celebrations when milestones have been met.

In summary, these activities will assist the team to clarify their vision and create a unique team-based culture.

It is incorrect for managers to assume that when an organisation is undergoing organisational transformation it eliminates boundaries altogether. Boundaries will likely reconceptualise at the team level (Yang & Louis, 1999). Managers are right to break down the boundaries that make the company rigid and unresponsive. However, they are wrong to think that they can restructure an organisation to have no tribal identities. Consequently, the appropriate question for managers is: How can we reconfigure boundaries to make the company more flexible and responsive to market forces?

Many new boundary-related activities emerge during system transformations and do require management attention. With an awareness of these three boundary protection strategies at the team level, managers have a useful framework for observing the development of superordinate identity in other organisational settings. From an employee's perspective, boundary spanning activity is natural and normal human behaviour and provides them with a sense of collective identity.

Elements of Project-Based Work

Similarly to the other seven values in the model, enhancing the value of Project-Based Work is a joint effort between employer and employee. Figure 8.1 illustrates the interaction of core elements associated with the value of Project-Based Work in an organisation.

Figure 8.1 illustrates the three core elements associated with moving from a functional-based to project-based work environment. The three

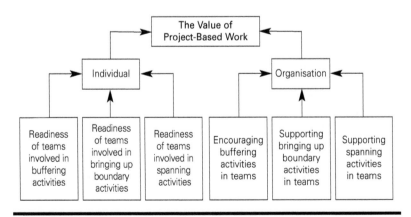

Figure 8.1 Elements of project-based work.

important issues are encouragement and support from management, a readiness on behalf of team members to engage in buffering and spanning, and bringing up boundary activities as outlined earlier in the chapter.

Cross-Functional Organisational Structures

Most organisational charts still illustrate their organisational structure as hierarchical and functional. Figure 8.2 below shows the typical functional formation.

This traditional organising approach creates two challenges. First, this functional arrangement creates 'silos' based on a departmental or divisional structure. These divisions are generally organised around functions such as operations, administration and sales as reflected in Figure 8.2. Each function traditionally has its own identity led by a functional leader and, as such, cross-functional communication is stifled. Through traditional boundary management activities, these functions insulate themselves from other functions within the company (Sethi, 2000).

The secondary dilemma faced by this hierarchical arrangement is that accountability for performance is contained within each function or discipline. In other words, the workforce in a particular department or division is answerable to a line manager or middle manager within that function and they, in turn, are answerable to their top manager. As a consequence, there is very little, if any, cross-functional accountabilities in these established structures. While

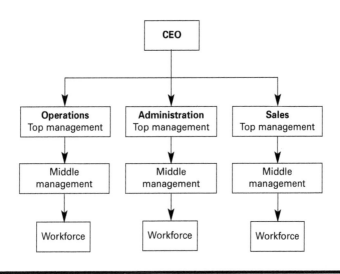

Figure 8.2 Traditional organisational structures.

this functional paradigm has been a successful organising process for at least a century, it has done more to impede customer-focused business performance improvement over the past 2 decades than any other single factor. For these reasons, a new organising structure is overdue to maximise the company's receptiveness to the rapidly changing external environment.

In contrast to Figure 8.2, Figure 8.3 illustrates a more flexible and responsive organisational structure, based on the cross-functional paradigm.

As Figure 8.3 shows, this structure still has functions, as illustrated by the spokes in the organisational wheel. However, there is an additional organising structure, which is illustrated as project-based teams. These teams are cross-functional entities whose members comprise representatives from several departments. Project-based teams strengthen cross-functional communication and disperse accountability beyond the functions. Moreover, instead of the traditional top-down hierarchy, the cross-functional paradigm is structured around the management team which promotes two dimensions of accountability: cross-functional as well as functional. Figure 8.3 illustrates this two-dimensional approach to organisational accountability. Note that in Figure 8.3 there are no spokes (functional boundaries) within the managerial space. This structure invites managers to think like organisational leaders rather than as heads of divisions, departments or business units.

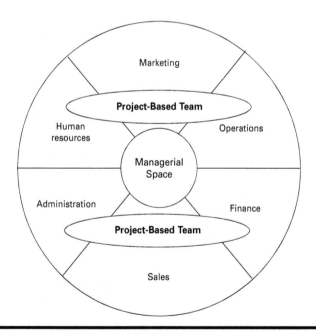

Figure 8.3 Cross-functional organisational structures.

Cross-Functional Teamwork

Aside from creating a new organisational structure, to maximise the potential of cross-functional teams, six important issues need to be addressed by managers and team members. These include:

- proper project-team membership
- a clear charter and purpose
- the right connections
- achievable, noticeable results
- understood and agreed-upon ground rules
- intensive team building upfront

Each issue is briefly explained below.

Proper Project Team Membership

Membership of any team is crucial to its success. Managers when selecting team members ought to consider three important questions:

1. Do potential members have expertise in the project the team must deal with?
2. Does the team have 'political pull' that can help them fulfil their charter?
3. Can they function effectively as a team?

The first question can be quite challenging. Expertise can be a 'sticky issue'. If all team members have substantial expertise in the problem area, they may not 'see the forest for the trees', yet a group of novices can make fundamental mistakes. The amount of expertise required for a group to be effective depends on the purpose of the team. If the purpose is to make incremental, small-scale change, then weighting the team with experts is probably the best strategy. If, on the other hand, the purpose is fundamental, large-scale change (re-engineering), loading the group with individuals with less experience is more appropriate. Large-scale change will require a broader perspective. Experts may find it difficult to empathise with people who do not share their expertise, experience or perspective.

Clear Charter and Purpose

One of the most frustrating experiences for team members is not having a clear team direction or purpose. Without clarity, the team may meander and waffle around and after a few overly long meetings, members stop showing up. Team members, their management and any other stakeholders should agree on the charter and purpose before the team starts on its project-based work. Once this charter has been established, it needs to be communicated clearly to the prospective team members.

The Right Connections

Not only should team members have some 'political pull' themselves, they benefit from also have access to bigger 'movers and shakers' within, and sometimes outside, the organisation. These connections would include senior departmental and divisional managers from the functions team members originate from and represent. As discussed earlier, reaching out to influential stakeholders is an important boundary spanning activity. Consequently, managers have a responsibility to facilitate a smooth access to these connections.

Achievable, Noticeable Results

Well-established departments tend to have fixed measures of success with clearly defined KRAs and KPIs. In the same way, cross-functional teams need to decide what results they expect to achieve, reasonably early in their formation. To make this task even more challenging for a newly appointed project team, it is likely that there is no established measure of success within the company to draw from. An ad hoc project team, for example, may want to reduce waste, or improve the delivery time of products or services to customers. However, the background information may not have been collected before and the team must develop a set of unique KRAs and KPIs specific to the problem they have been charged to solve. Simply put, a project team should understand from the outset what its primary focus is, and the yardstick by which it will be measured.

Understood and Agreed-Upon Ground Rules

These ground rules are the guiding norms for the team; for example, issues such as how conflict and consensus can be handled, who writes the minutes and facilitates team meetings, and the degree of formality in those meetings. Other practical issues need also to be addressed by the project team. For instance, how much time, money, and how many people will be available for the project, or who can the group turn to when it needs advice and support, or if management fails to follow through on promises, how will the team resolve this? These agreed-upon ground rules will assist to manage boundaries early on in the life of the project team.

Intensive Team Building Upfront

So often teams come together with good purpose, but through personal misunderstandings between team members, the team begins to unravel. Typically, consultants are then called in to 'fix the problem' after the damage is done. It is always better to prevent a problem from happening than committing to damage control. Upfront team building sessions, where members' concerns, problems and issues come out, are a constructive way of preventing problems arising through misunderstanding later on in the life of the project. These sessions can also deal with many of the issues described above. These team-building sessions are especially important in cross-functional teams. Otherwise it is quite possible (and is often the case) that entrenched department rivalries and personality clashes detract from the quality of cross-functional work.

Such team-building sessions serve two important purposes. The first purpose is to train the team in using tools and approaches they can use to resolve the organisational issues they have been formed to deal with in the first place. For instance, these techniques may include such things as problem-solving, statistical process control, and flowcharting. After an initial overview, this training is best delivered in a 'just in time' fashion, where trainers teach the members the specific tool just before they use it. For example, a team might receive a general overview of techniques in problem-solving as part of their initial team building, but specifically learn to develop process mapping just before the team needs to apply it to a work problem. The second purpose of team building involves some training in the usual set of group interaction skills such as meeting management, stages of group development, avoiding 'groupthink', and communication.

There are a variety of strategies for rewarding project-based work. Broadly, there are two types of rewards for teamwork: monetary and recognition.

Monetary Rewards

There are several challenges in implementing gain sharing reward structures. Gain-sharing programs allow team members to 'share the gains' of efforts made by a particular team. It therefore establishes an incentive to help co-workers achieve their shared goals. Three of the most common challenges in applying a gain-sharing program are:

- the difficulty of measuring precise cost savings or productivity gains
- the inability of team members to sometimes see the relationship between the performance of their team and the reward
- the issue of whether to reward people who provide essential support and service to the team but who may not directly contribute to the gain.

It is important for managers to be aware of these challenges when implementing a gain-sharing program.

For gain sharing to be effective, rewards must be directly related to team performance, so that if the team succeeds, all members will be rewarded for their contribution. Below are three of the most common forms of monetary rewards for team performance. These include:

- knowledge-based pay
- one-time bonuses
- team incentive system.

Knowledge-Based Pay

Knowledge-based pay encourages staff to learn new skills and acquire knowledge about the jobs of other team members, by offering incremental pay increases after the new skill is acquired. This method encourages collaboration among team members and facilitates process improvement, since team members can perform many tasks and can understand how the total process works. Knowledge-based pay systems allow the company to support the concept of team learning, while at the same time recognising outstanding individual performance. Behind this form of incentive is the assumption that the mastery of new skills will ultimately lead to improvements in organisational productivity. Knowledge-based pay systems have a direct application for the facilitation of flexible deployment as described in Chapter 5.

One-Time Bonuses

One-time bonuses can be offered to an ad hoc project team, formed for a specific purpose, who deliver goods or services on time (or ahead of schedule), achieve results under budget, or produce cost-saving ideas. As an illustration, Honeywell's Space Systems Group (Parker, 1994) had a chance to win a major contract for highly specialised computer chips, if it could design the best chip first. Intent on turning out perfect chips with reduced design time, the project manager implemented a 'bounty system'. He offered each engineer $150 if a chip passed the first design step on time and up to $1200 when three chips passed in one design cycle. The team could receive up to $4000 for similar passes. The team designed two perfect chips in the first cycle, putting Honeywell 9 months ahead of the competition.

Team Incentive System

The team incentive system is an ongoing reward system as distinct from the one-time bonus system. Specifically, cross-functional teams that shorten the time needed to bring new products to market may be paid a bonus by the company on more than one occasion. The team incentive and company expectation must be negotiated between the company and the team upfront.

These are some of the more common and successful gain sharing monetary approaches for encouraging the value of Project-Based Work.

Rewarding Through Recognition

So far, we have discussed reward programs that are tied to specific team outcomes, but it is also possible, and often desirable, to reward cross-functional teams for an unplanned or extraordinary effort. In other words, this is the recognition of unplanned and exceptional project-based work.

Who and What Should Be Recognised?

There are many variations. Some people appreciate recognition from an authority figure (such as a supervisor), while others value acknowledgment by colleagues and fellow team members. Alternatively, some employees appreciate public rewards, such as having their efforts being recognised in the company newsletter; others prefer intrinsic rewards, such as the opportunity to take on a challenging assignment. All the evidence suggests that people appreciate recognition, but vary in terms of their preference for the form that recognition takes.

Extrinsic rewards are quite different from intrinsic rewards. For example, recognition in a company newsletter or on a bulletin board is a form of external reward which appeals to people who respond to 'extrinsic motivation'. Other simple, practical and effective extrinsic ideas for recognising teams are:

- giving verbal praise at staff meetings
- inviting the team to present its work at a company conference
- prominently displaying a poster with team photographs and accomplishments
- sending the team on an outing, such as a boat ride or to a sporting event
- inviting the team to the CEOs home for a barbecue
- placing a photograph and story about the team in the company or community newspaper
- encouraging team members to speak at professional conferences by paying travel expenses
- asking the CEO to attend a team meeting to praise its performance
- sending a letter to the CEO detailing the team's work
- giving each team member a T-shirt, hat, or mug with his or her name (or the team's name) on it.

On the other hand, some people respond to intrinsic rewards that appeal to the 'inner self' of team members. Some simple and effective examples include:

- asking the team to accept a new challenge
- writing timely, thoughtful comments in the margin of the team's reports

- giving the team the opportunity to meet off-site
- giving the team improved resources, such as new equipment
- asking the team's opinion about tough problems or new business opportunities
- asking the team to help another team start up or solve a problem
- offering to pitch in and help the team directly
- empowering the team to act independently.

Both extrinsic and intrinsic rewards are effective in rewarding and reinforcing exceptional team performance. Their value will depend on the team's preference, the culture of the organisation, and the resources at the disposal of managers. A combination is often the most effective form of recognition.

Conclusion

In reference to the New Employment Relationship Model in Chapter 4, the appropriate individual response to the value of Project-Based Work is to accept and embrace yourself as a project-based worker rather than a functional-based employee. This mindset is likely to be characteristic of employees when there is evidence of boundary protection activity at the cross functional team level. From an organisational point of view, the mutual response is to focus on projects rather than organisational functions. Evidence of this from managers would include actively facilitating and encouraging boundary protection activity at the cross functional team level and reciprocally discouraging these activities between functional areas of the business. These responses are likely to be characteristic of an organisation culture that has moved from a value of Functional-Based to Project-Based Work.

■ Reflective Questions for Managers

The following questions relate to the case study on page 99.

1. If you were the manager responsible for overseeing this project team's performance, referring back to the section on boundary activities in Chapter 8, what would you do to facilitate a team identity?

2. Referring back to the section on cross-functional teamwork, how would you address the six important issues of functioning effectively as a team?

3. A lack of multiskilling is an issue in this team. How would you address this to ensure that there is a greater transfer of skills and knowledge?

4. What rewards and recognition might be appropriate to motivate this team to higher performance?

Consider how the following questions can be addressed in your own organisation:

5. Can an organisational structure operate effectively with both functional and cross-functional configurations similar to Figure 8.3? How can organisational leaders manage this cross-functional organisational structure?

6. What has your experience been with implementing successful and unsuccessful rewards and recognition programs to support teamwork? What has worked or not worked?

7. Consider some examples of boundary activities you have witnessed in teams. Are these examples constructive or destructive attempts at creating a team identity?

8. 'People are by nature tribal; that is, they naturally build alliances and associations with others.' Discuss this statement. Do you agree or disagree? Why?

9. What are the benefits to employees of accepting and embracing themselves as project-based workers rather than functional-based workers?

■ Top 10 Key Points from Chapter 8

1. The use of project teams, both short- and long-term, as distinct from functional work groups, provides organisations with adaptable and flexible structures.

2. A project-based team is a group of employees from various functional areas of the organisation who are all focused on a specific cross-functional project.

3. The development of a cross-functional team identity can replace functional identity.

4. The superordinate identity is concerned with where someone sees their association, or identity within the organisational structure.

5. These three generic boundary activities are Buffering, Spanning, and Bringing Up Boundaries.

6. Buffering is a strategy that protects the team from threatening outside influences.

7. Boundary spanning activities are designed to build useful alliances external to the team.

8. Bringing Up Boundaries is concerned with developing a team vision and shared team culture.

9. The six important issues associated with developing effective cross-functional teams are (1) proper team membership, (2) a clear charter and purpose, (3) the right connections, (4) achievable, noticeable results, (5) understood and agreed-upon ground rules, and (6) intensive team building upfront.

10. There are two types of rewards for teamwork: monetary and recognition.

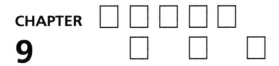
Employee Engagement
From Human Dispirit and Work to Human Spirit and Work

> Heightened expectations of work and the changing nature of the role work plays in people's lives creates a more significant connection between human spirit and work.

Several developments are contributing to a growing interest in the value of Human Spirit and Work. The downsizing movement in the 1980s and 1990s has alienated employees and, consequently, there is pressure to rectify the cynicism employees have for the motives of employers. Organisations are now viewed as a primary source of community with a general decline in connectivity in the wider community. Increasing interest in Eastern philosophies has focused attention on the concept of discovering one's spiritual centre in any activity, including work. The ageing workforce and their inevitable orientation to contemplating the meaning of life as they get older has bought into question the significance work has in their lives. Globalisation has shifted the emphasis to human rather than technical resources and correspondingly the human relations movement has become fashionable once again. The meaning of work is constructed at both the personal and interpersonal levels. It is therefore the joint responsibility of the individual and organisation to generate meaningfulness in work. Working conditions, the linkage between personal interests and jobs, and the belief in the capacity to find work meaningful are the key elements associated with the value of Human Spirit and Work. An employment engagement strategy is a recommended approach for developing this value in the workplace. The plan for this strategy should consider a hierarchy of employee engagement needs to prioritise necessary action steps.

Defining the Value of Human Spirit and Work

The quest to find meaning in work is not a new concept. Human relations scholars emphasise the notion of job satisfaction and employee happiness, although many might argue that belief in the assumptions of the human relations movement disappeared from the workplace with the downsizing and employee layoffs of the 1980s and 1990s. Some scholars are sceptical that the values of meaning, satisfaction and happiness were ever really part of organisational work in the first place. For instance, Terkel's (1995) extensive workplace research shows that many workers across many industries categorise their work as unhappy and dissatisfying, and describe their work experience as one that wounds their human spirit. Nonetheless, with the profound changes in the modern workplace, the notion of meaningful work comes into sharper focus.

Some writers believe that the idea of 'corporate spirituality' may well shape the new organisation (Wheatley, 1992; Zohar, 1997). It is important to clarify that spirituality at work has nothing to do with religion conversion, or getting people to accept a basic belief system. It is about employees having their spiritual needs nourished through their work. Moreover, it is about workers experiencing a sense of purpose and meaning in their work. This notion has been referred to as 'organisation-based self-esteem' (Tang, Furnham, & Davis, 2003). This sense of purpose goes beyond simply finding meaning in the performance of work-related tasks. The spirituality at work movement is concerned with the engagement between the human spirit and work. Spirituality in this context is also about people experiencing a sense of connectedness to one another and to their workplace community.

The spirituality at work movement is getting the attention of business leaders because of the recognition that nourishing an individual's spirit at work may be good for business (Ashmos & Duchon, 2000). This growing interest in spirituality at work can be understood in relation to several trends in Western society. These developments include:

Organisational Restructuring

Organisational restructuring in the form of downsizing, re-engineering, and layoffs over the past 25 years has turned the workplace into an environment where workers often feel demoralised (Brandt, 1996; Hamel & Prahalad, 1994) and where there is a growing inequality in wages (Beyer, 1999). This places pressure on companies to redress this sense of alienation employees feel.

Decline in Connectivity

Decline in connectivity within the community has placed pressure on organisations to fill the void. These days the workplace is being seen more often as a primary source of community for many people because of the decline in Western society of neighbourhoods, churches, civic groups, and extended

EMPLOYEE ENGAGEMENT
Not Just a Buzz Word!

'Employee Engagement' is one of those 'buzzwords' that you hear thrown about quite a bit ... but this is a buzzword that should be carefully thought about by every organisation.

A recent survey, reported by *Management Issues*, has some very interesting results pertaining to employee engagement. It reports the following findings:

A poll of 14,000 employees across 10 European countries by consultants Watson Wyatt has confirmed what a number of similar large-scale surveys have been suggesting over the past few years, namely that there is a vast reserve of untapped potential in the workplace in the form of uncommitted or actively disgruntled staff.

It also revealed that more than four out of 10 are actively considering leaving their current employer.

But whereas a 2007 poll of almost 90,000 workers by workplace consultancy Towers Perrin found that just 20% felt engaged with their work, Watson Wyatt found that only 13% (fewer than one in seven) displayed both strong commitment as well as having a good understanding of the part they could play in making their organisations successful, an understanding Watson Wyatt term 'line of sight'.

Only 13% of the workforce is fully engaged and trying to create value for their organisation. What are the other 87% of the workforce up to? Are they lazy? Incompetent? I highly doubt it; it's more likely that the organisation has done a poor job of describing how each person's contributions can affect the organisation.

The lack of employee engagement isn't just the fault of an organisation. There are people who are OK with doing 'just enough' to get by but an organisation should do everything in its power to ensure that employees are happy and that they understand how valuable they are to the organisation.

Whether you agree with the Towers Perrin study that found 20% engagement or Watson Wyatt's 13% engagement, I think you'd have to agree that there is a problem. How many co-workers/employees do you know that are actively seeking employment elsewhere? How many are really doing the best job that they can do?

How can an organisation engage employees? There is no simple answer. It takes long-term effort by both the organisation and the employee(s). I will provide a few basic thoughts on how to get started engaging more employees.

- Recruit and select right.
- Don't ask for (or expect) an employee to 'live to work' for you. Respect their life outside of the office.
- Hold all employees accountable. If an employee notices that there are 'sacred cows' that aren't accountable for their actions, their level of effort and engagement will drop.

- Offer flexible work hours.
- Offer job rotation opportunities. This would hold especially true to young/new employees. Keep people interested and don't let them get bored with their job.

Those are just a few thoughts. I'm sure there are many more.

Source: Brown, E.D. (2008), *Employee engagement — Not just a buzz word!* Retrieved June 15, 2008 from http://ericbrown.com/category/organization. Reproduced with permission.

families as principal places for feeling attached (Conger, 1994). For many, the workplace provides the only consistent link to other people and to the human needs of connection and contribution.

Rise in Eastern Philosophies

The rise in Eastern philosophies has encouraged Westerners to look at alternative forms of spirituality (Brandt, 1996). There is an increasing curiosity about Eastern philosophies. Philosophies such as Zen Buddhism and Confucianism, which encourage meditation and stress values such as loyalty to one's groups and discovering one's spiritual centre in any activity, are finding greater acceptance (Ashmos & Duchon, 2000).

Meaning of Life

Meaning of life is a core concern for older workers in particular. As ageing baby boomers move closer to life's greatest certainty — death — there is a growing interest in contemplating life's meaning (Brandt, 1996; Conger, 1994).

Global Competition

Global competition has shifted the focus from technical to human resources. The pressure of global competition has lead organisational leaders to recognise that employees' creative energies need a fuller expression at work as a way of combining 'head and heart' as a potential competitive advantage. Many workers want nourishment from their work as well.

From the perspective of employees, work increasingly defines their self-concept and connection to others (Bertram & Sharpe, 2000). Yet at the same time as 'new capitalism' alters the conditions of work, the individuals' connection to the workplace is becoming more tenuous (Sennett, 1998). Accelerated change and uncertainty is turning work from something that was once considered stable and predictable into a source of profound insecurity. People are now changing jobs more frequently, job security is an outdated concept of the last century and the workforce is becoming increasingly fragmented. So, on the one hand, people want more meaning from their work. On the other hand, employees are told there is 'no long-term'. These are undoubtedly confusing signals. So, while several trends in society have elevated the importance of the value of Human Spirit and Work, it does raise challenges for employees and employers and their respective pursuit of seeking and providing meaningful work.

Employees and Employers and Meaningful Work

Workers have a greater expectation of the role work plays in their lives. For a growing number of people, work is no longer simply a source of income, but also an important factor in generating and maintaining personal growth, and a source of wellbeing (Burton & Farris, 1999). The essence is that a job that provides only income, but no recognition, no learning, no compatibility with the rest of the social environment, is a job that cannot do much to enhance the wellbeing of the contemporary employee beyond 'paying the bills'. General wellbeing in work is associated with three broad conditions:

Working Environment
The foundation for the quality of working conditions is efficiency and justice in the allocation of resources. In particular, employees' perception of their immediate manager's trust in them can affect their job satisfaction (Lester & Brower, 2003).

Role in Production
Production in the organisation's goods and services and the role employee's play has a huge bearing on their well-being. Put simply, if workers feel their role is significant in generating productivity, this is likely to have a positive impact on their welfare. Alternatively, if they feel no connection with the organisation's productivity through their job, employees are more likely to see their work as insignificant.

Social Significance of Work
The social significance of work is becoming increasingly important. Work and the way it fits in with, and serves, other social activities contributes to meaning beyond financial rewards.

Heightened expectations of work, and the changing nature of the role work plays in people's lives, creates a more significant connection between the concepts of 'Human Spirit' and 'Work'. It is more important therefore for managers now to understand the specific conditions necessary for fostering wellbeing at work. This means maintaining working conditions that are safe and pleasant and creating jobs that contribute to individual and social wellbeing.

How do People Construct Meaning in Their Work?

Employees gain meaning from work on three levels (Isaksen, 2000).

Level 1: Role of Work

The first level concerns the abstract meaning of work. A general evaluation of the meaningfulness of work is concerned with the question: What is the meaning of work? From an employees' perspective, it maybe conceptualised as: What is the role work plays in creating meaning for me in my life?

Level 2: Role of a Specific Type of Work

The second level concerns the general meaning in a specific type of work. For example: What is the meaning of being a nurse?

Level 3: Role of a Specific Job

The third level is the personal meaning associated with work. For example: Do you find your work as a nurse meaningful?

The general and personal meanings in work in the second and third levels do not necessarily have the same content or the same depth. For example, a nurse may find the nursing profession meaningful as such (Level 2), and at the same time, find their own job as a nurse (Level 3) absolutely meaningless because the demands of their particular job tax his or her own capacity for working. Broadly speaking, workers bring to an organisation a general meaning about their vocation and through their interaction with a work environment develop a personal meaning about their day-to-day work.

According to Isaksen's (2000) meaningful work construct, the provision of adequate working conditions in a company cannot guarantee that staff will find their work meaningful. For instance, Isaksen (2000) researched workers performing highly repetitive work in a catering company, using three criteria: first, meaning through attachment to the workplace and its procedures; second, meaning through engagement in the social relations; and third, meaning through regarding work as a necessary part of a larger meaningful context. One of Isaksen's findings suggests that meaning or meaningless are not simple outcomes of some specific working conditions. Isaksen found that the construction of meaning was the result of workers' spontaneous and continuous effort and will. The creation of meaning was shaped by workers regardless of the kinds of workplace conditions they had to endure. All 28 employees in Isaksen's sample faced the same hindrances in their work. They had more or less the same type of repetitive work. Despite these obstacles, some still experienced work as meaningful overall, whereas others did not. Does this imply that companies should not bother making their organisations more conducive to stimulating and meaningful work? Will employees generate their own meaning independent of their working conditions?

There is little research evidence to support the direct relationship between satisfactory working conditions and the creation of stimulating and meaningful work. However, before managers start slashing their budgets, they should consider this: poor working conditions will create a level of frustration within the workforce. And this level of frustration will potentially lower the number of people who actually experience meaning in their work. In other words, staff who have few and very narrow interests when they start a job in a company that provides poor working conditions, are more likely to become disenchanted in their personal efforts to create meaning. Poor working conditions limit the potential for workers to develop meaning through their specific job. If individuals have low expectations of the likelihood of constructing meaning in any job beforehand, workers will tend to experience even greater difficulty obtaining it in a working environment that is rigid and lacks stimulation.

The degree of fit between individual and organisation depends partly on the aspirations for meaning the individual brings to the job. But also, just as importantly, is the degree of help or hindrance in the working climate and conditions provided by the company employing the individual. Put simply, meaning in work is derived from the interaction between worker and their workplace. It is important for managers to recognise that meaningfulness is not an inherent characteristic of a specific type of work or place of work. It is a subjective judgement made by an employee in his or her interface with a particular workplace.

Both the conditions of the workplace and personal characteristics of the employee have to be considered to understand why some people construct meaning, whereas others do not. Some people have personality traits that predispose them towards easily constructing meaning, whereas other people have personal characteristics that make it difficult for them to construct meaning in some or all types of work. Likewise, some workplaces offer optimal working conditions that facilitate the creation of meaning. Other workplaces offer poor working conditions that hinder the development of meaning.

Elements of Human Spirit and Work

As with the other seven values in the model, constructing the value of Human Spirit and Work is a cooperative endeavour between employer and employee. Figure 9.1 illustrates the interaction of core elements associated with the value of Human Spirit and Work in an organisation.

Figure 9.1 displays the three core elements associated with moving from a value of Human Dispirit and Work to a value of Human Spirit and Work. The three key responsibilities for an individual to find meaning in their organisational work are: a willingness to appreciate good working conditions, the capacity to find meaning in their daily work, and matching their interests with their job. From the perspective of the organisation, the value of Human Spirit and Work involves: the provision of good working conditions, opportunities for workers to construct meaning in their daily work, and policies and procedures that match worker interests with their job.

Conversely, managers need to be mindful that not fulfilling these elements is likely to have the potential to inhibit a meaningful work mindset in the workplace they are responsible for. Simply put, meaning in organisational work can be repressed from:

- poor working conditions
- a poor fit between worker's interests and job opportunities, or
- a lack of belief from managers in their capacity to provide employees with meaning in their work.

It is therefore important for managers to strategically intervene on these three levels as a starting point for enhancing the prospects that workers could be more likely to construct meaning, or at least not to be deterred from finding meaning in their work.

Is it possible for managers, operating from a traditional employment relationship mindset, to misuse this knowledge about the elements associated with the value of Human Spirit and Work to exploit workers? In other words, just give the employees a sense of meaningfulness and then exploit workers in other ways such as reducing wages and expect employees to work harder. Not likely (Isaksen, 2000). Employees sense exploitation quickly and this leads to a negative perception of the working environment, which results in a poor fit between person and environment, and consequently a lower sense of meaning in work. Nonetheless, a workplace operating out of a

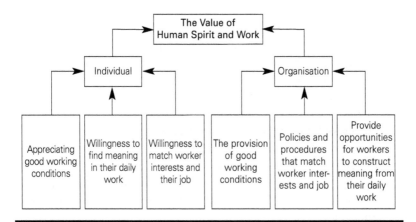

Figure 9.1 Elements of human spirit and work.

genuine quest for a new working relationship can invest in improving working conditions in a way that supports some workers' will to construct meaning in work and get at least some of this investment back in terms of a higher level of job fulfilment and employee engagement.

It is the employees' responsibility to find work that is stimulating and meaningful. As Noer (1997) puts it, 'there is power, excitement, and amazing productivity when our work is congruent with our personal mission and values'. Organisations, on the other hand, have an obligation to provide workers with the opportunities to participate in meaningful, stimulating tasks and projects wherever possible. As Noer (1997) states:

> If organisations can provide the spark that ignites [employees'] reservoir of human spirit and allow [them] to apply it to work that [they] perceive as meaningful, [the organisation has] unleashed a powerful competitive weapon of creative energy. (p. 217)

An important element associated with human spirit and work is a degree of flexibility, optimism, and creativity in matching organisational work to the individual's needs and interests.

Fully Engaged Employees

For more than 25 years, managers have been looking at the organisational factors that engage (or disengage) employees. Research studies have been conducted to determine the link, if any, between an engaged workforce and organisational performance. While some research remains inconclusive, there is a growing body of work suggesting a link between employee engagement and organisational performance. For instance, Buckingham and Coffman (1999) found employees who responded more favourably to survey questions on engagement, also worked in business units with higher levels of productivity, profit, retention, and customer satisfaction. Buckingham and Coffman also found significantly that the manager, not the remuneration and benefits, was the key to building and sustaining an engaged workforce.

Before addressing ways of implementing an employee engagement strategy, it would be helpful to define what the term 'engaged employee' means and how it is different from a 'disengaged employee'. Below are six descriptors of fully engaged employees:

1. Fully engaged employees are more dedicated and tend to exhibit that dedication through their work practices that are directed towards achieving the organisation's mission and goals.
2. Fully engaged employees are less likely to leave for other employment opportunities because they enjoy what they are doing and find their work meaningful.

3. Fully engaged employees like their work environment and the people they work with.

4. Fully engaged employees tell others about the organisation and are more likely to refer good employment candidates.

5. Fully engaged employees have a sense of pride and ownership in what they do within the organisation.

6. Fully engaged employees are more productive and contribute more significantly to the organisation's success.

In summary, there is a link between an organisation that values Human Spirit and Work and a fully engaged workforce.

Disengaged employees, on the other hand, are more likely to be costly to the organisation. For instance, disengaged employees are more likely to be absent from work for more frequent and longer periods of time, are less productive on average and therefore more of a liability to the company. While it is difficult to quantify the cost of disengaged employees, it is likely that they have a significantly negative impact on quality, safety, customer satisfaction, number of days off work, and missed opportunities in increased productivity.

Employment Engagement Strategy

One way to foster the value of Human Spirit and Work in a workplace is the implementation of an employee engagement strategy. To apply this strategy, the first step is to measure the current level of engagement within the company. Reputable employee engagement surveys can be a good tool for measuring the level of engagement of employees in an organisation. These kinds of surveys serve several useful purposes:

Communication of Values

The kind of surveys adopted by management communicates to the workforce the values that are considered important in that particular company. Employee engagement surveys signal to the workforce the importance and relevance of capturing the hearts and minds of workers in their organisational association.

Useful Data

Well-constructed and administered surveys have the potential to provide useful data. Employee engagement surveys can provide information to help employers understand the level of engagement between employees and the company. This information can be used to put in place strategies to improve employee commitment.

Benchmarking

Apart from being a useful source of data, survey results provide organisations with benchmarks. These benchmarks can be used to monitor annual progress towards predetermined goals. Externally, benchmarks provide baseline, historic and normative contrast so that the organisation can be compared with other organisations within and outside their particular industry.

Employee surveys, no matter how well crafted, do not in themselves create fully engaged employees. Effective feedback, action planning, implementation and follow-up of the survey results are the critical steps in formulating and executing an employment engagement strategy. By collecting survey data from an organisational setting, there is a raised expectation from survey participants that something constructive will be done with the results. Done properly, survey results can be a catalyst for change and organisational development.

The use of employee surveys as a management tool has significantly increased over the past 50 years. While most organisations are likely to see the value of implementing an employee survey process, many companies fail to obtain significant and sustainable value from surveying their staff. This is usually because they fail to follow through on the data collected.

In terms of administering the survey, all members of the organisation should be given the opportunity to participate. The survey should be structured to compare the perspectives of the three organisational strata: top management, middle management and workforce. For example, top management may collectively hold the view that employees are given ample opportunity to grow and develop. However, the workforce perspective could collectively hold a contrary view and the middle management perspective may be split on this issue. This kind of result should be a 'wake-up call' to top management that their growth and development strategies are not being perceived positively by the group they are intended for — the workforce. Therefore, by stratifying the organisation, survey results can be compared horizontally (between functions) and vertically (between organisational layers).

Action Planning

Action planning is the critical component of any survey process. Without following through and implementing action plans, managers fall short of identifying important opportunities to improve the overall health of the workforce. Some managers do not know what to do with the survey results, understand where to start, or how to identify important priorities for action planning.

An employee engagement strategy is an action planning approach that categorises survey items based on different levels of employee engagement. The tiers of engagement are based on well-founded motivational theories that suggest that certain factors need to be met before employees can achieve a level of satisfaction with their job and the company.

Survey items can be divided into three progressive tiers, each tier addressing higher individual and organisational needs in the context of the value of Human Spirit and Work. Well-established models of human functioning and employee motivation, such as Maslow's (1954) Hierarchical Theory of Needs (physiological, safety, belonging, esteem and self-actualisation), Alderfer's (1969) ERG Model (existence, relatedness and growth) and Herzberg's (1966) Two Factor Theory (hygiene and motivators) form the basis for making sense of the data from a employee engagement survey. All three theoretical models describe different levels of fulfilment starting with basis or 'necessary for survival' needs. While the employee engagement strategic model does not mirror these theorists' ideas directly, it does apply the same principle of a hierarchical structure and the need for fulfilment or satisfaction along different dimensions.

Figure 9.2 illustrates the employee engagement strategy model. Explanations of the three dimensions (basic, intermediate and advanced) of employee engagement in Figure 9.2 are outlined below.

Basic Engagement Needs: Working Conditions

The first tier is the categorisation that addresses basic needs in a job to enable engagement. These basic needs are the starting point for instilling the value of Human Spirit and Work from an organisational perspective. Basic items are fundamental to any reasonable job in an organisation and range from safe working conditions to being treated fairly. Most employees take these basic engagement issues for granted, however, if left unmet or unfulfilled, employees are likely to become fundamentally dispirited with their work and the company.

Basic engagement factors provide a solid foundation for action planning. Organisational leaders can use the results of their employee survey to work on established survey dimensions such as quality, job satisfaction, environment, health and safety, communications and management practices.

Intermediate Engagement Needs: Growth and Development

The second tier is a categorisation of items that addresses the growth and development needs of the individual. These items make up the intermediate category of engagement. Once the basics have been met, employees are likely to focus on these intermediate factors. They range from learning and performance development to pride in the company's products and service. If intermediate

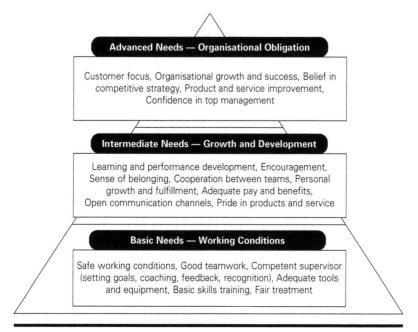

Figure 9.2 Dimensions of employee engagement model.

factors are fulfilled, employees' engagement with their work and the company has the potential to improve beyond the basic level.

The value of Human Spirit and Work is therefore likely to be more deeply embedded within the culture of the organisation once growth and development needs of the individual have been identified and fulfilled.

Advanced Engagement Needs: Organisational Obligation

The third tier is a categorisation of items that addresses organisational obligation needs. These items make up the advanced engagement category. To exceed employees' expectations of gaining meaning from their work, advanced factors need to be addressed. They range from customer focus to confidence in top management. An important distinction between the first two tiers and the advanced tier is the focus of the employee. In the basic and intermediate needs, the focus is on the individual and his or her welfare. These needs are fundamental to all jobs and the growth and development of the individual as a person and employee. The advanced needs, on the other hand, are focused on external factors such as the customer and the employee's relationship with the organisation-at-large.

A complete commitment to the value of Human Spirit and Work cannot ignore the surroundings of the employee. His or her relationship with the customer and top management is likely to have a significant bearing on the extent to which they find meaning in their working environment.

While this employee engagement strategy follows the hierarchical structure of theories of motivation, one level does not need to be completely fulfilled before moving on to the next level. It simply identifies three tiers of employee engagement. However, in order to improve survey results, managers need to take a look at the basic items first and, if low scores or deficiencies are evident, begin working on those items. For instance, demonstrating how much a company is doing for a community cause (advanced item) is fine, but it will not help to engage employees if their work equipment does not function properly or if the employee does not feel valued and respected. Eventually a deficiency in the basic tier will mean that the employee will either leave the company or retreat in some other way, such decreasing productivity or increasing absenteeism. Strategically, it makes sense to work on the basic tier needs first in terms of priority.

The use of the three tiers of employee engagement assists the organisation to organise their priorities in terms of employee engagement. Therefore, low scores on basic items should receive a higher priority for action planning. Action plans to counter low scores on intermediate issues should be dealt with once basic items have been largely addressed. Advanced items should receive priority once basic and intermediate items had been addressed. Companies with fully engaged employees devote time and resources to improving the items in the advanced tier because most of the items in the basic and intermediate tiers have already been fulfilled and appear as strengths in the survey results. So this tiered approach is a convenient way for managers to strategise their employee and organisational needs. The end result is to embed the value of Human Spirit and Work within the culture of the company.

A project-based team should be set up to analyse the data and make recommendations. As defined in Chapter 8, a project-based team should be a cross-functional team that is reasonably representative of the organisation-at-large. The 'Employee Engagement Project Team' has an important role to play in advancing the value of Human Spirit and Work within the organisation.

Conclusion

For the value of Human Spirit and Work and in line with the New Employment Relationship Model in Chapter 4, the appropriate individual responsibility is to find work that is meaningful. This mindset is likely to be present when employees appreciate good working conditions when they are present in the workplace, a willingness to match their interests with job opportunities, and motivation to find meaning in their daily work. From the organisational perspective, the responsibility is to provide work (wherever possible) that is meaningful. By fulfilling the developmental needs of the employee, the organisation is accounting for their role. These elements are likely to contribute to an organisation that values human spirit and work.

■ Reflective Questions for Managers

In relation to the case study on pages 116–117, consider the following questions:

1. How do these two survey results compare with your organisation?

2. What can managers do to improve what Watson Wyatt terms 'line of sight'?

3. Is a happy employee necessarily an engaged employee? Discuss.

4. What else can you add to Brown's list to contribute to employee engagement?

Consider how the following questions relate to your own career:

1. Describe a time in your career when you felt very highly engaged in your work. What was it that caused you to feel that way? What were the important factors?

2. Describe a time in your career when you felt actively disengaged from your work. What was it that caused you to feel that way? What were the important factors?

3. Isn't it inevitable that employees will generally become more and more disengaged with their organisation?

4. If an employee has a negative view of work in general (corresponding with Isaksen's Level 1), is there anything an organisation can do to engage that employee?

5. In practical terms, what can managers do to match worker interests with organisational work?

6. Is it true that unskilled workers are generally likely to be more disengaged than skilled workers?

7. What influence do you think skills in managing people have in creating engagement? Give examples.

■ Top 10 Key Points from Chapter 9

1. Spirituality at work is about employees having their spiritual needs nourished through their work.

2. This growing interest in spirituality at work can be understood in relation to several trends in Western society.

3. For a growing number of people, work is no longer simply a source of income, but also an important factor in generating and maintaining personal growth, and a source of wellbeing.

4. General wellbeing in work is associated with three broad conditions: working environment, role in production, and the social significance of work.

5. People construct meaning from work on three levels: (1) role of work, (2) role of a specific type of work, and (3) role of a specific job.

6. Both the conditions of the workplace and personal characteristics of the employee have to be considered to understand why some people construct meaning.

7. The three elements associated with the value of Human Spirit and Work are good working conditions, the capacity for employees to find meaning in their daily work, and matching interests with the job.

8. One way to foster the value of Human Spirit and Work in a workplace is the implementation of an employee engagement strategy.

9. An employee engagement strategy serves several useful purposes, namely, it communicates the particular values associated with Human Spirit and Work, it can provide useful data, and it provides a set of benchmarks to measure against.

10. An action plan can categorise employee requirements in hierarchical formation between basis, intermediate, and advanced needs.

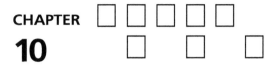
Commitment Replacing Loyalty
From Loyalty to Commitment

> Today, employees not only do not expect to work for decades for the same company, they do not necessarily want to.

The value of Commitment is not the same as the value of Human Spirit and Work. Although they share similar characteristics, they have different emphases. Organisational loyalty has been largely replaced by organisational commitment in the new employment relationship paradigm. Employees need, more than ever, to continually develop their career skills to remain employable. Simultaneously, companies can use these newly gained employee skills in the short term to maintain and enhance their performance in the increasingly competitive marketplace. The value of Commitment can therefore be conceptualised as a practical exchange process between individual and organisation. From the employees' point of view, organisational commitment can be based on the psychological attachment associated with desire to stay, the cost of leaving, or the obligation to remain with the organisation. A number of practical strategies can be applied by managers to generate these emotional states in their staff. Some of these approaches include:

- aligning career and organisational goals
- designing work that has variety and autonomy
- nurturing good relationship with colleagues and organisational leaders
- matching individual and organisational values
- assisting employees to balance their work and home responsibilities.

Specific working conditions in these areas can be negotiated and made part of an enterprise agreement.

Commitment Replacing Loyalty

On the surface, it seems apparent that the value of Human Spirit and Work and a meaningful work construct (discussed in Chapter 9) is the same thing as the value of Commitment. Even though there are elements that overlap, the values of Human Spirit and Work and Commitment have different emphases. The value of Human Spirit and Work stresses the relationship between the individual and his or her work and its associated conditions. More broadly, the value of Commitment is concerned with the link between the individual and the organisation. To illustrate the distinction, an employee may find their work meaningful but still not be committed to the organisation. Conversely, a person can have a sense of commitment to the organisation, but not find their work particularly meaningful. It is in the best interests of individual and organisation to cultivate both values.

Few business leaders would deny the importance of organisational loyalty; perhaps fewer still believe they can achieve it the way they once did. After all, the lifetime contract between the individual and organisation expired long ago. Employees who have embraced the mindsets of the new psychological contract are more likely to display loyalty to their careers first before their current employer.

Today, employers not only do not expect to work for decades for the same company, they do not necessarily want to. Progressive thinking employees are largely disillusioned with the very idea of loyalty to organisations. But, at the same time, they do not really want to shift employers every 2 to 3 years for their entire careers. Similarly, companies would grind to a halt if they had to replace large portions of the workforce on a similar schedule.

So where does this leave the employer/employee partnership? Is there a way for both employers and employees to strike a new agreement when it comes to the notion of loyalty; one that gives organisations the focus and expertise they need to compete in the marketplace and one that gives employees the career development opportunities they demand? The answer to this question is yes, but only if companies are willing to rethink how they define loyalty and how they manage people.

Employers require focused and skilled employees. Employees require the capacity to maintain their employability through career development opportunities. The two concepts of organisational performance and career focus are not mutually exclusive. This is especially so when the skills that a person masters to further his or her own career are also what the company needs in the short-term. Sentimental loyalty must give way to pragmatic commitment.

The value of Commitment is a more practical value than a value of Loyalty in the modern workplace. They do not mean the same thing, nor are they interrelated. A person can be committed to something or someone

Assessing Employee Commitment

Use this diagnostic tool to assess your employees' commitment levels. You can administer this brief survey to all employees who have spent more than a year working in your company. The instructions on administering the survey are at the beginning of the questionnaire, and the process of interpreting the survey ratings is explained at the end of the survey.

Hello colleague,

We're doing a study as part of a feedback exercise to understand how well we're doing in our business growth.

- This survey needs to be filled out anonymously. Don't write your name or identify yourself.
- Honestly and rapidly rate the 20 statements below by applying each statement to your own perception.
- Rate these statements by considering the current situation prevailing in the company — *not* what you think should be the situation.
- Return the survey after covering all the statements.

Statement	Tick if applicable			
	True	True sometimes	True rarely	Not true
1. I believe that leaders in our organisation encourage participation at multiple levels.				
2. I see that leaders frequently communicate about how the work being done by the company is connected to a larger market trend.				
3. I believe that leaders and managers take the lead in motivating employees toward reaching goals.				
4. Leaders are candid — I hear them talking about their professional failures, and they illustrate these with lessons learned.				
5. Leaders have tolerated and encouraged objective analysis of my professional failures.				
6. I find that lack of commitment is treated sensitively and uniformly at first and firmly later if not successful.				
7. I feel assured of my market worth; I see a clear roadmap to my career aspirations if I decide to move out of this company.				

Statement	Tick if applicable			
	True	True sometimes	True rarely	Not true
8. I believe that employees feel charged to achieve goals set.				
9. We participate in setting our goals.				
10. I think most of the employees are happy about the company and would like to continue here even if the career growth is slower.				
11. The company assesses us on what else we can do, and we are encouraged to undertake such activities.				
12. I regularly find that leaders and managers maintain high activity levels within the company to keep the employees charged.				
13. I believe leaders and managers proactively work toward building positive publicity on the company through the media.				
14. I feel like talking about my team and company at my home and with my industry friends.				
15. I strongly recommend that my industry colleagues apply for jobs in my company.				
16. I think most of the employees are happy about the career opportunities that the company offers and don't feel the need to look outside for a similar career or role.				
17. I would be comfortable representing my company or team in external forums.				
18. I see that employees have grown well in the company.				
19. I am happy about the career opportunities I have and the company's growth and the nature of its teams.				
20. I believe the reward and recognition systems in the company have been fair to me.				

Thank you! Please return this form to the administrator.

RATING COMPILATION KEY:

- If the respondent has ticked in 'True,' count 20 points.
- If the respondent has ticked in 'True sometimes,' count 15 points.
- If the respondent has ticked in 'True rarely,' count 7 points.
- If the respondent has ticked in 'Not true,' count 4 points.

Based on the above, provide the points and add them all to arrive at a total.

If the total is:

- More than 320, group the employee under the category of 'Committed' employee.
- Between 250 and 320, group the employee under the category of 'Concerned' employee.
- Between 175 and 250, group the employee under the category of 'Emotionally Separated' employee.
- Less than 175, group the employee as a 'Lost Case' employee.

At an organisational level, measure the percentage of employees falling under the above categories. A typical indicative benchmark for healthy commitment is indicated below. Gauge your employee commitment levels against this benchmark:

For an organisation to exhibit healthy employee commitment levels:

- The percentage of 'Committed' employees should be more than 60%.
- The percentage of 'Concerned' employees should be no more than 15% to 20%.
- The percentage of 'Emotionally Separated' employees should be no more than 10% to 15%.
- The percentage of 'Lost Case' employees should be no more than 10% to 15%.

Source: Tech Republic (2008). *Diagnostic tool for assessing employee commitment.* Used with permission of TechRepublic.com. Copyright © 2009. All rights reserved.

without being loyal. For example, a student can be committed to completing a university degree without being loyal to the institution bestowing the degree. Similarly, a person can display loyalty without commitment. For example, someone can be faithful and devoted to a person without committing to a particular course of action they may adhere to. In other words, a person may claim loyalty to someone, but can at times break their promises to them. This, of course, occurs regularly. It therefore follows that the idea of displaying organisational loyalty does not necessarily translate into a strong commitment to achieve organisational outcomes. Equally, if an employee demonstrates commitment to achieving organisational outcomes, it does not necessarily follow that they are loyal to the institution or company. Given a choice between the values of Loyalty and Commitment, managers should choose committed employees to assist the firm to achieve its organisational outcomes. At the same time, it is in the best interests of the employee to seek commitment from the company to support them to achieve their personal objectives.

Another mistaken assumption is that loyalty means 'forever'. But even when companies cannot retain a top talent, it does not mean that the departing employee was not committed to the company in the short term. As a university student expressed it: 'It's like dating: You can be faithful to the person you're seeing now while you're involved with him or her, but that doesn't mean you won't move on to dating someone else later'. In a similar way, a company should not (and increasingly cannot) strive to keep all employees forever. Instead of loyalty, modern corporations ought to be cultivating mutual commitment between employer and employee, albeit, for a limited timeframe.

Defining the Value of Commitment

The value of Commitment is defined as the employee's psychological attachment to the organisation. It can be contrasted with other work-related attitudes such as Job Satisfaction (an employee's feeling about their job) and Organisational Identification (the degree to which an employee experiences a 'sense of oneness' with their company). Although they are all different concepts, there is some relationship between commitment, satisfaction and identification.

Organisational scientists have developed many definitions of organisational commitment, and numerous scales to measure it. Exemplary of this work is Meyer and Allen's (1991) model of commitment, which was developed to integrate numerous definitions of commitment that had proliferated in the literature. According to Meyer and Allen's model, there are three states of mind that can characterise an employee's commitment to the organisation. These can be summarised as:

Affective Commitment (Desire)

Affective Commitment is defined as the employee's emotional attachment to the organisation. As a result, he or she strongly identifies with the goals of the company and desires to remain a part of the organisation. In other words, the employee commits to the organisation because he or she 'wants to'. When firms help workers acquire new skills that support their professional and personal advancement, they can potentially win the commitment from those employees to achieving organisational goals. The transaction is also likely to be attractive to potential employees. Paradoxically, employers can instil a sense of commitment from workers by helping them 'grow out' of their jobs, into new ones within the same company, or in another company.

Continuance Commitment (Cost)

Continuance Commitment is defined as the employee's attachment to the organisation because of the perceived costs of leaving to work somewhere else. The individual commits to the organisation because he or she sees high personal costs of losing organisational membership, including economic losses (such as superannuation accruals) and social costs (membership ties with co-workers). Simply put, the employee remains with a company because he/she 'has to'.

Normative Commitment (Obligation)

Normative Commitment is defined as the employee's attachment, due to obligation. The individual commits to and remains with a company because of feelings of indebtedness. For instance, the company may have invested resources in training an employee who then feels a sense of obligation to put forth effort on the job and stay with the organisation to 'repay the debt'. It may also reflect an internalised norm, developed before the person joins the organisation through family or other socialisation processes, that one should be loyal to one's organisation. In other words, the employee stays with the organisation because he or she 'ought to'.

In summary, Meyer and Allen's model shows that the value of Commitment can be characterised by different mindsets: desire, cost and obligation. Employees with a strong Affective Commitment stay because they want to, those with strong Normative Commitment stay because they feel they ought to, and those with strong Continuance Commitment stay because they have to.

Elements of Commitment

In line with the other seven values in the model, applying the value of Commitment is a joint venture between employer and employee. Figure 10.1 shows the three core elements involved with the value of Commitment.

Figure 10.1 illustrates the three core elements in making the transition from a value of Loyalty to Commitment. The three key individual mindsets are: a desire to acquire organisationally-sponsored professional and personal skills, a perceived cost in leaving the organisation, and a sense of obligation to the organisation. From the organisation perspective, the appropriate response is a commitment to providing professional and personal skills opportunities, financial and social inducements, and investing resources in developing employees.

These elements of the value of Commitment are not mutually exclusive from an employee's point of view: an individual can simultaneously be committed to an organisation in an affective, normative, and continuance sense, at varying levels of intensity. This idea led Meyer and Herscovitch (2001) to

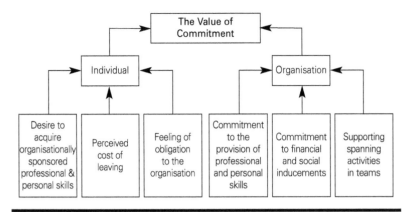

Figure 10.1 Elements of commitment.

argue that at any time, an employee has a 'commitment profile' that reflects high or low levels of all three of these mindsets, and that different profiles have different effects on workplace behaviour such as job performance, absenteeism, and the chance that they will leave.

Their research shows that employees who want to stay (Desire) tend to perform at a higher level than those who do not. Employees who remain out of obligation also tend to outperform those who feel no such obligation, but the effect on performance is not as strong as that observed for Desire. Finally, employees who have to stay primarily to avoid losing something of value (Cost — e.g., benefits, seniority) often have little incentive to do anything more than is required to retain their position. So, not all forms of commitment are alike.

What are some practical steps managers can take to increase the level of the various dimensions of commitment from employees?

Aligning Career Growth with Company Goals

Aligning career growth with company goals can be an effective way of impacting on Affective, Normative, and Continuance Commitment. When a company helps its employees' develop expertise that furthers their professional and personal development, research suggests that employees generally feel a sense of obligation and perhaps desire to assist the organisation to achieve its outcomes (Eisenberger, Fasolo, & Davis-La Mastro, 1990; Shore & Wayne, 1993; Wayne, Shore, & Liden, 1997). If the program of study is ongoing, the employee may also perceive a significant cost in leaving before the development program is completed. As such, a properly executed and relevant skills development program has the potential of aligning employee career development and organisational commitment.

How does an organisation achieve this alignment? A practical starting point is a genuine discussion between the manager and his or her staff on the employee's career goals. It is also helpful, wherever possible, for managers to assist their people to identify a link between their own professional and personal goals and the company's goals. When people understand the larger business framework in which the company is operating, they can potentially more easily define ways to advance their own careers within the context of the organisation.

It should also be acknowledged that frank and frequent dialogue about careers can decrease commitment. Employees may part ways with their employer when they discover that they cannot achieve their career goals. However, on balance, honest and regular dialogue between managers and staff is more likely to be beneficial to both the individual and organisation.

Some companies use assessment tools and career coaches to identify employees' strengths and decide how to best leverage those talents for the company's good. These companies also encourage employees to initiate conversations about how their strengths and talents might be best used in the organisation. When employees are using their strengths, they find their work more satisfying, and feel that they are supporting their own career paths. As an illustration, a staff accountant at Choctawatchee Electric Cooperative, Inc. (CHELCO), a Florida-based electricity cooperative benefited from assessment tools and career coaching (Johnson, 2005). When the accountant expressed interest in a management position, her coach reminded her that her assessment indicated strengths in areas other than management. The accountant then acknowledged that her interest in management stemmed primarily from the managerial position's earning potential. She could not see any other way to increase her earning capacity beyond leaving to work somewhere else. Based on her interest and commitment to furthering her career, as well as on her educational background and strengths, including attention to detail, adherence to company policies and procedures, the company offered her the position of revenue analyst. In this new role, she provided more value to the organisation and took on new challenges. She also increased her earning potential because the new position rated several grades higher than her former position as an accountant. Aligning career goals with company goals has the potential to positively affect all three forms of Meyer and Allen's Commitment model.

Design Work With Variety and Autonomy

Jobs that provide variety and the freedom to make decisions and mistakes can engender commitment from those filling them. Allowing staff to take ownership of projects gives them the opportunity to develop new skills and, just as importantly, the chance to demonstrate what they are capable of. Designing work with variety and freedom takes some organisational discipline. Still, at the very least, managers ought to let employees know how and when they can exercise choice in their work role. As a simple and practical illustration, a public relations firm may use their weekly staff meeting to share responsibility. They can use the meeting to invite expressions of interest from staff to project manage key accounts. This strategy provides staff with variety and choices in the work that may interest them.

Focus on Relationships

For many employees, commitment is fostered through good relationships with supervisors and colleagues. Anecdotal evidence suggests that one of the main reasons that people leave a company is not inadequate pay or benefits; it is usually due to their difficult day-to-day relationship with their immediate superior. Managers would do well to realise that positive working relationships with employees is a cornerstone for instilling a sense of commitment from employees. Moreover, fostering supportive relationships among employees in a team or unit can generate a sense of obligation towards the organisation. Apart from the manager/staff relationships, peer relationships can, and often do, have a major bearing on Continuance Commitment for employees.

Matching Individual and Organisational Values

The reconciling of employee and organisational values is another way to increase organisational commitment. A good example of linking staff and organisational values occurs at Medtronic, a medical device developer in Minneapolis (Johnson, 2005). Medtronic broadcasts to its 30,000 employees worldwide stories of patients who have benefited from the company's products. In the words of a senior executive:

> Our people end up feeling personally involved in our company's mission to restore people to full life. They can see the end result of their work. Many of them are profoundly moved by the patients' stories.

The matching of personal and organisational values builds Affective Commitment. To quantify Affective Commitment, by putting a human face on its mission, Medtronic has achieved employee-retention rates above the industry average. The company gets an impressive 95% favourable response rate to the employee survey item: 'I have a clear understanding of Medtronic's mission', and a 93% favourable response to another statement: 'The work I do supports the Medtronic mission'. Of course, a company's mission is especially compelling when patients' lives are at stake. But companies in any industry can find creative ways to help employees see how their daily work has a personal impact on their lives of their customers. Employees in these circumstances commit to the organisation because they 'want to'.

Work–Life Balance

Another important area impacting more and more on organisational commitment is addressing challenges associated with balancing work and home responsibilities (Stephens & Feldman, 1997). Put simply, implementing practical strategies to overcome conflict between work and home is a means by which companies can retain their core employees (Capelli, 2000). Although career scholars have long been writing that career success cannot be measured simply in terms of advancement (Schein, 1978), it is only relatively recently that a significant number of employees are beginning to define career success in terms of work–home balance rather than hierarchical rank (Stephens & Feldman, 1997). Some organisations are notable for their efforts in providing flexible scheduling, childcare facilities and other support services, although most companies have generally not developed an overall policy for dealing with the changing nature of employees' time demands. Future-orientated organisations are likely then to develop comprehensive programs to assist employees to manage work–home conflicts, rather than cobble together ad hoc experimental initiatives. After all, this shift is in keeping with the current realities of a market-driven workforce and the imperative to attract and keep top performers (Capelli, 2000).

Advantages to Employers and Employees

Given what managers are aware of increased worker mobility, it is challenging for companies to gauge just how much effort they should put into promoting the idea of organisational commitment. Notwithstanding this dilemma, it is beyond doubt that a committed workforce saves the firm money in the form of lower recruiting costs, fewer stranded clients, and less downtime. Individuals and organisations are both more likely to benefit from encouraging knowledge acquisition and sharing. Organisations are motivated to foster commitment in their employees as a way of achieving stability and reduce costly turnover. It is commonly believed that committed employees will also work harder and be more likely to 'go the extra mile' to achieve organisational objectives.

From a pragmatic point of view, the more unique and organisationally relevant a person's expertise, the greater the likelihood that a staff member will be able to exert influence within that organisation. The ability to exert influence is likely to be appealing to self-motivated employees.

In summary, increased Affective, Continuance and Normative employee commitment is based on number of employment factors. These factors include, but are not limited to:

- sufficiency of pay, benefits and rewards
- family oriented policies and actions
- quality of the supervisory relationship
- favourable developmental training and experiences
- promotions
- clearly stated guidelines defining appropriate work behaviour and job demands
- participation in goal setting
- receipt of performance feedback
- supportive communications with immediate supervisors and upper management
- procedural justice in performance-appraisal decisions
- evaluative and objective measures of performance.

Of course the reverse is true; commitment will erode if these factors are violated in some way by managers.

Enterprise Agreement

From an organisational perspective, the key question for employers is: 'What can we as an enterprise do to help employees become more committed to assisting us to achieve organisational goals?' From an employee's perspective, the answer to this question may be: 'I am willing to commit to these goals if the organisation is committed to assisting me to achieve my personal objectives'. This exchange process can formulate the basis of an Enterprise Agreement (EA) between the employees and the organisation.

Any of the factors listed above are open for negotiation between employees and their employer at the enterprise level. There are widely differing systems of bargaining over pay and conditions throughout the industrialised world. However, despite these differences there is a widely observed trend towards the decentralisation of bargaining; that is, bargaining and agreement at the business level. Decentralised bargaining structures are also typically argued to be conducive to more flexible employment arrangements (Wooden & Sloan, 1998).

An EA consists of an industrial agreement between either:

- an employer and a trade union acting on behalf of employees, or
- an employer and employees acting for themselves.

On the one hand an EA, at least in principle, benefits employers, as they allow for improved flexibility in such areas as ordinary working hours, flat rates of hourly pay, and performance-related conditions. On the other hand, industrial agreements benefit workers, as they usually provide higher pay, bonuses, additional leave and enhanced entitlements than an award does.

A worthwhile EA should address some, or all, of the issues listed above. If the EA is perceived fairly by both the individual and organisation, it is likely to enhance commitment from both parties in the employment relationship. In exchange terms, the employee commits to assisting the organisation achieve its output goals, and, in return, receives the opportunity to achieve specified favourable pay and working conditions.

Conclusion

With reference to the New Employment Relationship Model in Chapter 4, the matching individual accountability for the value of Commitment is to commit to assisting the organisation achieve its outcomes. This mindset is likely to be present when employees have a desire to acquire organisation-ally-sponsored professional and personal skills, perceive a loss in leaving, and feel a sense of obligation to the organisation. From the organisational per-spective, the accountability is to commit to assisting employees to achieve their personal objectives. This can be achieved by committing to the provi-sion of a professional and personal skills program for employees, providing financial and social inducements, and investing resources in developing employees. These individual and organisation responsibilities are the elements that contribute to an organisational culture that values Commitment over Loyalty.

■ Reflective Questions for Managers

1. Do you think it is easier in some industries or cultures to engender loyalty from staff? Can you give examples?

2. What has your experience been with enterprise agreements? Have those experiences been positive or negative?

3. Which of the three elements of the value of Commitment (Desire, Cost, Obligation) do you think is the easiest and hardest to culti-vate in staff? Explain.

4. Some organisations accept that people will not be committed and that high staff turnover is a fact of life in the modern workplace. In response to this, managers implemented systems and processes that made it easier for new employees to be inducted

into the business at minimum time and cost. Do you accept this proposition?

5. Can you think of an example where an employee has stayed with an organisation because of the professional and personal development they are receiving from the company?

6. Do you think that the erosion of organisational loyalty is a reflection of contemporary society in general?

■ Top 10 Key Points from Chapter 10

1. The value of Commitment is concerned with the link between the individual and the organisation.

2. When the skills that a person masters to further his or her own career are sponsored by the organisation and fulfils the company's needs in the short-term then this benefits both entities in the employment relationship.

3. The value of Commitment is a more practical value than Loyalty in the contemporary workplace.

4. The value of Commitment is defined as the employee's psychological attachment to the organisation.

5. There are three kinds of Commitment: Affective, Continuance, and Normative.

6. Affective Commitment is defined as the employee's emotional attachment to the organisation.

7. Continuance Commitment is defined as the employee's attachment to the organisation because of the perceived costs of leaving to work somewhere else.

8. Normative Commitment is defined as the employee's attachment due to obligation.

9. There are several ways to gain greater commitment from employees to the organisation. These include: aligning career growth with company goals; design work with variety and autonomy; a focus on relationships; matching individual and organisational values; and addressing challenges associated with balancing work and home responsibilities.

10. An enterprise agreement is a useful way of negotiating and agreeing on ways to create a more compatible fit between the individual and organisation.

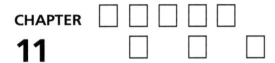

11

Developing the Whole Person
From Training to Learning and Development

> A multidimensional approach to learning and development is more likely to meet the growth needs of workers and, at the same time, assist in contributing to organisational outputs.

Although all eight values in the model embrace components of HRD, the value of Learning and Development is about the philosophical orientation of a company's approach to learning and development. There are three prominent theoretical positions on HRD. The most common perspective, likely to predominate in traditional organisations, is the production-centred approach. This strategy is concerned with the development of job-specific skills and competencies. The person-centred approach, on the other hand, is an HRD philosophy that espouses that learning should be primarily about developing the person. By focusing on the person rather than the job, this personal development approach will develop the individual and probably indirectly enhance job and organisational performance. The third dimension of HRD is referred to as the principled problem-solving approach. This strategy is based on equipping employees with the necessary skills and knowledge to solve unanticipated predicaments arising from their work. Each approach has strengths and shortcomings. It therefore follows that a multidimensional approach has the capacity to emphasise the strong points of each orientation and minimise their weaknesses. Also, an adherence to a broad HRD framework is likely to align the needs and interests of the individual and organisation. This eclectic orientation moves the organisation beyond a value of Training to a value of Learning and Development.

Defining the Value of Learning and Development

There are elements related to HRD in all eight values of the model. Specifically, the value of Learning and Development cuts across the values of Flexible Employment, Customer Focus, Performance Focus, Project-Based Work, Human Spirit and Work, Commitment, and Open Information. The discussions on the other seven values are primarily concerned with operation-related learning and development interventions. However, the overall philosophical dimension of HRD is an important consideration for a company. So this chapter is about the overarching strategic perspective of people development. In other words, the chapter explores the overriding assumptions of HRD in an organisational context. A company's viewpoint about HRD can explain its premise about human nature.

The literature advocates three predominant philosophical approaches to HRD. These three dimensions are commonly referred to as the:

- production-centred approach
- person-centred approach
- principled problem-solving approach.

Each approach has a particular orientation and has certain advantages and disadvantages.

Production-Centred Approach

The traditional method commonly adopted in most organisations is the production-centred approach (Kuchinke, 1999; Maitland, 1994; Rummler & Brache, 1990; Stryker & Statham, 1985). A production-centred approach emphasises the performance perspective for organisationally-sponsored learning and development programs. The rationale for this approach stresses a direct link between training that focuses on enhancing current job skills and organisational performance. Consequently, the primary motive for a company adopting this approach is to develop employees' current job skills to directly improve overall production and productivity. Of the three approaches to HRD, the production-centred approach is the one most directly related to the specifics of an employee's job performance.

For example, training programs that improve a worker's mastery of the use of machines, technology, or processes that are connected directly to the job an employee does are production-centred. Production-centred learning is likely to have a direct pay-off in terms of increasing the productivity of the employee. It therefore follows that the motive is a direct return on investment in terms of increasing the efficiency and effectiveness of employees in their day-to-day job function. The measure of success of training based on the production-centred approach is whether or not the learning experience directly translates into a more technically proficient employee.

CASE STUDY

Catering Corporation

Catering Corporation is a medium-sized enterprise employing approximately 250 people. It provides pre-prepared fresh and frozen foods to establishments that have a catering or food service function. The range of clients includes fast-food chains, family restaurants, supermarkets, hospitals and nursing homes. Its product range includes prepared vegetables, salads, soups, sauces and wet dishes (casseroles, stews etc.).

There is a five-person management team: general manager, sales manager, production manager and scientific services manager.

The production area has recently negotiated its second workplace agreement in which the staff agreed to productivity increases generated by changes in work practices. It is due to be effective in 3 months time. The major change is the introduction of multiskilled career paths, with steps in the career path tied to the acquisition of work-related competencies that facilitate multiskilling. The general manager and production manager had intended that the multiskilling concept be applied to the production crew only. The staff in the stores department believed they could also multiskill across into production, and this was negotiated into the agreement by the union. The enterprise agreement also indicated that the production staff would move into a team-based approach to work. The manager is keen to implement this team approach as soon as possible as it will enable him to remove the positions of leading hand/supervisor and shift supervisor, resulting in obvious cost savings. The union saw no problem with this move, provided that the new multiskilled career path enabled the displaced to recoup their lost pay through progression based on competencies. The final agreement enabled all staff to build their competencies to full multiskilled status through access to appropriate recognised training. Hypothetically, through training, all production staff will be able to access the highest pay point in the career ladder. The appeal of the new agreement to the production manager is his idea that he will be able to reduce staff, believing that multiskilled staff will reduce the need for total staff numbers — he hopes that 40 positions can be saved in the first year of the new enterprise agreement's operation.

The HR manager is concerned that a key problem in building effective teams on the production floor is the diverse ethnic mix and the language problems. She also has concern about the literacy level on the basis of the forms she has people fill in from time to time: overtime claims, leave forms, and so on. She would also like to see the sales staff work in a more integrated way with the scientific services staff. She suspects that the innovative ideas that clients suggest to sales reps are not being conveyed to the test kitchens. In discussions she has had with their stores manager they have often raised the idea of integrating sales and delivery processes to improve client service. She would also like to have the sales staff take over full responsibility for dealing with clients' problems so that she can focus on the HR aspects of the business.

The scientific services manager is concerned that members of the sales team promise the clients things that are technically impossible, and that the production manager doesn't control quality sufficiently in the preparation areas. The result is a higher than acceptable number of client complaints that everybody blames on her team, which, in her opinion, is a model that the rest of the organisation should follow. The scientific services team has developed an understanding of the important contribution that each member plays in the work processes, and has also made significant attempts to understand the problems faced by production in turning their recipes into production realities. They have also offered to accompany sales reps when dealing with 'problem' clients, but their offer has been declined.

Source: Kellie, D. (1999). Human resource development: Improving performance at Catering corporation. In G. Dessler, J. Griffiths, B. Lloyd-Walker, & A. Williams (Eds.), *Human resource management: Theory, skills application* (pp. 378–379). Melbourne: Prentice Hall.

Author's Note: All reasonable attempts to locate the copyright owner have been unsuccessful. Any reasonable claims by the copyright owner will be settled in good faith.

From the employee's point of view, the primary incentive for undertaking production-centred training is greater technical mastery of their current job. In other words, the primary attraction for workers to this HRD approach is based on helping them complete their organisational tasks with greater skill. This approach and its attraction to both employer and employee has been embraced and argued passionately by theorists and practitioners, particularly those in the competency-based movement.

Person-Centred Approach

A second philosophical perspective on learning and HRD is the person-centred approach (Aktouf, 1992; Barrie & Pace, 1999; Berger & Luckman, 1966; Elliott, 2000; Fisher & Torbert, 1995; Nader, 1984). The emphasis of this approach is on the development of self. A person-centred approach is based on the personal development of employees. Person-centred learning stresses an indirect link between the learning experience and organisational performance.

The primary motive for the employer to invest in personal development learning is to enhance employees' personal qualities. This ultimately has a positive impact on overall work performance. Unlike the production-centred approach, the person-centred approach has a more tenuous link to performance. It is based on the theory that capable people make capable employees in a variety of contexts.

For example, training programs that improve people's mastery of themselves, such as courses on goal-setting, personal motivation, time management and emotional intelligence can have a resultant payoff in terms of increased productivity. The incentive to sponsor personal development programs for the manager is based on the premise that by developing the most precious organisational resource: people, the company is likely to stimulate them to be more proficient in their current and future work practices. Over the last quarter of a century, the growing popularity of this HRD approach would suggest that this premise is well founded.

From the employees' perspective, the motivation to undertake person-centred learning is the opportunity to develop themselves and thus improve and enrich their career prospects. In other words, the attraction for employees is broadening the scope of their skills sets beyond their technical competence. In concert with production-centred training, person-centred learning has the potential to instil a sense of commitment from employees to the organisation as discussed in the previous chapter. Of the two approaches, the person-centred approach has traditionally been less appealing to employers because of the weaker connection between the learning experience and current job outputs.

Principled Problem-Solving Approach

The third school of HRD thinking is referred to as the principled problem-solving approach (Anderson, 1995; Argyris, 1964; Bandura, 1997; Kincheloe, 1995; Kohlberg & Mayer, 1972; Lawler, 1992; Lawler, Mohrman, & Ledford, 1995; Watkins & Marsick, 1993). The focus of this approach is on the development of problem-solving capabilities. As a consequence of superior problem-solving capacities, the principled problem-solving approach improves the employee's ability to make more effective decisions on the job. The rationale for this approach is the direct and indirect connection between problem-solving capability and organisational performance. In other words, the primary motive for organisational leaders to invest in problem-solving learning is to improve employees' decision-making aptitude to deal with unpredictable challenges in their jobs.

This HRD approach is based on the theory that individuals are likely to make better decisions in their day-to-day work if they have the necessary knowledge, skills and mindsets to analyse random problems. Consequently, employees are likely to exercise greater autonomy in dealing with ambiguous issues affecting their work. This is likely to result is less dependence on their supervisor. For example, topics such as creative problem-solving techniques, research skills, or analysis of typical workplace case studies can develop problem-solving ability.

The motive for managers to use the principled problem-solving approach is based on the idea that by developing employees' problem-solving capacities, the organisation is likely to stimulate faster and better quality decision-making throughout the organisation. Quicker and improved execution of daily challenges is likely to result in better customer service. Apart from this attraction for managers, greater employee self-sufficiency is likely to place less strain on managerial resources.

From an employee's perspective, the motivation to learn problem-solving skills is that they will become less reliant on their boss to make decisions affecting their daily work. Workers therefore have more freedom and confidence to make decisions. Furthermore, employees can be attracted to problem-solving learning opportunities to improve their overall employability. It is not surprising, therefore, that this HRD approach is gaining more prominence in an increasingly complex and less predictable working environment.

The Shift from Training to Learning and Development

How is the value of Training (characteristic of the traditional employment relationship) different from the value of Learning and Development? The fundamental difference is that the value of Learning and Development takes a multidimensional approach to HRD. Training, on the other hand, is one-dimensional and based essentially on the production-centred approach. Missing in traditional HRD programs is the person-centred and principled problem-solving approaches. The traditional employment relationship has a performance orientation that is based on directly enhancing the technical job skills of employees. Yet the unpredictability associated with the contemporary marketplace and the increasing focus on the customer has elevated the reliance on problem-solving and decision-making. To be flexible and able to think autonomously is now a core capability of the modern employee. Also, the dimension of personal development and its impact on overall workplace performance is now more widely understood and accepted. The new workplace needs a more sophisticated approach to HRD beyond a reliance on technical training.

Multidimensional Approach

Notwithstanding the fact that there are strong advocates for all three approaches, the most effective approach in terms of aligning the needs and interests of the individual and organisation is an eclectic approach. A multidimensional strategy is a more comprehensive approach to learning and development that brings together the strengths of each HRD perspective. It is not really a question of which philosophical approach is the best. A better question is: What does each approach have to offer individual and organisation?

A multidimensional approach is likely to benefit both entities in the employment relationship. An assorted HRD strategy is able to consider the dimensions of the individual (person-centred), organisation (production-centred), and situation (problem-solving). Put another way, an eclectic approach to HRD consists of three aspects: skill development, personal development and problem-solving capabilities.

More specifically, the development of skills assists the organisation to achieve its work-based objectives. Personal development assists the employee to achieve his or her career objectives. The learning of problem-solving capabilities assists both the individual and organisation to deal with an ambiguous, unpredictable and fast-paced marketplace. A multidimensional approach to learning and development is more likely to meet the growth needs of workers and, at the same time, assist in contributing to company outputs.

Elements of Learning and Development

Similar to the other seven values in the model, applying the value of Learning and Development is a joint responsibility between employer and employee. Figure 11.1 illustrates the three core elements involved with the value of Learning and Development.

Figure 11.1 shows the three core elements in changing from a value of Training to a value of Learning and Development. From the perspective of the organisation, the three key elements are the provision of a balanced HRD program inclusive of job, problem-solving and personal development HRD opportunities for employees. From the individual perspective, the corresponding key elements are a willingness to participate in these three types of learning opportunities.

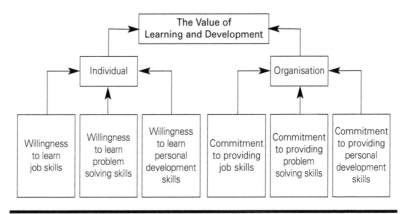

Figure 11.1 Elements of learning and development.

Benefits of a Multidimensional Approach

This mixed framework is likely to enhance the legitimacy of the corporate HRD function within an organisation by broadening its capacity to influence the culture of a workplace. Apart from emphasising the strengths of each dimension, a multidimensional approach can also minimise the weaknesses inherent in each HRD perspective. In this way, HRD can have a greater overall influence on organisational performance.

The fundamental weakness of the production-centred approach is that it subordinates the individual's needs and interests to the charter of the organisation. A purely production-centred approach is based on the notion that individuals play a role in organisations and can therefore be viewed as abstract and anonymous job-holders or performers. The overriding assumption is that employees passively react to stimuli in the organisational environment. It is true that the worker does gain skills development through this approach that may assist them in their careers. However, these job skills are based primarily on the needs and priorities of the organisation. The needs of the individual worker are a secondary consideration.

Regardless of the rhetoric of the person-centred approach, in reality this strategy can also subordinate the individual to organisational needs and interests. For example, the employee attending a personal development training program is often placed in a position where he or she is required to follow an organisationally sponsored trainer and curriculum. It is often the case that the trainee simply follows what the trainer says (there being no logical requirement to engage in independent thinking). In this way, the trained person simply acts on the basis of orders from the trainer or on the contents of a training manual. These personal development courses are often 'how to' or procedurally driven. For instance, how to complete a 'to do' list is a process-driven set of instructions as part of a 'time management' personal development course. Undoubtedly, procedural knowledge gained this way is necessary for some tasks. However, too much attention on procedural knowledge training has the potential to undercut the capacity for real personal development of the individual. So, in certain circumstances, the person-centred approach can undermine an individual's fundamental and inherent self-determination. In practice, both the product- and personal-centred approaches can reinforce traditional mindsets that consider the organisation's needs and interests above those of the individual.

For this reason, the principled problem-solving approach needs to be jointly considered with the person- and production-centred perspectives. In today's world, the ability to think laterally, creatively and flexibly is critical to success in any work. The pressure of global competition means that the customer's needs must be treated uniquely and stock standard problem-solving approaches are not always going to work, or be suitable. Being able to take an exceptional situation and be able to deal with it efficiently and effectively is a skill-set that is invaluable to all parties.

In positive terms, understanding the basis of each approach can lead managers to be more informed about their choices. For example, a manager who is faced with the challenge of overturning lagging work performance might deal with this issue from any one or collection of the three theoretical perspectives. From the person-centred perspective, names of top performers could be posted on the luncheon bulletin board and monthly award ceremonies for these employees could be held to instil pride in individual performance. This strategy promotes the personal development of the individual. From a production-centred perspective, pay-for-performance systems with the support of organisationally-sponsored skill-based training programs may provide incentives and skills needed to increase productivity. Viewed from a principled problem-solving perspective, a management strategy could be proposed to investigate the causes of poor performance, including problem-solving and brainstorming meetings with, and between, workers. This strategy promotes 'lateral thinking' to solve the problem. A manager who can select from a number of different perspectives to solve HRD challenges has a potentially wider array of possible solutions than one who is only applying one philosophical approach to solving learning and development issues. It therefore stands to reason that the manager is more likely to be successful in resolving challenging HRD issues.

In terms of managing the HRD multidimensional approach, it is suggested that approximately one third of the HRD budget should be devoted to each approach. Specifically, a third of the budget can be committed to the self-development of workers (person-centred approach), a third for specific training to carry out organisation roles with greater skill and competence (production-centred approach), and a third to developing problem-solving capabilities (principle problem-solving approach). This mix of learning and development approaches can reinforce the legitimacy of HRD, contribute significantly to balancing the developmental needs of individual and organisation, and provide managers with a broader framework for solving organisational issues.

Conclusion

In terms of the New Employment Relationship Model outlined in Chapter 4, the individual corresponding accountability for the value of Learning and Development is to be committed to lifelong learning. This mindset is present when there is a willingness to learn job skills, problem-solving skills, and personal development skills. From the organisational perspective, the corresponding accountability is to enter into a partnership for employee development. This is likely to be accomplished with a commitment to provide job, problem-solving and personal development learning opportunities. These elements and the matching individual and organisational responses are likely to modify the culture of the organisation from a value of Training to a value of Learning and Development.

■ Reflective Questions for Managers

The following scenario and questions relate to the case study on pages 146–147. The HR manager has suggested to the general manager that she'd like some outside help in moving towards resolving the issues. He'd agreed to allow an external HR development consultant to work with the HR manager in defining an appropriate resolution to the issues, but wants to see a tangible outcome in the form of training as a matter of urgency.

1. What process(es) would you recommend to identify the organisation's requirements?

2. On the facts as presented, what do you consider to be the key issues related to learning and development?

3. What additional information would you need to validate your response to question 2?

4. How would you recommend the organisation address the learning and development needs associated with moving to a multiskilled environment?

5. How would you recommend the organisation address the learning and development implied by the move to team-based production?

Consider how the following questions can be addressed in your own organisation:

6. The author advocates a balanced approach to HRD between the production-centred, person-centred, and principled problem-solving approach. Do you think this balance would vary depending on the industry? Can you give examples?

7. Which of the three approaches to HRD do you personally favour? Why?

8. Do you agree with the author's proposition that the person-centred approach can 'also subordinate the individual to organisational needs and interests'? Give reasons.

9. Apart from legitimising HRD, balancing the learning needs of the individual and organisation, and providing managers with more scope to solve organisational issues, what other benefits can you think of?

■ Top 10 Key Points from Chapter 11

1. All eight values in the model have operational components of learning and development.

2. The value of Learning and Development is based on the philosophical orientation of HRD.

3. An organisation's approach to a strategic HRD explains management's beliefs about human nature.

4. There are three predominant approaches to HRD, namely, the production-centred, person-centred, and principle problem-solving orientation.

5. The production-centred approach, a traditional organisation strategy, is based on the development of technical skills related to a specific job.

6. The person-centred approach is based on the personal development of the employee.

7. The principle problem-solving approach is based on the development of problem-solving capabilities.

8. A multidimensional approach, encompassing all three perspectives, builds on the strengths and minimises the limitations of each strategy.

9. The three key elements of the value of Learning and Development are a willingness and provision of organisationally based, individually based, and problem-solving based learning from the individual and organisation respectively.

10. A multidimensional approach to learning and development strengthens the authority of HRD, helps to balance the needs and interests of the individual and organisation, and gives managers an extensive framework for solving organisational issues.

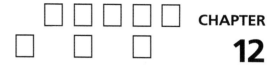

Conquering the Initiative Paradox
From Closed to Open Information

How can managers constrain employees' independent judgment and, at the same, encourage initiative?

The importance of opening information channels between employer and employee is well documented in the literature, has commercial advantages for organisations, and is generally desired by modern employees. By communicating information flow in a structured way, this can resolve the dilemma of when employees should display enterprising behaviour in their work. This dilemma is referred to as the 'initiative paradox'. Four approaches can overcome the initiative paradox, and are referred to as goal alignment, communication of boundaries, information sharing, and dynamic accountability. Each method has particular strengths and weaknesses, and can be used in different work contexts. By using all four approaches, or a combination of approaches, managers are able to define and confine the enterprising behaviour of employees. There are many strategies that can be used to boundary manage employee initiative. These approaches comprise the elements of the value of Open Information.

Importance of Open Information
The value of Open Information is part of the model for four reasons. These are briefly outlined below.

References in Literature
The literature pertaining to the psychological contract and organisational change generally points out the importance and relevance of opening the information channels within organisations (see Guest & Conway, 2002; Denis et al., 2001; Hyman & Mason, 1995; and Pickard, 1993). So one of the

reasons for the inclusion of the value of Open Information is its frequent reference in the literature.

Commercial Advantages

There are commercial advantages in having a flexible, adaptable and responsive organisational structure (see Chapters 3 and 8). These characteristics are likely to come from a culture that is willing to share information cross functionally. It is this sharing and communicating of information that assists employees to make better quality decisions.

Participative Values

There has been renewed interest in participative values, cultures, and everyday practices of organisations as they operate in an increasingly competitive global market (see Chapter 9). This can only be achieved through an opening of the communication channels in a company.

Employees Want More Autonomy

Closely associated with participative values is evidence supporting the notion that the majority of enlightened employees want to have more autonomy and show more initiative and participation in organisational decision-making processes (see Chapters 3 and 10). To be more involved in their work, employees need a flow of quality information from their managers to inform them of when and where they can display their initiative. These four factors legitimise the value of Open Information in the model.

The Initiative Paradox

The line between employee initiative and managerial responsibility is referred to by Campbell (2000) as the initiative paradox. The initiative paradox is defined as managing the extent and limits of worker participation in decision-making. It is therefore concerned with the flow and quality of information that will provide a responsive environment to enable appropriate participation by employees in organisational decision-making. The drive to empower employees is becoming stronger (see Chapter 2). As a consequence, the challenge of resolving the initiative paradox involves greater numbers of workers and organisational leaders across more and more industry groups. If modern companies are to flourish in this volatile global environment and meet challenges such as geographical dispersion, electronic collaboration, and cultural diversity, they need to encourage open information systems.

From the perspective of the employee, opening up communication systems promises to assist organisational members to become more knowledge intensive, radically decentralised, participative, adaptive, flexible, efficient, and responsive to rapid change. The value of having employees

CASE STUDY

Southwest Airlines

How does an airline succeed in an industry that struggles to make profits and keep employees and customers happy? A profile of Southwest Airlines (United States Chamber of Commerce, 2008) reports that it has been profitable for an industry-record 33 years with a total market value that exceeds all the other Fortune 500 airlines combined.

By prioritising a happy workforce, it believes that its 32,000 satisfied employees will keep customers coming back. The co-founder and current board chairman Herbert D. Kelleher and president Colleen Barrett believe the company values of concern, respect, and caring for employees and customers define its culture and reputation. The importance of building and sustaining strong internal relationships, promoting from within, and providing employees the opportunity to grow and learn from one another means that everyone at Southwest understands the role each individual plays and how each and every employee contributes to the company's success. There is a free flow of information between employees and leadership, which is significant achievement when over 85% of the workforce is unionised.

Managers and front-line staff are empowered to act as 'problem-solvers', to make decisions on the spot that can save the relationship with a customer. In this industry, the customer's perception is that a company is only as good as their last travel experience. Southwest's senior vice president for corporate communication, Ginger Hardage, recently told participates at a conference a story about a Southwest pilot:

'On September 11, 2001, after terrorists had brought the planes down, all other planes that were already in the air were grounded. A Southwest plane was directed to land at an airport that Southwest did not serve, and the passengers and crew were put up in a hotel. When Southwest management called the hotel to enquire about the passengers and crew, they were told that no one was there — the pilot had taken everyone from that plane out to the movies.

'There's no manual from which to learn that,' said Hardage. 'At Southwest, employees are encouraged to make decisions from the heart, and in turn, these proactive gestures provide positive benefits to the customers and the company.'

In a recent survey, 76% of Americans think that a company's treatment of its employees is a major factor in whether customers will purchase from that company. As Southwest makes its employees the top priority, Southwest is really making its customers come first, too.

Results

As reported in the United States Chamber of Commerce profile, Southwest Airline's performance results speak for themselves:

- In 2005, Southwest reported its 33rd year of consecutive profitability — a record unmatched in the aviation industry.

- Since 1987, Southwest has received the fewest overall customer complaints, as published in the Department of Transportation's 'Air Travel Consumer Report'. In 2005, Southwest again ranked first in customer satisfaction.
- Among all industries in 2006, Fortune has listed Southwest Airlines as number three among America's Top 10 Most Admired corporations.
- Southwest has spent 3 years on Fortune's '100 Best Companies to Work For' list.
- For the fifth year in a row, Business Ethics magazine listed Southwest in its '100 Best Corporate Citizens' ranking.

Open Information at Southwest Airlines

The corporate cultures like Southwest's commit from the boardroom down to the frontline employees, as a way of life, rather than 'programs' or 'tactics'.

Hardage notes the following points about the role of communications in fostering a positive corporate culture.

- 'Companies must provide the level of knowledge and information that allows employees to 'act like owners'. Southwest Airlines provides daily news updates via its intranet, the CEO records a weekly telephone message for all employees, and the company communicates detailed financial information called 'Knowing the Score' on quarterly earnings. More than 14% of outstanding shares of stock are held by Southwest employees.
- Southwest communicates with employees every day through news on their intranet, every week through a telephone news line, every month with a 32-page magazine, and every quarter through the financial Knowing the Score message, and every year through a series of town hall meetings.
- Communicators must nurture their corporate cultures so that employees understand how their behaviour contributes to how their organisations are judged. In its monthly newsletter LUVLines, Southwest features employees who have been nominated by their peers for 'Winning Spirit' recognition. These outstanding employees are modelling the type of proactive behaviour that results in a remarkable vs. ordinary experience for a customer or fellow employee.'

Source: United States Chamber of Commerce (2008). Southwest's secret to a positive corporate culture: Its employees. Retrieved June 24, 2008, from http://www.uschamber.com/bclc/profiles/southwest.htm

participate in implementing projects and programs has been emphasised in settings such as information systems, manufacturing, total quality, and small groups, as well as internationally. Managing worker initiative is therefore an ongoing concern for all organisations.

Nonetheless, there are still plenty of examples of inconsistencies in terms of managing this initiative paradox across a range of organisational settings. For example, in a retail franchise business, employees will often talk about ownership when they refer to their involvement in retail outlets. They are often (by necessity) multiskilled in all the tasks associated with the function of their retail store, which may comprise six to eight employees. These same employees will often question what they perceive to be unnecessary interference by head office in the running of 'their' store in areas such as recruitment and selection, policy making, customer interface, purchasing, stock control, and systems and procedures. This creates a tension between head office and individual franchises. The tension is characterised by frustration from employees that their initiative to make decisions at the 'coalface' is being sabotaged by head office. Conversely, senior managers also become frustrated by workers 'in the frontline' who they perceive as lacking initiative and relying too heavily on them to make decisions that they consider to be operational matters.

One of the outcomes of the initiative paradox is employees failing to show initiative when they need too. This results from a perception on behalf of employees that managers will interfere in their areas of influence, so they become less resourceful. Accordingly, this lack of resourcefulness by staff is viewed by managers as a sign they cannot, or will not, take the initiative when required to do so. The manager therefore feels reluctantly justified to make decisions in operational matters. This 'vicious cycle' leads to frustration from both employees and managers. The cycle can be broken by adopting Cambell's initiative paradox model. The application of Campbell's model involves opening up the channels of communication between managers and staff in a variety of ways.

How can managers constrain employees' independent judgment and, at the same time, encourage initiative? It is a perpetual challenge for managers. Managers have tried to implement company rules, regulations, policies, and guidelines as a way of resolving the initiative paradox. Some strategies have been successful but many have failed. Campbell's model is designed to manage most contexts of workplace initiative. It contains four potential resolution strategies. These include:

- goal alignment
- communication of boundaries
- information sharing
- dynamic accountability.

Campbell's model outlines the limitations and specific recommendations for the usage of each approach. Each strategy is defined below, and how it may be applied to open information channels.

Goal Alignment

This strategy is about aligning the viewpoints of workers and managers. Where a considerable agreement exists between the motives of employer and employee, it is less likely that the exercising of the judgment of employees will not be in conflict with their manager. Conversely, where there is nonalignment between both entities, employee initiative is likely to result in unwelcome consequences by management. The assumption reinforcing the goal alignment approach is that conflict is not the consequence of the enterprising qualities of employees, rather it is the result of a misalignment between the organisation and the individual. Given the complexities of organisational environments, this resolution is often easier to suggest than to accomplish.

Frequently, this misalignment between individual and organisation is the result of poorly thought out and implemented reward systems. Inappropriate performance-measurement processes can create confusion and conflict. For instance, a company that values teamwork on the one hand, but rewards individual performance on the other, is likely to create nonalignment between the employee and the organisation. For example, shop attendants in a retail outlet who receive bonuses for the sale of products or services are likely to favour individual sales activity over teamwork. So, supportive proactive behaviours such as exchanging sales leads between shop attendants in that store are less likely to occur. Performance management systems can discourage initiative deemed appropriate by managers. Reward systems have the potential to encourage or discourage goal alignment.

Goal alignment between employees and management can be created by implementing and communicating a rewards and bonus system that aligns their purpose. Getting back to the above example, if the company truly values teamwork over individual performance, it would reward shop attendants for exchanging leads, irrespective of whether it led to a successful sale or not. By rewarding the actions that lead to a sale, rather than the sale itself, team behaviours are more likely to be encouraged. In this way, the outcome is likely to foster goal alignment.

Aside from formal recognition, managers can informally foster or discourage goal alignment. A manager can send mixed signals in their casual discussions with staff. For example, a manager may insist on being kept informed about all interactions with customers on the one hand, and expect them to show initiative on the other. When informed about an approach made by an employee to a customer, the manager chastises them for their particular approach. This may inadvertently create confusion in the mind of the staff member. If the manager criticises the staff member for the approach without praise for showing initiative, the staff member may interpret this as criticism for being proactive. The outcome is goal misalignment, the opposite result to what may be desired by the manager.

Communication of Boundaries

A second approach to resolving the initiative paradox is through the manager's careful communication of the kind of initiative desired, and the limits surrounding this initiative. This strategy is about clarifying the extent and limits of an individual's authority to display initiative. Explaining when, where and how initiative is expected, spells out to employees the boundaries of enterprising behaviour. If these boundaries are not communicated, employees will be confused and indecisive about displaying their initiative in their organisational role. The assumption underpinning this strategy is that in certain situations it is appropriate and expected that employees demonstrate enterprising behaviour. In other circumstances, it is inappropriate that staff show initiative. Like goal alignment, given the complexities of organisational environments, this resolution is often easier to suggest than to accomplish. Nonetheless, when employees are confused about the extent and limits of displaying initiative, it is usually because managers have not clarified and communicated these boundaries.

What is more, these boundaries are not static. They can change with time and situation. The essence of good management in these circumstances is to be aware of these potentially changing situations and circumstances and to communicate their expectations to staff when there are variations. Apart from communicating these boundaries on a regular basis, managers should use a variety of approaches to explain the boundaries of appropriate enterprising behaviour. These communication strategies may include staff meetings and discussions, coaching individuals, inducting new staff, using critical incidents and cases as examples to clarify their expectations, and written instructions.

To illustrate, consider a common and unanticipated dilemma facing an airline. In a circumstance where an airplane has been grounded due to unforeseen mechanical difficulties, what are the roles and responsibilities of all staff? To clarify and communicate boundaries with staff in this situation, a workshop could be organised by management. Participants may consist of a functional cross-section of the company including pilots, flight attendants, engineers, customer service, sales, and operational crew. In discussing this scenario, the focus would be on the various functional areas and how they would communicate and minimise damage to customers on board, and get the plane in the air as soon as possible. This case study approach encouraged participants to clarify when, where and how each function could, and should, show initiative in resolving the problem.

Since the approach of communicating boundaries works by limiting employees' enterprising qualities to highly defined situations, this resolution is especially attractive to those managers who feel uncomfortable with placing heavy reliance on the judgment of employees. On the other hand, this approach may hold little appeal in situations where managers wish to tap employees' initiative more broadly.

Information Sharing

A third approach to resolve the initiative paradox centres on managerial information sharing and trust building. This approach concentrates on minimising unshared expectations by providing employees with the same information, perspective and frame of reference that the manager uses in managing their area of responsibility. The underlying assumption of this approach is that by sharing information, and therefore trusting each other, employees and managers will have a similar perspective. This method encourages employees to channel their enterprising qualities based on an appropriate flow of information from organisational leaders.

Information sharing is a particularly useful approach in the areas of strategic planning and continuous improvement. For example, a manager, using the services of a professional and independent facilitator, organises a staff retreat. The purpose of the retreat is to facilitate a process of developing a five year plan for the department, involving all staff. The manager may share his or her vision, mission and values with the team and invite them to operationalise these in a structured five year plan. The facilitator works with departmental staff to develop several goals that encompass the manager's vision. Further, the staff work on developing strategies, plans-of-action, accountabilities and timelines. By sharing information with the staff, the manager can encourage them to be involved in, and initiate, a strategic plan.

Another practical illustration for initiating continuous improvement is simple and effective. A group of employees are invited to document an issue that they believe needs improvement within the area of their control. They are then invited to vote on the issue they believe to be the most pressing or relevant. The top issues are prioritised, and employees are invited to work in project teams to develop improvement strategies using a template. These plans are then documented. For this process to be workable, managers share information that assists the project teams to develop practical improvements. By sharing information, the end result in the process of developing a continuous improvement plan is likely to be an alignment of perspectives between managers and staff.

In these two examples, the manager essentially shares the managerial role with the staff. Through the information sharing processes, individuals understand the manager's perspective on important issues, procedures, and policies. This alignment of thinking comes from the manager freely sharing and exchanging work unit information and strategies with staff. This ongoing dialogue is characterised by openness and mutual influence. Such openness and sharing can mean that the manager is to some extent exposed and more dependent on staff. Because of this, the information sharing strategy requires a high degree of trust between the manager and employees.

Dynamic Accountability

The fourth approach involves an understanding between managers and staff that organisational members can exercise initiative and judgment, but only at their own risk. In other words, if the result of employee initiative is unacceptable to management, it can adversely affect the career of the initiator. This kind of strategy is typically commonplace in bureaucratic and authority-focused organisations, such as the military. These kinds of organisations rely on a clearly defined chain of command for decision-making. Management in these hierarchically structured organisations recognises, nonetheless, that from time to time, employee initiative is inevitable.

For example, consider an employee in charge of buying product in a large corporation with very stringent purchasing rules and regulations. One of those policies may be to order in products at a specified time of the month. But the employee may have advanced notice that the company has won a large contract with a customer. This customer requires immediate delivery of the product. The employee elects to order outside the normal ordering cycle to respond to the immediate needs of the customer. This enterprising behaviour exhibited by the employee violates a major company policy. It is, nevertheless, in the interests of the customer, so no negative consequences may occur for this staff member.

Consider another case in a military context. A squad leader may refuse a potentially illegal order from a direct superior. For example, if the superior ordered the subordinate to cover up the details of a murder before an official investigation took place. By not doing so, the squad leader is violating a command. While the subordinate may suffer initially from insubordination from the commanding officer, they are probably unlikely to suffer negative consequences beyond the confines of the military unit. To cover these kinds of circumstances, the organisation wants employees to use independent judgment, but with the associated knowledge that the organisation treats errors in such judgments harshly.

Dynamic accountability is the least effective of the four approaches in promoting enterprising behaviour. Using this strategy, the organisation purposely avoids attempts to define the conditions calling for employee initiative, while simultaneously conceding that employees will occasionally encounter such exceptional circumstances. This ambiguity in the boundaries of enterprising behaviour effectively allows the organisation to shift the problem to the individual, who cannot be certain that the organisation will support their judgment. In other words, should employees strongly believe that a situation requires initiative and actually elects to take such action; the organisation remains the final arbiter of their enterprising behaviour. Managers can evaluate such decisions dynamically, on a case by case basis, with hindsight knowledge of the ultimate consequences of the decision. Using this approach, the resolution of the initiative paradox has several organisational advantages, but holds few benefits for employees. Under these conditions, it is likely that employees will limit their initiative to extraordinary circumstances.

In summary, the use of Campbell's (2000) model has the potential to overcome two significant challenges in encouraging and managing enterprising behaviour. The first is to motivate individuals to use their initiative in decision-making. In particular, the test is to ensure that employees' enterprising behaviour is aligned with organisational needs and interests. Second, the specific solutions used to address this predicament vary in their emphasis. All four strategies attempt to limit undesirable, unintended consequences of employee enterprise. Communication of Boundaries and Dynamic Accountability do this by carefully constraining employee initiative. Alternatively, Goal Alignment and Information Sharing overcome the initiative paradox by creating shared perspectives and common frameworks. Managers should therefore carefully consider when and where to use each of these four approaches. Used correctly, these approaches have the potential to encourage appropriate employee initiative.

Elements of Open Information

Like the other seven values in the model, the accountability for developing a value of Open Information is a combined effort from individual and organisation. Figure 12.1 highlights the four elements associated with the value of Open Information.

Figure 12.1 illustrates the four core elements in moving from a value of Closed Information to a value of Open Information. These four key elements are associated with the appropriate individual and organisation response to goal alignment, boundary communication, information sharing, and dynamic accountability.

Open Information Strategies

Well-managed firms are likely to use a combination of techniques to address the initiative paradox. For instance, managers wanting to encourage initiative could put strategies in place that align individual and organisation goals

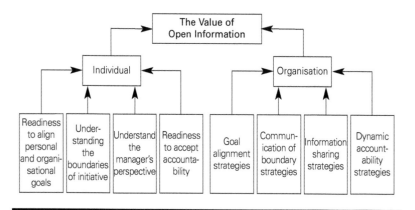

Figure 12.1 Elements of open information.

(Goal Alignment). To do this, managers need to share particular information with staff (Information Sharing), since that technique has the potential to bring into line individual and organisational objectives. For companies wishing to restrict employees' initiative, highlighting the limits of enterprising behaviour (Communication of Boundaries) and the consequences of inappropriate initiative (Dynamic Accountability) are natural pairings, and most likely would be used together. Other combinations are also possible (but less likely) and specific situational or job circumstances would determine those particular mixes.

Figure 12.2 summarises workplace opportunities for implementing the four elements of the value of Open Information.

Below is a brief overview of each strategy corresponding with the four approaches mentioned in Figure 12.2.

Goal Alignment Strategies

Clearly Defined Formal Performance Bonus System

A performance bonus system that is directly linked to desirable enterprising behaviours is most likely to encourage appropriate employee initiative and so contribute to the alignment of goals between individual and organisation.

Role Modelling by Management

If managers are not 'walking the talk', then it is likely that staff will follow their pattern of behaviour. For example, if the senior management team is not operating as a cohesive team, then it is likely that other teams in the organisation will not display good team work.

Approach	Goal of the Approach		Strategies
Goal alignment =	The alignment of individual and organisational goals.	+	• Clearly defined formal performance bonus system. • Role modelling by management. • Consistent informal communication. • Performance appraisals that focus on aligning individual and organisation goals. • Succession planning.
Communication of boundaries =	The clarification of when, where and how initiative can be exercised.	+	• Use of process mapping. • Use of critical incidents. • Coaching and mentoring. • Documenting boundaries. • Rewarding appropriate initiative.
Information sharing =	The sharing of information to align the perspectives of management and staff.	+	• Strategic planning workshops. • Continuous improvement workshops. • Democratic problem solving approaches. • Regular whole staff meetings.
Dynamic accountability =	The accountability for initiative is with the individual, not the organisation.	+	• Workplace investigations. • Showing initiative against unethical behaviour. • Reporting unlawful behaviour. • Crisis management.

Figure 12.2 Approaches to open information

Source: Campbell, D.J. (2000). The proactive employee: Managing workplace initiative. Academy of Management Executive, 14(3), 52–66.

Consistent Informal Communication

The consequences of what managers say to staff in informal conversations are often underestimated by organisational leaders. For instance, if two managers give out inconsistent messages to the same staff member, it will undoubtedly create confusion and consequently, goal misalignment.

*Performance Appraisals That Focus on Aligning
Individual and Organisation Goals*

A fair amount of a performance appraisal discussion should be devoted to matching an employee's skills set and interests to assisting the organisation achieve its outcomes. This is an important element of the value of Human Spirit and Work (see Chapter 9).

Succession Planning

Wherever there is potential, managers should look at grooming junior employees for more senior positions within the organisational structure.

Communication of Boundaries Strategies

Use of Process Mapping

Process mapping is a potent way of identifying and obtaining agreement on where, when, and how employee's, can and should, display their initiative. Figure 12.3 shows a simple example of a process map illustrating a florist's online ordering process.

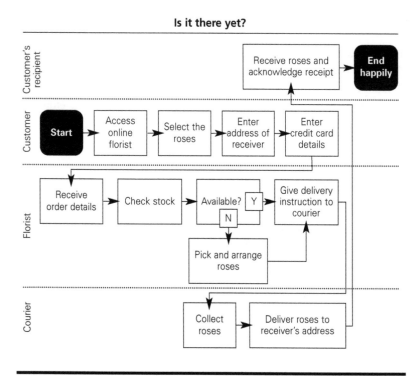

Figure 12.3 Florist's online ordering process.

Using a visual representation of a business process, such as the example shown in Figure 12.3, can be a vehicle for pinpointing opportunities to demonstrate enterprise.

Use of Critical Incidents
Using a critical incident or a real life case can assist managers and staff to clarify suitable opportunities to exhibit initiative in comparable situations in the future.

Coaching and Mentoring
All one-on-one coaching and mentoring opportunities present ideal conditions to explain to the employee the parameters of initiative in their work.

Documenting Boundaries
Documenting situations when initiative should be displayed can be outlined in the company handbook or intranet site. This can be helpful for employees.

Rewarding Appropriate Initiative
When enterprising behaviour has been exhibited by an employee, an effective way to reinforce the value of this behaviour is by rewarding or recognising the person for their efforts.

Information Sharing Strategies
Strategic Planning Workshops
Annual retreats for all staff in a department or organisation to review the year and plan for the future can be an effective way to align employer/ employee perspectives.

Continuous Improvement Workshops
Getting an organisational department, function, or team together to review its processes and systems is potentially a highly effective way of bringing into line the views of managers and staff.

Democratic Problem-Solving Approaches
Problem-solving meetings with staff and management can get both parties 'on the same wave length'.

Regular Whole Staff Meetings
Whole staff meetings once a month or once a quarter are useful forums for sharing information.

Dynamic Accountability Strategies

Workplace Investigations

Workplace investigations that take into account all factors associated with staff initiative can determine the merits or otherwise of the enterprising behaviour.

Showing Initiative Against Unethical Behaviour

Employee's careers can sometimes be adversely affected by not conforming to unethical workplace behaviour or practices. However, in the majority of cases, showing appropriate initiative in these circumstances is deemed valid and reasonable.

Reporting Unlawful Behaviour

Employees who are prepared to report corruption and discriminatory behaviour are exercising initiative and this, if done appropriately, is generally considered reasonable grounds for exercising initiative.

Crisis Management

During a crisis, it is appreciated and encouraged when employees exercise prudent initiative as these predicaments are usually unique and without precedent.

Conclusion

With regard to the model in Chapter 4, the individual parallel response to the value of Open Information is to be willing to contribute to the organisational decision-making processes. To display this mindset, the individual needs to be willing to align their personal goals with those of the organisation. In addition, the individual makes every effort to understand the parameters of, and be willing to exercise, enterprising behaviour. Also, they should be prepared to understand their manager's point of reference, and be ready to accept their responsibility in being involved in the decision-making processes. To be able to do this, the organisation needs to provide employees with access to information about organisational goals, needs, and HR systems. Specifically, this means putting in place strategies to align individual and organisational goals: define, communicate and encourage appropriate enterprising behaviour; share useful information; and discourage initiative in certain areas by making the employee accountable for improper enterprise. These elements and the right responses from both entities in the employment relationship will go a long way towards shifting from a value of Closed Information to a value of Open Information.

■ Reflective Questions for Managers

The following questions relate to the case study on pages 157–158.

1. As discussed in Chapter 1, there needs to be a degree of caution applied when reading these sorts of accounts of high performing workplaces. Nevertheless, the results of Southwest Airlines are undeniably impressive. Of the four approaches to overcoming the initiative paradox discussed in Chapter 12, which seems to predominate at Southwest?

2. According to the survey in the article, 76% of Americans think that a company's treatment of its employees is a major factor considered by customers in determining whether to purchase from that company. Why do you think this is becoming such an important factor in purchasing decisions? Or, do you think it has always been an important factor?

3. What influence do you think employee shareholdings have in encouraging staff to 'act like owners'?

Consider how the following questions can be addressed in your own organisation:

4. It was probably easier to define the boundaries of enterprising behaviour in the traditional employment relationship because the employees' role was more clearly defined. Discuss.

5. Some employees do not want to take any initiative and some managers do not want employees to be proactive. How can these two entities be managed in an environment that should be promoting proactive employee behaviours?

6. From your own experience, can you give an example of when each of the four approaches should be used?

7. How would you start implementing a rewards and recognition program for enterprising behaviour? How could you ensure that it was fair and equitable?

8. Which of the four approaches is the easiest to implement in your opinion? Why? Which is the most challenging to implement? Why?

■ Top 10 Key Points from Chapter 12

1. The value of Open Information is part of the model for several reasons: it is well documented in the literature, has commercial advantages for company, and is generally desired by modern employees.

2. The initiative paradox is defined as managing the extent and limits of worker participation in decision-making contexts.

3. There are four approaches to resolving the initiative paradox: goal alignment, communication of boundaries, information sharing, and dynamic accountability.

4. Goal alignment is an approach that aligns the needs and interests of the individual and organisation.

5. Communication of boundaries is an approach that clarifies the extent and limits of an individual's authority to display initiative.

6. Information sharing centres on managerial information sharing and trust building.

7. Dynamic accountability involves an understanding between managers and staff that organisational members can exercise initiative and judgment, but only at their own risk.

8. This use of the four approaches has the potential to motivate individuals to use their initiative in decision-making and provide specific solutions to address the initiative paradox.

9. Communication of boundaries and dynamic accountability are natural pairings that constrain employee initiative.

10. Goal alignment and Information sharing are natural pairings that create shared perspectives and common frameworks.

PART III

□ □ □ □ □ **APPLYING**
□　 □　 □ **THE MODEL**

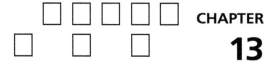

Bottom-Up Transformation
Corporate Culture Change Cycle

> The purpose of the Corporate Culture Change Cycle is to appraise how closely the individual and organisation entities are aligned to the New Employment Relationship Model.

The Corporate Culture Change Cycle described in this chapter is a distinctive and plausible means of appraising the perceptions of organisational members in relation to the New Employment Relationship Model. It is also a useful benchmarking tool and method for transforming the employment relationship. The process uses a 360-degree instrument to analysis data from a structured organisation-wide survey. An analysis of the survey results identifies the extent of alignment in thinking between the individual and organisation. This feedback is the basis for creating a series of priorities for an ongoing project team to tackle. As a representative sample of the organisation, the project team is charged with the responsibility to verify the 360 degree analysis, and come up with practical suggestions for improving the organisation's culture. This bottom-up approach has been very effective in bringing about change in several organisations. The Corporate Culture Change Cycle has also been the methodology used in a doctoral research project (Baker, 2005), and therefore has been thoroughly appraised. As a process, this mix of methods is both unique and credible.

Corporate Culture Change Cycle

The eight-step Corporate Culture Change Cycle is a vehicle for transforming the culture of the organisation, with respect to the employment relationship. The process begins by surveying the entire workforce. Its purpose is to gather data about the perceptions organisational members have about the elements of the eight values in the model. Once the results have been collected, they are analysed from three organisational perspectives: Top Management (TopMgt), Middle Management (MidMgt), and Workforce (Workers). Through this stratification, a comparative analysis between the three perspectives is undertaken, using a 360-degree instrument. The 360-degree tool analyses the extent of agreement or disagreement between the three organisational perspectives. From the 80 items in the survey, 16 elements are then prioritised for further investigation by an ongoing project team. This project team is a representative slice of the organisation. Practical recommendations are then made based on the team's consideration of the multisource perspectives in the survey analysis. As distinct from the traditional top-down method, the Corporate Culture Change Cycle is based upon a bottom-up approach to change. The success of this approach is measured cyclically.

To provide an illustrative overview of the Corporate Culture Change Cycle, Figure 13.1 shows the eight steps in the cycle.

In particular, three aspects of the Corporate Culture Change Cycle need further explanation. These include: the survey schema and its relationship to the model, how the results of the survey guide and inform the project team, and the make-up and charter of the project team. These steps will be discussed in greater detail.

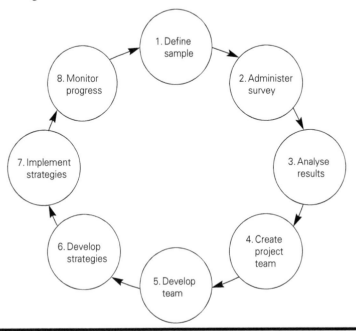

Figure 13.1 Corporate culture change cycle.

EXTRACT
Project Team Discussion

The author facilitated a project team discussion at Flight Centre Limited (FCL) to assist the company to transform the employment relationship. The company was written up in the early part of the decade as a high performing workplace (Blake, 2001). FLC is an Australian-based international travel retailer, specialising in the sale of discount international airfares, holiday packages and domestic travel operating in the United States, Great Britain, South Africa, Canada and New Zealand.

This is an extract from transcripts of the project team discussion on the survey statement: 'I find my work meaningful' (an element of the value of Human Spirit and Work). The matching organisation statement is: 'Employees find their work meaningful'.

The analysis illustrated strong, favourable agreement between the three perspectives (TopMgt, MidMgt, Workers). In the project team discussions, four themes validated the survey results. These themes were:

- 'selling people's dreams',
- growing and developing as a person,
- employee benefits, and
- respect from other people.

Selling People's Dreams

Several team members indicated that their meaning in work was based on the satisfaction of assisting their customers. One worker put it this way: 'Sending someone on their holiday, their honeymoon, it's a good feeling'.

Another team member representing the MidMgt strata expanded on this 'good feeling':

> You are giving the people their dreams, they may only do one or two big trips away in their life and whether that be to go as far as Sydney for the first time or getting on a plane for the first time, or doing that grand tour of Europe or Africa, you're giving the people their dreams and at the end of the day it comes down to what you do has a direct influence on how they are going to enjoy their holiday.

A TopMgt participant reinforced this message: 'We do say that they're selling people's dreams; you know they're out there helping people live their dream and open the world to people'.

Growing and Developing as a Person

Some team members across the three perspectives talked about attaining meaning from personal growth and development.

For instance, a worker explained that when one of their colleagues started at FCL, they knew 'nothing about business and that when they do leave FCL, as they may, they have developed and grown as a person and we've given them a lot more skills to go out into the world then what they walked in with'.

A MidMgt participant remarked that meaning can be associated with progress within FCL: 'there are people who enjoy what they are doing and especially as they go up the ladder you get to enjoy it more because you have more control over what you're doing and where you are going'.

Employee Benefits

Other participants commented on the several favourable employee benefits of working for FCL. For example, a worker identified some of these fringe benefits:

If you are really, really good you can make some decent money but I think it's more the other benefits of the role, the opportunity to travel, the company is very good in the fact that it gives you the opportunity to purchase shares, they have areas that can help you get healthy, or unhealthy. They have financial advisers; they have people that can help you get home loans.

Respect from Other People

Some individuals found meaning in their work from the respect they received internally from their colleagues and externally from their friends. For instance, a TopMgt participant stated that:

FCL has created a real community in the sense of you're always interested in how other people are performing and people do generally find a meaning in their work and that the longer someone stays the more meaning they find in what they're doing and especially when they feel a sense of accomplishment that they've achieved something.

Apart from admiration from colleagues internally, a MidMgt participant conceptualised meaning in their work as social status: 'Meaning for me is respect from colleagues, respect for myself for what I do and also respect for just going out socially and meeting people and saying this is what I do'.

Another MidMgt participant emphasised the value they placed on social status by giving the following example: 'If you're at a party and someone says what do you do and you say, I'm a branch manager of a travel agency it just doesn't gel with anyone, I guess travel doesn't really have the same respect'.

Source: Baker, T.B. (2005). *Towards a new employment relationship model: Merging the needs and interests of individual and organisation.* Unpublished doctoral dissertation, Queensland University of Technology, Brisbane, Australia.

Step 1: Define Sample

All organisational members should be given the opportunity to be sampled. It is obvious that the larger the sample, the more likely it is to be representative of the organisation. For geographically dispersed organisations, separate samples for each cite may be considered.

Step 2: Administer Survey

The survey can be administered online and should take no more than 20 minutes to complete.

There are 80 statements in the survey, with 10 representing each of the eight values in the model, in random order, without identifying which value they relate to. There are five statements referring to the organisational accountability and five for the individual accountability for each value. For example, consider one of the elements for the value of Performance Focus: team-based behaviour or teamwork (see Chapter 7). The provision of incentives for team-based behaviour is the matching organisational accountability and willingness to exhibit team-based behaviour is the related individual accountability. So, the organisational statement in the survey is: 'The organisation recognises and rewards team-based behaviour'. This is the statement that TopMgt and MidMgt answer. The corresponding Workers statement is: 'I have seen examples of the organisation recognising and rewarding team-based behaviour'. Meaning the same thing from different viewpoints, this forms one statement in the survey. Each element has two statements represented in the survey, expressed slightly differently, from the individual's and organisational viewpoint. All eight values in the model have three of four elements, so this makes up for six or eight statements out of 10.

The additional statements to make up the 10 for each value, are negatively worded, and are reflective of the traditional employment relationship. For example, using the same team-based element, it would be expected that in a traditional organisation, recognition and rewards for teamwork would not be prevalent. So the negatively worded organisational statement is: 'The organisation does not recognise and reward team-based behaviour'. This would be the statement that TopMgt and MidMgt respond to. The matching negatively worded statement for the individual (Workers) is: 'I have never seen an example of the organisation recognising and rewarding team-based behaviour'. In summary, the structure of the survey balances values, individual and organisation accountabilities, associated elements, and positive and negatively worded statements.

Step 3: Analyse Results

An analysis of the survey results is done across three perspectives: TopMgt, MidMgt, and Workers. TopMgt represents the organisational perspective, Workers represents the individual perspective, and MidMgt takes into account a third perspective.

There are three reasons for including a third perspective of MidMgt in the analysis of the survey results. The first reason is that the viewpoint of middle managers are often excluded, or devalued in organisational survey results of this nature. There is often an overemphasis on the importance of senior management and workers' views. By including this stratum, it recognises an additional and significant viewpoint.

Second, it is debatable whether the collective MidMgt point of view should be part of the organisational or individual perspective. For instance, a senior accountant in an organisation may have some supervisory responsibility across the workplace for overseeing accounting practices, budgeting, and production planning. Then again, they do not have any direct reports, yet spend the majority of their time completing tasks as a worker. It is difficult then to classify such a position as either management or workforce. So, it is sensible to have a separate perspective because of this uncertainty for particular organisational roles.

The third reason why MidMgt are treated as a distinct stratum in the analysis is their communication link between TopMgt and Workers. Because of this link between organisational and individual perspectives, MidMgt is in an exceptional position to appreciate neither, either, or both the TopMgt and Workers' viewpoints. Put simply, middle management is the 'meat in the sandwich'. As a collective stratum, MidMgt may then validate either or both the individual and organisational responses, or provide another entirely different perspective. For these three reasons it is advisable to separate the MidMgt perspective in the survey analysis.

Responses from the survey are analysed using a 360-degree instrument; this sorts the data into three perspectives: TopMgt, MidMgt, and Workers. The particular tool used in this analysis provides both graphical and descriptive statistical representation of the degree of agreement between the three organisational perspectives. Specifically, this 360-degree analysis method is referred to as the Holistic Imaging Profiling SYStem (HIPSYS) (Christie, 2005).

The survey gives participants three options. They can agree, disagree, or neither agree or disagree (neither) with each statement. With three perspectives, and three choices and their combinations, this generates seven possible outcomes in a HIPSYS analysis. Figure 13.2 illustrates these seven potential outcomes for the HIPSYS.

The three circles in Figure 13.2 represent the three strata: TopMgt, MidMgt, and Workers. A, B, C, D, E, F, and G signify the possible outcomes for each statement. In summary, these results can mean the following:

- A represents a view shared exclusively by TopMgt.
- B represents a view shared exclusively by MidMgt.
- C represents a view shared exclusively by the Workers.
- D represents a view shared by TopMgt and MidMgt but not the Workers.
- E represents a view shared by MidMgt and the Workers but not TopMgt.
- F represents a view shared by the Workers and TopMgt but not MidMgt.
- G represents a view shared by all three perspectives.

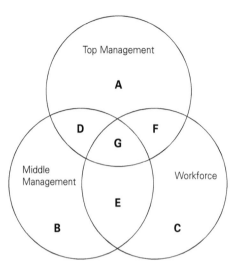

Figure 13.2 Potential outcomes of the survey analysis.

All seven results can be significant. For instance, an aggregate agree or disagree result by all three perspectives (represented as G in Figure 13.2) would suggest overwhelming or underwhelming evidence that the element described in the statement is part of the organisation's culture. For example, consider an aggregate agree result (represented as G in Figure 13.2) for the statement relating to the team-based element, that is, 'The organisation does not recognise and reward team-based behaviour' (organisation accountability), and 'I have never seen an example of the organisation recognising and rewarding team-based behaviour' (individual accountability). This would suggest a strong perception of the team-based element being present in the culture of the organisation because there is aggregate agreement from all three perspectives. To the contrary, a collective disagree result from the three perspectives for the same statement would point to an overwhelming opinion that the team-based element is not present.

Consider another example: an A (a view shared exclusively by TopMgt) outcome for the same element. An A outcome indicates that MidMgt and Workers do not share the same aggregate perspective as TopMgt. One explanation of this result could be that MidMgt and Worker collectively either believe that the organisation does not reward and recognise team-based behaviour (MidMgt), or they have never seen an example of this (Workers). Yet, TopMgt collectively believe that the organisation does have rewards and recognition for team-based behaviour. Which is the correct interpretation?

There are, of course, many possible explanations for this result. This interpretation then becomes a topic for further investigation in the project team.

Profiles from the HIPSYS do not explain the reason for agreement or disagreement between three perspectives; they merely show the degree of agreement or disagreement. The analysis provides the basis for developing an agenda for further investigation by the project team.

Two graphic representations are generated in a HIPSYS analysis. For example, Figure 13.3 is the HIPSYS Venn diagram representation for the value of Performance Focus.

In Figure 13.3, the plus signs (+) in the cross-hatched area represents aggregate positive agreement between the MidMgt and Workers perspective. The minus signs (–) represent disagreement by TopMgt (grey), or collective disagreement between TopMgt and MidMgt (dotted), or disagreement by Workers (black). A (o) symbolises a polarised response, that is, there is an equivalent number of agree and disagree responses to a particular statement. In Figure 13.3, five split results (polarised) are recorded in TopMgt (grey), one in MidMgt (white), one between MidMgt and Workers (cross-hatched), or one in Workers (black).

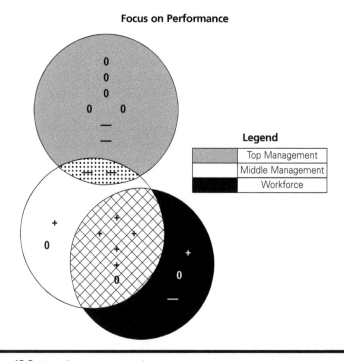

Figure 13.3 Venn diagram representation.

Data are also represented in histogram format (Figure 13.4). Figure 13.4 shows the same data as in Figure 13.3, but displayed a different way. The histogram gives an overview of the percentage of aggregate agreement and disagreement responses from each perspective. Unlike the Venn diagram, the histogram does not indicate where the agreement and disagreement occurs. These two representations provide an overview of responses for each of the model's eight values.

A statistical representation for each element provides more specific data. Figure 13.5 below illustrates a statistical representation for one element of the value of Performance Focus.

The statistical representation in Figure 13.5 shows a comparison of responses between the three perspectives for one of the 80 statements in the survey. In the above example, there is aggregate agreement between MidMgt and Workers, but the TopMgt response is polarised. The reason for this can once again be explored in the project team deliberations.

A HIPSYS report forms the basis for developing an agenda for change. An even-handed representation of evidence is critical. Ideally, all 80 items should be discussed by the project team, but in reality this is likely to take too much time and place an unreasonable strain on organisational resources. Three criterion are therefore used to prioritise the report.

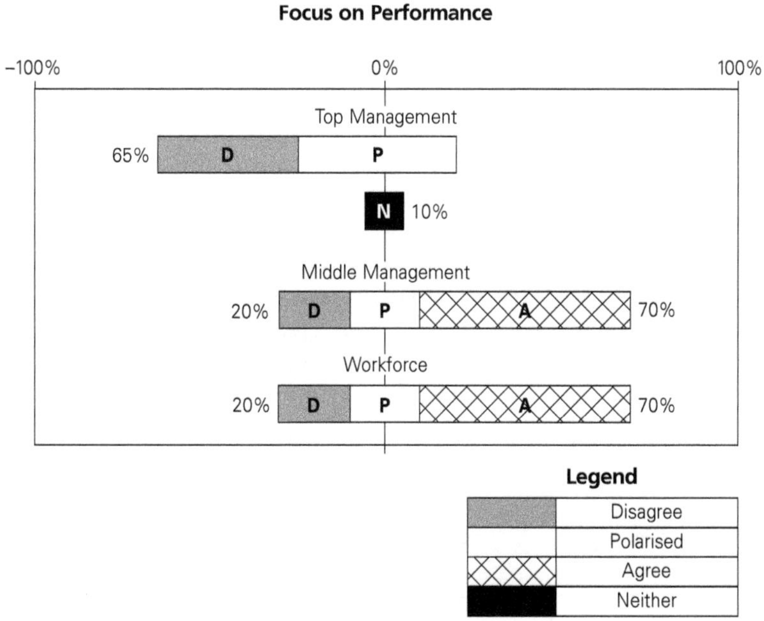

Focus on Performance

Figure 13.4 Histogram representation.

The first criterion applied is to ensure that all eight values are evenly covered. To do this, two issues for each value are selected, making a total of 16 elements for the agenda.

Balancing individual and organisational accountabilities is the basis for the second criterion. An organisational and an individual accountability are chosen to represent each value.

One polar example for the individual and organisational accountability is the third criterion for inclusion in the agenda. In other words, one item with the greatest statistical aggregate agreement and one item with the greatest statistical aggregate disagreement are selected, using the statistical representations in the report (see Figure 13.5). The justification for this selection condition is based on identifying the most favourable and unfavourable response for each accountability. Since two extreme examples are selected for each value, the two most acute cases offer a counterbalance, and arguably a broader representation for that value. In summary, the selection of the 16 statements from the HIPSYS report is based on balancing values, accountabilities, and elements.

Table 13.1 shows an example of an agenda for the project team. The agenda is the framework for further analysis, discussion, and resolution by the project team.

Step 4: Create Project Team

The composition of the project team is critical for its success. There is one essential criterion for selection. This condition is that the membership is as representative as possible of the entire organisation. The structure of the project team is based on a proportionate stratification of the company. Put simply, it should be a small replica of the organisation-at-large. To illustrate, the project team, depending on the size of the organisation, may consist of a maximum of

Focus on Performance

Q19   The organisation rewards and recognises good performance.

TOPMGT:	Polarised	Agree:	50%	(3/6)
		Neither:	0%	(0/6)
		Disagree:	50%	(3/6)
MIDMGT:	Agree	Agree:	50%	(4/8)
		Neither:	37%	(3/8)
		Disagree:	13%	(1/8)
WORKERS:	Agree	Agree:	73%	(11/15)
		Neither:	7%	(1/15)
		Disagree:	20%	(3/15)

Figure 13.5 Statistical representation.

three members of TopMgt strata, six MidMgt participants and 12 members of the Workers strata, a total of 21 members. A minimum may include one TopMgt representative, two MidMgt participants and four members of the Workers, a total of seven members. Proportional representation, rather than size, is the most important structural consideration.

Table 13.1

Agenda for Change

Issue No.	Survey No.	Value	Related Elements	Accountability	Overall aggregate result
1	76	Flexible Deployment	The provision of incentives for multiskilling	Organisation	Disagreement
2	34		Preparedness to learn and take on new tasks	Individual	Agreement
3	13	Customer Focus	A willingness to enhance customer service skills	Individual	Agreement
4	2		The clarification of customer service role priorities	Organisation	Disagreement
5	57	Performance Focus	Incentives for innovative ideas	Organisation	Disagreement
6	18		Willingness to be innovative and entrepreneurial	Individual	Agreement
7	1	Project-Based Work	Readiness of teams involved in activities characteristic of boundary spanning	Individual	Disagreement
8	7		Support for bringing up boundary activities in teams	Organisation	Agreement
9	33	Human Spirit and Work	An appreciation of good working conditions	Individual	Agreement
10	27		The provision of good working conditions	Organisation	Disagreement
11	29	Commitment	A feeling of a sense of obligation to the organisation	Individual	Agreement
12	14		A commitment to financial and social inducements for employees to stay	Organisation	Disagreement
13	77	Learning and Development	Commitment to providing problem-solving skills training	Organisation	Disagreement
14	62		Willingness to learn job skills	Individual	Agreement
15	6	Open Information	Understanding the boundaries for enterprising behaviour	Individual	Agreement
16	50		Organisational strategies in place for information sharing	Organisation	Disagreement

In addition to replicating the three organisational strata, consideration needs to be given to ensure that the various functions of the business are embodied in the team. For instance, generic functions such as finance, administration, marketing and sales, human resources, and operations should have representation in one or more of these strata. In other words, to be effective, the cross-functional project team should be a miniature reflection of the company.

This mirroring of the organisation is critical because, as the project team, they are charged with the responsibility of verifying the survey analysis. A project team analysis should therefore be as reflective as possible of the overall organisational outlook. It ought to also be stressed that a representative team is likely to be in a stronger position to gain legitimacy for their recommendations.

Step 5: Develop Team

As pointed out in Chapter 8, it is important for the success of a newly-formed team to undergo some form of team development. There are many team development models available. One that is recommended is the Margerison-McCann Team Management Systems (TMS) Model.

The TMS model is illustrated in Figure 13.6 and identifies eight critical tasks or functions associated with the process of achievement in a team context. By completing an online diagnostic, team members identify their preferred team role(s). Together, these team roles provide an overview of the team profile. The exercise of team development is designed to make the most of the role contributions of team members. Team development ensures that the team members maximise their potential to function effectively as a team during their interactions.

Step 6: Develop Strategies

After the successful completion of the team development workshop, the next focus for the project team is to tackle the 16-element agenda for change. In doing this, the objectives for the second workshop are threefold:

- to validate the survey results,
- offer strategies for culture change to better reflect the model, and
- to agree on a process for working together as an ongoing project team.

To achieve the first two outcomes, the project team is principally charged with the responsibility of responding to three key questions for each of the 16 agenda items:

1. What are the factors contributing to the result in the report?

2. What are some practical examples that support this result?

3. What are some strategies that will improve or build upon this result?

The outcome of this discussion culminates in a documented action plan. To illustrate this action plan, Figure 13.7 is an extract from one of these reports for a division of a well-known multinational corporation.

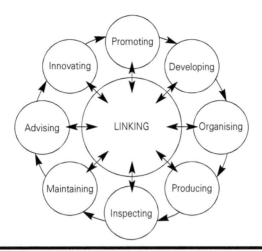

Figure 13.6 TMS model. (Margerison and McCann, 2009). Reproduced with permission.
Source: Margerison, C. & McCann, D. (2009). *Team Management Systems Model.* Retrieved June 1, 2009 from
    http://www.tms.com.au/tms03.html

The HIPSYS results at the top of Figure 13.7 show aggregate disagreement between TopMgt and Workers on the issue of whether management encourages workers to find meaning in their work (organisational accountability) (Q.8). There was agreement between the three perspectives on the individual accountability, that is, that employees find their work meaningful (Q. 48). The project team speculated what the results mean, gave some workplace examples, and finally made some practical recommendations to positively enhance these perceptions from organisational members.

In summary, the final report from the project team deliberations covers the following important aspects of their discussions:

1. Executive Summary
2. The New Employment Relationship Model
3. Agenda for Culture Change
4. Recommendations
5. Role of the project team
6. Where to from here?
7. Personal impressions of the workshop.

Step 7: Implement Strategies

Once the report has been documented, the project team, in consultation with management, is in a position to implement strategies that aim to positively alter the views from the report. This implementation process can be done in a variety of ways, from small incremental change to large-scale systemic transformation.

EXTRACT

Value of Human Spirit and Work

Q8   Management encourages staff to find meaning in their work.

TOPMGT:	Disagree	Agree:	33%	(1/3)
		Neither:	0%	(0/3)
		disagree:	67%	(2/3)
MIDMGT:	Agree	Agree:	60%	(6/10)
		Neither:	20%	(2/10)
		Disagree:	20%	(2/10)
WORKERS:	Agree	Agree:	53%	(9/17)
		Neither:	29%	(5/17)
		Disagree:	18%	(3/17)

Q48   Most employees find their work meaningful.

TOPMGT:	Agree	Agree:	67%	(2/3)
		Neither:	33%	(1/3)
		disagree:	0%	(0/3)
MIDMGT:	Agree	Agree:	60%	(6/10)
		Neither:	30%	(3/10)
		Disagree:	10%	(1/10)
WORKERS:	Agree	Agree:	53%	(9/17)
		Neither:	23.5%	(4/17)
		Disagree:	23.5%	(4/17)

1. **What are the factors contributing to the result in the report?**
    - Are senior management disconnected from the 'coalface'?
    - Only 53% of staff feels they are encouraged to find meaning in their work, therefore 47% do not find meaning in their work because they are too reactively driven instead of proactive.
    - These results could be a consequence of 'throwing people in at the deep end'.
    - People are generally too busy or stressed to find meaning in their work.
    - People define meaningful work in multiple ways.
    - We are working in a dynamic fast moving business. Everyone is very busy.
    - This result varies across the business, that is, more input from CSO people would have affected the result.
    - Most work (except for CSO) has a degree of variety.

2. **What are some practical examples that support this result?**
    - Sales reps are 'buzzed' when they win a deal; this excitement needs to resonate to the rest of the group.
    - WinWire mentions some departments but may not mention CSO and they are not celebrated.

3. What are some strategies that will improve or build upon this result?
   - Need to have an ultimate focus (THE CUSTOMER), so if we get a good customer satisfaction result we should all celebrate.
   - Each business unit should have a mission and a vision to achieve the overall goals of the organisation.
   - Fortnightly WinWire Dial in to celebrate all our wins as a team.
   - Link PBC to our ultimate mission and vision to make it more relevant to our day-to-day activity.
   - Visual countdown to targets (Revenue/Customer satisfaction/ Market share) so that people can 'see and live and breathe' their contribution every day.
   - Create a stress-free, fun, high-performance, customer-friendly environment to work in.
   - Need clear understanding of how the individual and organisation is tracking against targets weekly or monthly.
   - Invite customers to 'kick on's' to hear good stories, or a customer to give us feedback on how well we perform compared with our competition.
   - Encourage customers to provide positive feedback as well as negative feedback
   - Project based improvements in process involving all departments
   - Living the company's mission and vision every day with visual reminders everywhere; for example, on the back of ID cards and posters.
   - Consistent signature on emails and when answering the phone.

Figure 13.7 Extract from develop strategies report.

Chapter 14 provides a strategic framework for putting into practice some of the proposed interventions from the project team report. Implementing strategies for one element of the model will inevitably involve other secondary elements and related values because of their interdependence. The final chapter considers the interrelationship between the eight values and their associated elements.

Step 8: Monitor Progress

The monitoring progress ought to occur annually. In other words, the organisation or organisational unit should repeat the Corporate Culture Change cycle every 12 months. For an effective comparative analysis to take place, it is recommended that the membership of the project team remain the same, or as close as possible. A 12-monthly review will provide the vehicle for the organisation to benchmark is progress or otherwise). This is done by comparing the 'before and after' analyses. By so doing, the Corporate Culture Change Cycle is a mechanism for monitoring the transition from the traditional to new employment relationship outlined in Parts I and II.

Conclusion

The Corporate Culture Change Cycle is a vital aspect of organisation development. This bottom-up approach to change relies heavily on the commitment of an ongoing cross-functional project team. The purpose of the Corporate Culture Change Cycle is to appraise how closely the individual and organisation entities are aligned to the New Employment Relationship Model (Chapter 4). This review is based on the aggregate perceptions of organisational members. A positive appraisal would suggest that elements of eight values are evident within the current employment relationship. On the contrary, a lack of congruence between the perceptions organisational members hold at the time of appraisal would imply elements of the model have yet to be embedded within the organisational culture. Irrespective of the outcome, the Corporate Culture Change Cycle can provide a useful benchmarking mechanism for monitoring the employment relationship within an organisational setting. Put simply, this analysis gives a 'before and after snapshot' of the state of the psychological contract.

■ Reflective Questions for Managers

The following questions relate to the extract on pages 177–178.

1. Meaning in work came from four factors in this discussion. Finding meaning in their work at FCL came from the satisfaction of assisting customers, personal growth, employee benefits, and the esteem from colleagues and friends. Which of these four factors do you think has the greatest impact on finding meaning in work? Why?

2. Based on the extract, what recommendations would you make to enhance the element of finding meaning in work?

3. How would you ensure that one participant does not dominate the project team discussions? How would you ensure that everyone in the team has a fair input in the discussions?

4. If you were facilitating the project team discussions, how would you determine whether a view expressed by a participant is a minority view, or one shared across the organisation?

Consider how the following questions can be addressed in your own organisation:

5. How would you get 'buy-in' across the organisation to get a great response to completing this survey?

---

6. How would you go about creating a project team that is as representative as possible of the organisation? What techniques and strategies could you use?

7. What has your experience been with 360-degree feedback? Has it mostly been positive or negative?

8. What would your approach be as a manager once the project team had completed its report? How would you engage with the team to maximise the potential for positive results?

9. As a manager, what support would you give the project team to undertake its task, as described in this chapter?

■ Top 10 Key Points From Chapter 13

1. The Corporate Culture Change Cycle is a vehicle for transforming the culture of the organisation, with respect to the employment relationship.

2. The Corporate Culture Change Cycle can provide a useful benchmarking mechanism for monitoring the psychological contract within an organisation setting.

3. Using the Corporate Culture Change Cycle, the business is adopting a bottom-up change process, as distinct from the traditional top-down approach.

4. The structure of the survey balances values, individual and organisation accountabilities, associated elements, and positive and negatively worded statements.

5. An analysis of the survey results is done by dividing the organisation into three strata: TopMgt, MidMgt, and Workers.

6. Responses from the survey are analysed using a 360-degree feedback instrument; 360-degree analyses sorts the data into three perspectives: TopMgt, MidMgt, and Workers.

7. Profiles from the HIPSYS do not explain the reason for agreement (or disagreement) between three perspectives; they merely show the degree of agreement or disagreement.

8. The 360-degree analysis provides the basis for developing an agenda for further investigation by the project team.

9. The structure and composition of the project team should be a small replica of the organisation-at-large.

10. The focus for the project team is threefold: to validate the survey results, offer strategies for change to better reflect the New Employment Relationship Model, and agree on a process for working together as an ongoing project team.

CHAPTER

14

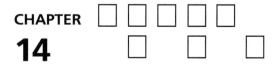

The Roadmap
A Strategic Framework for Change

A review of the interdependencies of the eight values in
the New Employment Relationship Model offers a practical
roadmap to navigate the transformation from a traditional
to new employment relationship in a company.

This final chapter provides a strategic framework for change. The purpose
here is to give managers, project teams, and management researchers a structure for each of the eight values. The structure illustrates and explains the
interdependency between the values in the New Employment Relationship
Model. So far, each of the eight values have been defined as separate entities.
This has been done to offer a clear explanation of each value, the challenges
associated with implementing each value, its associated elements, and their
relevance from the perspective of both the employee and employer. Even the
analysis in the Corporate Culture Change Cycle in Chapter 13 is done by
treating each value as a single unit of study. However, within the complexities
of a workplace, there is an interconnection between these values. So, by
attempting to implant one value in a company's culture, it will inevitably
affect several other values. Knowing the interrelationship between the values
and elements of the model offers a useful strategic framework. This roadmap
is a constructive guide for change agents interested in transforming the
employment relationship in an organisational context.

Each of the eight figures in this chapter relating to each value illustrates the
interdependencies with the other values in the model. The left hand column
shows the appropriate individual accountability and the right hand column
shows the organisational accountability for each primary and secondary
element associated with the particular value being discussed. Row 2 is the
broad descriptor related to the primary value for both entities from the

model in Figure 4.1, Chapter 5. Following the individual and organisation accountabilities are the primary and secondary elements. These elements have been thoroughly discussed in Part II. As a result, the eight figures show the linkage between the values in the model. The ensuing discussion explains these related values and their associated elements.

The Value of Flexible Deployment

Figure 14.1 illustrates the individual and organisation accountabilities associated with the primary and secondary elements for the value of Flexible Deployment.

With reference to Figure 14.1, there are seven secondary elements for the value of Flexible Deployment. These seven secondary elements combined with the three primary elements also illustrated in Figure 14.1, are characteristic of a workplace culture with a flexible approach to staff deployment. In broad terms, the elements in the left-hand column in Figure 14.1 contribute to an employee's enthusiasm to work in a range of work situations and organisational settings. For instance, employees who are eager to improve their customer relations skills, particularly those who's current role does not have direct contact with customers, are demonstrating an interest in broadening their work role (Customer Focus). More generally, individuals who are ready to enhance job or non-job skills are also displaying a flexible mindset to their employment (Performance Focus). Individuals who are prepared to try and match their personal interests with the organisational work are apt to try a range of roles at work (Human Spirit and Work). People with these attitudes probably have a wish to gain available organisationally sponsored HRD programs (Commitment). An HRD program that includes technical, personal and problem-solving dimensions is going to be appealing for employees who have a motivation to rotate and sample a variety of work-related roles (Learning and Development). All of these individual accountabilities of the secondary elements are additional contributing factors in an appropriate functionally flexible employee mindset.

The right-hand column in Figure 14.1 shows the organisation accountabilities for the same elements of the value of Flexible Deployment. These organisation elements, if met by the employee, will undoubtedly encourage employees to work in a variety of workplace roles and circumstances. For instance, the availability of relevant customer-service training will give individuals wanting to try customer service roles newly acquired capabilities (Customer Focus). An organisationally sponsored incentives program for the learning of new job and non-job skills is going to be appealing to individuals with a flexible deployment mindset (Performance Focus). Managers that help individuals to match their preferences and interests with work tasks are likely to be more flexible in their

The Value of Flexible Deployment

Individual	Organisation

Accountability
Work in a variety of organisational settings.

Accountability
Encourage employees to work in other organisations or organisational units within the same organisation.

PRIMARY ELEMENTS

- Prepared to take on new tasks
- Open to incentives to learn new skills
- Prepared to learn more quickly

+

- Increase task responsibilities
- Incentives for skills development
- Implementing a multiskilling program

+ SECONDARY ELEMENTS **+**

Secondary Value: Customer Focus
- Willingness to enhance customer service skills

+

Secondary Value: Customer Focus
- Customer service training

+ **+**

Secondary Value: Performance Focus
- Willingness to enhance job- and non-job skills

+

Secondary Value: Performance Focus
- Incentives to enhance job- and non-job skills

+ **+**

Secondary Value: Human Spirit and Work
- Willingness to match worker interests and their job

+

Secondary Value: Human Spirit and Work
- Policies and procedures that match worker interests and job

+ **+**

Secondary Value: Commitment
- Desire to acquire organisationally-sponsored professional and personal skills

+

Secondary Value: Commitment
- Commitment to the provision of professional and personal skills

+ **+**

Secondary Value: Learning & Development
- Willingness to learn job skills
- Willingness to learn problem-solving skills
- Willingness to learn personal development skills

+

Secondary Value: Learning & Development
- Commitment to providing job skills
- Commitment to providing problem-solving skills
- Commitment to providing personal development skills

Figure 14.1 Value of flexible deployment.

use of staff capabilities (Human Spirit and Work). A commitment to assist employees to develop skills that will assist them in their careers may be reciprocated by employees' readiness to rotate and sample different job tasks (Commitment). Finally, organisations that support a production-centred, person-centred, and problem-solving HRD approach will undoubtedly better equip their workforce for flexible deployment (Learning and Development). These secondary elements are additional factors that help to move the company from a specialist employment mindset to a flexibly deployed mindset.

The Value of Customer Focus

Figure 14.2 shows the individual and organisation accountabilities linked with the primary and secondary elements for the value of Customer Focus.

Referring to Figure 14.2, there are seven secondary elements for the value of Customer Focus. These seven secondary elements combined with the four primary elements also shown in Figure 14.2, are characteristic of a customer-focused organisation. The elements in the left-hand column in Figure 14.2 combine to create a mindset that the customer is the organisation's central priority. For instance, customer workers who are willing to find a sense of meaning in their work are more likely to be focused on meeting the needs of their customers (Human Spirit and Work). To be effective in servicing the needs of their customers, customer workers need good problem-solving capabilities and the capacity to grow and develop as a person. Consequently, motivated customer workers are likely to be enthusiastic about their personal development and the expansion of their problem-solving capabilities (Learning and Development). Also, to be effective at serving the needs of customers, customer workers have to exercise their initiative from time to time. To do this, they need to understand the extent and limits of their initiative (Open Information). Employees with these additional attributes are apt to be customer focused.

From the organisational perspective, several elements beyond the primary elements will help in providing information, skills and incentives to encourage the customer worker to focus externally. For instance, organisational processes that match workers' interests in dealing with customers will assist in cultivating an external focus (Human Spirit and Work). Assisting customer workers to develop personally and to solve inevitable customer problems and dilemmas assists them to focus with confidence and skill on the needs of the customer (Learning and Development). The four elements connected with the value of Open Information, are likely to give the employee the autonomy to exercise their initiative when needed with their customers. These additional elements of the model are important considerations beyond the primary elements, and will further strengthen the focus on the needs of the organisation's customers.

The Value of Customer Focus

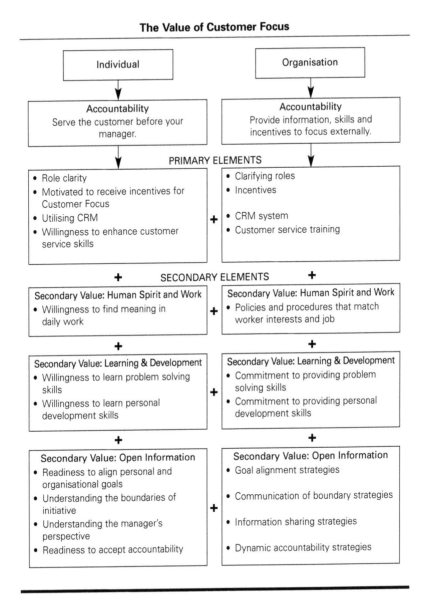

Figure 14.2 Value of customer focus.

The Value of Performance Focus

Figure 14.3 illustrates the individual and organisation accountabilities associated with the primary and secondary elements of the value of Performance Focus.

With regard to Figure 14.3, there are 14 secondary elements for the value of Performance Focus. These 14 secondary elements combined with the three primary elements also shown in Figure 14.3, are characteristic of a performance-focused organisation. The elements in the left-hand column in Figure 14.3 join to produce an individual emphasis on the work they do, being more important then where you work. For instance, a performance-focused individual is probably prepared to take on new tasks, be open to learn new skills, and able to learn quickly (Flexible Deployment). These same individuals are likely to want to develop their customer relationship skills to boost their internal and external service (Customer Focus). The same individual almost certainly makes an effort to match their personal interests with their work (Human Spirit and Work). Performance-oriented employees have a desire to obtain professional and personal skills from the company, when these opportunities are available. In so doing, they are likely to have a sense of obligation to their employer (Commitment). These employees have a holistic approach to learning and are therefore keen to undertake personal and problem-solving learning opportunities, as well as technical training (Learning and Development). This worker knows when and how to show initiative because they are keen to align their perspective with their manager's. They also accept accountability when necessary and understand the boundaries of enterprising behaviour (Open Information). Employees with these additional mindsets are likely to be more performance oriented than job oriented.

From the organisational perspective, several factors, beyond the primary elements, will help to shift the focus from organisational dependence to organisational performance. With reference to Figure 14.3, managers need to broaden the scope of task responsibilities, provide incentives for skill acquisition, and put into practice a multiskilling program (Flexible Employment). Managers should extend customer service training to all staff to improve internal and external customer service (Customer Focus). Wherever possible, managers ought to attempt to match job tasks with people's preferences as a means of increasing performance (Human Spirit and Work). A commitment to investing resources in training employees to help them grow and develop assists in performance improvement (Commitment). In particular, a multidimensional approach consisting of skills, personal and problem-solving learning broadens performance beyond the current job role (Learning and Development). Applying the four elements to conquer the initiative paradox is likely to encourage appropriate enterprising behaviour (Open Information). These management approaches, in

The Value of Performance Focus

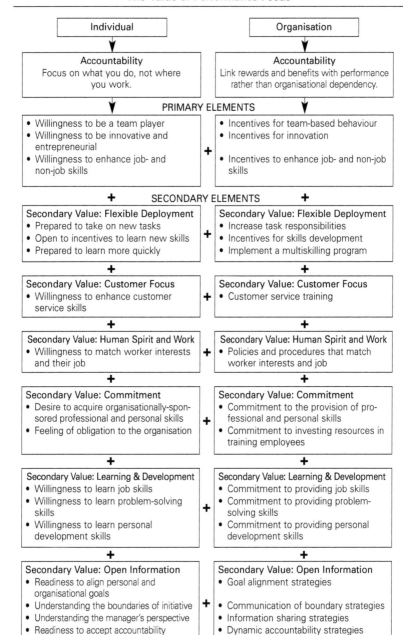

Figure 14.3 Value of performance focus.

concert with the elements for performance, will most likely create the right culture for a focus on performance rather than a focus on the job.

The Value of Project-Based Work

Figure 14.4 shows the individual and organisation accountabilities associated with the primary and secondary elements of the value of Project-Based Work.

As Figure 14.4 indicates, there are nine secondary elements for the value of Project-Based Work. These nine secondary elements in concert with the three primary elements also displayed in Figure 14.4 are attributes of a project-based organisational structure. The elements in the left-hand column in Figure 14.4 indicate an employee mindset that is project-based rather than functional-based. Apart from the primary elements, evidence of a project-based work attitude is a willingness to learn new skills quickly. This preparedness is an important requisite for project teams to become self-sufficient and buffer themselves from outside influences (Flexible Deployment). Apart from a readiness to boost their skill-base, individuals also need to be team players and innovative to effectively work in project teams (Performance Focus). Team oriented employees may feel a sense of obligation to the organisation via their close relationships with team members (Commitment). A willingness to learn problem-solving skills will also assist in maintaining a degree of autonomy in a team context or, on the other hand, knowing where and how to seek out support from outside the team (Learning and Development). A team member is likely to be enterprising if he or she knows the boundaries of his or her authority (Open Information). In addition to the primary accountabilities, individuals with these secondary accountabilities are likely to see themselves as team-based more than departmentally-based employees.

Looking at these nine elements from an organisational perspective, managers are generally attempting to shift the priority from organisational dependence to organisational performance. A cross-functional multiskilling program has the potential to challenge the 'silo' mentality of an organisation (Flexible Deployment). A further emphasis on the importance and value of project-based work can be encouraged by the provision of incentives for mul-tiskill development, innovation, and team-based behaviours (Performance Focus). Managers who commit to investing resources in training staff at the team level are likely to encourage individuals to feel a sense of obligation to their team members (Commitment). Increased growth and development, and in particular problem-solving capabilities, are likely to encourage stronger team work (Learning and Development). These management approaches, in concert with the primary elements for project work, will most likely put the attention on projects, rather than functions.

The Value of Project-Based Work

Individual	Organisation
↓	↓
Accountability Accept and embrace yourself as a project-based employee.	**Accountability** Focus on projects rather than organisational functions.

↓ PRIMARY ELEMENTS ↓

• Readiness of teams involved in buffering activities • Readiness of teams involved in bringing up boundary activities • Readiness of teams involved in spanning activities	• Encouraging buffering activities in teams • Supporting bringing up boundary activities in teams • Supporting spanning activities in teams

+ SECONDARY ELEMENTS **+**

Secondary Value: Flexible Deployment • Prepared to learn more quickly	**Secondary Value: Flexible Deployment** • Implement a multiskilling program

+

Secondary Value: Performance Focus • Willingness to be a team player • Willingness to be innovative and entrepreneurial • Willingness to enhance job- and non-job skills	**Secondary Value: Performance Focus** • Incentives for team-based behaviour • Incentives for innovation • Incentives to enhance job- and non-job skills

+

Secondary Value: Commitment • Feeling of obligation to the organisation	**Secondary Value: Commitment** • Commitment to investing resources in training employees

+

Secondary Value: Learning & Development • Willingness to learn job skills • Willingness to learn problem-solving skills	**Secondary Value: Learning & Development** • Commitment to provide job skills • Commitment to providing problem-solving skills

+

Secondary Value: Open Information • Understanding the boundaries of initiative • Understanding the manager's perspective	**Secondary Value: Open Information** • Communication of boundary strategies • Information sharing strategies

Figure 14.4 Value of project-based work.

The Value of Human Spirit and Work

Figure 14.5 illustrates the individual and organisation accountabilities linked with the primary and secondary elements of the value of Human Spirit and Work.

As Figure 14.5 illustrates, there are 15 secondary elements linked with the value of Human Spirit and Work. These 15 secondary elements in combination with the three primary elements also displayed in Figure 14.5 are characteristic of an organisation where meaningful work is sought by employees and, wherever possible, provided. The elements in the left-hand column in Figure 14.5 all contribute towards a willingness by individuals to find meaning in their organisational work. An individual employee, who wants work that is meaningful, is likely to feel like learning more rapidly and have an open-mind to incentives for learning (Flexible Deployment). For customer workers in particular, they need to be enthusiastic about the organisation's CRM system. This technology can be conceptualised as part of the organisation's working conditions. And one of the primary elements associated with individuals that find work that is meaningful is an appreciation of good working conditions (Customer Focus). As well as a preparedness to learn and grow, individuals with the appropriate mindset are likely to be innovative and want to be team players (Performance Focus). It stands to reason that a worker who finds their work meaningful is also likely to feel a sense of obligation to the company. Their engagement to the organisation could come from any of the three elements in Figure 14.5 associated with the value of Commitment. Engaged employees are also likely to have an eclectic approach to their learning and development needs, covering the spectrum of technical, personal, and problem-solving capabilities (Learning and Development). Also, a worker who wants to find meaning from their work is likely to want to show enterprise and display initiative (Open Information). Employees with these additional mindsets are more likely to find their work meaningful.

The reciprocal responses in Figure 14.5 will contribute to an organisational environment that cultivates the value of Human Spirit and Work. For instance, an organisation that actively promotes a flexibly deployed working environment is providing some opportunity for workers to construct meaning in their work. Multiskilling may also provide opportunities for employees to match their interests with their organisational work (Flexible Deployment). A good quality CRM system is part of the provision of good working conditions and is therefore likely to appeal to customer workers who appreciate good working conditions (Customer Focus). Managers who have an incentives system in place for performing beyond the boundaries of workers' job descriptions are likely to promote a broader sense of performance including teamwork, innovation, and learning (Performance Focus). A company that is committed to assisting

The Value of Human Spirit and Work

Individual	Organisation
↓	↓
Accountability Find work that is meaningful.	**Accountability** Provide work (wherever possible) that is meaningful.

↓ **PRIMARY ELEMENTS** ↓

Individual		Organisation
• Appreciating good working conditions • Willingness to find meaning in daily work • Willingness to match worker interests and their job	**+**	• The provision of good working conditions • Provide opportunities for workers to construct meaning from their daily work • Policies and procedures that match worker interests and job

+ SECONDARY ELEMENTS **+**

Secondary Value: Flexible Deployment • Open to incentives to learn new skills • Prepared to learn more quickly	**+**	**Secondary Value: Flexible Deployment** • Incentives for skills development • Implement a multiskilling program

+   **+**

Secondary Value: Customer Focus • Utilising CRM system	**+**	**Secondary Value: Customer Focus** • CRM system

+   **+**

Secondary Value: Performance Focus • Willingness to be a team player • Willingness to be innovative and entrepreneurial • Willingness to enhance job- and non-job skills	**+**	**Secondary Value: Performance Focus** • Incentives for team-based behaviour • Incentives for innovation • Incentives to enhance job- and non-job skills

+   **+**

Secondary Value: Commitment • Desire to acquire organisationally-sponsored professional and personal skills • Perceived cost of leaving • Feeling of obligation to the organisation	**+**	**Secondary Value: Commitment** • Commitment to the provision of professional and personal skills • Commitment to financial and social inducements • Commitment to investing resources in training employees

+   **+**

Secondary Value: Learning & Development • Willingness to learn job skills • Willingness to learn problem-solving skills • Willingness to learn personal development skills	**+**	**Secondary Value: Learning & Development** • Commitment to providing job skills • Commitment to providing problem-solving skills • Commitment to providing personal development skills

+   **+**

Secondary Value: Open Information • Readiness to align personal and organisational goals • Understanding the boundaries of initiative • Readiness to accept accountability	**+**	**Secondary Value: Open Information** • Goal alignment strategies • Communication of boundary strategies • Information sharing strategies

Figure 14.5 Value of human spirit and work.

employees develop their career goals has the potential to receive a mutual sense of obligation from employees. This commitment from employees may contribute to a sense of engagement in their work (Human Spirit and Work). The HRD program ought to include personal and problem-solving dimensions. This assists employees to use these capacities meaningfully in their daily work (Learning and Development). A lack of autonomy in work is most probably going to stifle employee engagement to some extent. So, apart from the other elements, encouraging appropriate autonomy, initiative, and enterprising behaviour is helpful in providing work that is meaningful (Open Information). These management approaches, with the elements for engagement, are most likely to create the right culture for employees to draw meaning from their organisational work.

The Value of Commitment

Figure 14.6 shows the individual and organisation accountabilities linked with the primary and secondary elements of the value of Commitment.

There are 19 secondary elements associated with the value of Commitment illustrated in Figure 14.6. Specifically, the left-hand column in Figure 14.6 displays the particular primary and secondary characteristics for an individual who is committed to assisting the organisation to achieve its organisational outcomes. A committed employee by this definition will want to take on new tasks, be open to incentives to learn new skills, and be prepared to make learning new skills a priority. These elements are likely to help attain company goals (Flexible Deployment). A dedicated customer worker will no doubt be very focused on the needs of the customer. To do this, they are clear about their role, willing to improve their customer relational skills, and enthusiastic about receiving incentives for good service (Customer Focus). A committed employee is likely to go beyond the confines of their position description. In other words, they will be innovative and entrepreneurial, a team player, and seek out learning and development opportunities (Performance Focus). They will probably accept and embrace themselves as a project-based rather than a functional-based worker. And as such, their behaviour is likely to help define, protect, and resource the project team (Project-Based Work). A devoted worker is likely to be an engaged worker. In other words, they seek out meaning in their daily work by linking their interests with the work they do wherever possible, and appreciate good working conditions (Human Spirit and Work). Finally, a committed worker is someone who is prepared, under the right circumstances and with the right information, to be enterprising in the interests of assisting the organisation to achieve their outcomes (Open Information). These are all important factors in defining the committed employee.

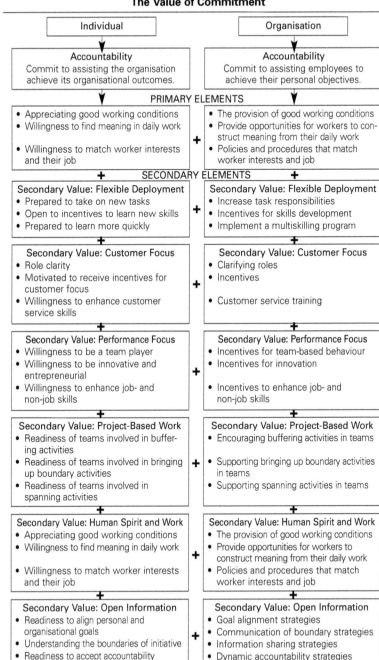

Figure 14.6 Value of commitment.

The manager's corresponding response will reinforce the value of Commitment. Figure 14.6 illustrates these responses in the right-hand column. For instance, by developing a flexible deployment program, with incentives to learn new skills, managers are helping employees to achieve their personal career objectives (Flexible Deployment). Customer service training opportunities, clear role descriptions, and incentives for superior customer service, are likely to help both the individual and organisation to obtain a sense of dedication from customer-service workers (Customer Focus). Since organisational performance is a broader concept than job performance, managers who encourage teamwork, innovation, and skill development through incentives are assisting the broader career goals of most employees (Performance Focus). Supporting project teams to create and develop their own identity is also in the best interests of the individual and organisation. Consequently, the company is more flexible in responding to the marketplace and employees are likely to benefit in the development of cross functional capabilities (Project-Based Work). Creating a more meaningful work environment by providing good working conditions, offering work assignments that are challenging, and matching people's interests with their work helps to instil a sense of obligation (Human Spirit and Work). Autonomous and committed workers need to be able to make decisions and show initiative to achieve the outcomes of an organisation. Therefore, strategies to conquer the initiative paradox are helpful to encourage this behaviour in employees (Open Information). All of these secondary elements combined with the primary elements, will go a long way to fostering employee commitment to achieve organisational objectives because, in exchange, these company initiatives help the individual achieve their personal career goals.

The Value of Learning and Development

Figure 14.7 illustrates the individual and organisation accountabilities associated with the primary and secondary elements of the value of Learning and Development.

As Figure 14.7 shows, there are 10 secondary elements for the value of Learning and Development. The primary and secondary elements in Figure 14.7 are characteristic of an employee who is devoted to lifelong learning. For instance, a dedication to lifelong learning will see an individual wanting to be multiskilled and prepared to learn constantly. They are therefore going to be responsive to incentives that are linked with learning new skills (Flexible Deployment). Customer workers with a commitment to lifelong learning are going to want (and even expect) their customer-service skills to be updated regularly (Customer Focus). In order to boost performance, a lifelong learner is

The Value of Learning and Development

Individual	Organisation
Accountability Be committed to life-long learning.	**Accountability** Enter into a partnership for employee development.

PRIMARY ELEMENTS

• Willingness to learn job skills • Willingness to learn problem solving skills • Willingness to learn personal development skills	• Commitment to providing job skills • Commitment to providing problem solving skills • Commitment to providing personal development skills

+   SECONDARY ELEMENTS   +

Secondary Value: Flexible Deployment • Prepared to take on new tasks • Open to incentives to learn new skills • Prepared to learn more quickly	**Secondary Value: Flexible Deployment** • Increase task responsibilities • Incentives for skills development • Implement a multiskilling program

+   **+**

Secondary Value: Customer Focus • Willingness to enhance customer service skills	**Secondary Value: Customer Focus** • Customer service training

+   **+**

Secondary Value: Performance Focus • Willingness to enhance job- and non-job skills	**Secondary Value: Performance Focus** • Incentives to enhance job- and non-job skills

+   **+**

Secondary Value: Project-Based Work • Readiness of teams involved in buffering activities	**Secondary Value: Project-Based Work** • Encouraging buffering activities in teams

+   **+**

Secondary Value: Human Spirit and Work • Willingness to match worker interests and their job	**Secondary Value: Human Spirit and Work** • Policies and procedures that match worker interests and job

+   **+**

Secondary Value: Open Information • Readiness to align personal and organisational goals • Understanding the boundaries of initiative • Readiness to accept accountability	**Secondary Value: Open Information** • Goal alignment strategies • communication of boundary strategies • Information sharing strategies

Figure 14.7 Value of learning and development.

going to be constant in improving their job and non-job skills (Performance Focus). Buffering activities are likely to improve the efficiency and relevance of a team. To do this, a common buffering activity is the sharing and development of the skills within the team. An individual dedicated to lifelong learning is likely to share and be receptive to buffering activities in a team (Project-Based Work). The pursuit of lifelong learning is about attempting to match personal interests with the job. An employee with this trait will probably find some sense of meaning from their work (Human Spirit and Work). To be continually in a learning mode, an employee is likely to take calculated risks on the job by showing an appropriate level of initiative. They would therefore be expected to seek out information from their manager so that they can understand the boundaries around enterprising behaviour (Open Information). All of these individual accountabilities of the secondary elements are additional contributing factors in having a lifelong learning mindset.

The organisational accountabilities for the primary and secondary elements of the value of Learning and Development in the right-hand column are characteristic of the organisation entering into a partnership with employees to assist them to grow and develop. In terms of secondary elements, the flexible deployment of staff in an organisation provides enthusiastic individuals with an opportunity to grow and develop in a way that is likely to be beneficial for the individual and organisation (Flexible Deployment). The provision of customer-service training will help all staff to grow, particularly frontline staff dealing directly with the customer (Customer Focus). Companies that are prepared to offer incentives to employees who develop their portfolio of skills are essentially working cooperatively with staff to help them to grow and develop (Performance Focus). Managers that allow (or even assist) teams to share knowledge within the team to strengthen their identity and relevance, are encouraging employee growth (Project-Based Work). Organisations that attempt to match the interests and capabilities of workers with organisational roles are, in other words, partnering employee growth (Human Spirit and Work). By opening up the information channels to support initiative and enterprise from employees, it encourages individuals to learn and grow on the job (Open Information). These secondary elements are additional factors that facilitate a company's move towards a learning and development culture. In particular, these organisation accountabilities, when met, help the employee develop their capabilities to become more employable in the open marketplace.

The Value of Open Information

Figure 14.8 shows the individual and organisation accountabilities for the primary and secondary elements pertaining to the value of Open Information.

The Value of Open Information

Individual	Organisation

Accountability
Be willing to contribute to the organisational decision-making processes.

Accountability
Providing employees with access to information about organisational goals, needs, and HR systems.

PRIMARY ELEMENTS

- Readiness to align personal and organisational goals
- Understanding the boundaries of initiative
- Readiness to accept accountability

+

- Goal alignment strategies
- Communication of boundary strategies
- Information sharing strategies
- Dynamic accountability strategies

+ SECONDARY ELEMENTS **+**

Secondary Value: Flexible Deployment
- Prepared to take on new tasks
- Prepared to learn more quickly

+

Secondary Value: Flexible Deployment
- Increase task responsibilities
- Implement a multiskilling program

+ **+**

Secondary Value: Customer Focus
- Role clarity
- Motivated to receive incentives for customer focus
- Utilising CRM system
- Willingness to enhance customer service skills

+

Secondary Value: Customer Focus
- Clarifying roles
- Incentives
- CRM system
- Customer service training

+ **+**

Secondary Value: Performance Focus
- Willingness to enhance job- and non-job skills

+

Secondary Value: Performance Focus
- Incentives to enhance job- and non-job skills

+ **+**

Secondary Value: Project-Based Work
- Readiness of teams involved in buffering activities

+

Secondary Value: Project-Based Work
- Encouraging buffering activities in teams

+ **+**

Secondary Value: Human Spirit and Work
- Willingness to match worker interests and their job

+

Secondary Value: Human Spirit and Work
- Policies and procedures that match worker interests and job

+ **+**

Secondary Value: Learning & Development
- Willingness to learn problem-solving skills

+

Secondary Value: Learning & Development
- Commitment to providing problem-solving skills

Figure 14.8 Value of open information.

In reference to Figure 14.8, there are 10 secondary elements for the value of Open Information. These secondary elements combined with the four primary elements also illustrated in Figure 14.8, are characteristic of a workplace culture with an open approach to sharing information. In particular, the individual elements in the left-hand column in Figure 14.8 are indicators of a mindset of wanting to have a say in the organisational decision-making process. For instance, an individual prepared to learn quickly, and willing to take on new tasks in a company, is probably also wanting to be involved in making decisions (Flexible Deployment). Customer workers who are eager to service the needs of their customers, and therefore fulfilling the four secondary elements in Figure 14.8, are likely to be displaying initiative and making enterprising decisions for the well-being of the customer (Customer Focus). It follows that if an employee is ready to be innovative and entrepreneurial, then they are probably also wanting to be involved in the organisational decision-making processes (Performance Focus). Most buffering activities discussed in Chapter 8 require employees to take greater responsibility at the team level and consequently demonstrate a desire to be more involved (Project-Based Work). If employees are keen to match their interests with their job, they are also more likely to want greater administrative accountability (Human Spirit and Work). And finally, if an individual has an inclination to learn to problem-solve, they are likely to be prepared to make decisions beyond the scope of their current job (Learning and Development). All of these individual accountabilities are further contributing factors in the pursuit of the value of Open Information.

The right-hand column in Figure 14.8 shows the organisation accountabilities. These organisation accountabilities, if met, are likely to provide employees with access to information about organisational goals, needs, and HR systems. For instance, to create a flexibly deployed workforce, information needs to be disseminated throughout the organisation (Flexible Deployment). Customer workers, in particular, need systems and processes to help them to focus on the needs of the customer. To do this, the manager needs to clarify expectations, provide incentives and technological support, and support customer-service training (Customer Focus). To be innovative and entrepreneurial, employees may possibly respond favourably to incentives from management (Performance Focus). Managers who encourage teams to be self-directed are apt to encourage decision-making at the team level (Project-Based Work). Actively aligning the interests of the individual with the needs of the organisation is a further way of promoting greater employee decision-making (Human Spirit and Work). And finally, a commitment to providing employees with problem-solving skill development is another method of encouraging greater initiative from workers (Learning and Development). These secondary elements are additional factors that help to overcome the initiative paradox by giving employees more information to help them to be involved in a wider range of decisions.

Conclusion

A review of the interdependencies of the eight values in the New Employment Relationship Model offers a practical roadmap to navigate the transformation from a traditional to new employment relationship in a company. With more than 200 years of conditioning, the challenges of changing the mindsets supporting the traditional employment relationship should not be underrated. Nonetheless, it has been argued in Chapter 1 that there is a need to alter these traditional mindsets wherever they may exist. The costs to both the organisation and individual are too great to continue with a 'them and us' employment relationship mentality, characteristic of the traditional employment relationship.

The 8 Values of Highly Productive Companies has given managers and management researchers a research-based model of the new psychological contract and workplace culture. The framework put forward is a creditable substitute for many outdated HRD strategies. These traditional HRD approaches often fail to take into account the revolution in individual and organisational paradigms over the past 25 years. Also, the traditional top down approach to managing change that avoids the changing psychological contract is likely to continue to be flawed in bringing about transformation in companies. The model and change process discussed in this book should be viewed as an up-to-date program for selected and carefully targeted HRD strategies to be applied in altering the way employee and employer thinks about their working relationship. This new approach promises to align the changing needs and interests of individuals and organisations.

■ Reflective Questions for Managers

1. Consider each of the eight values and associated elements and their related values and secondary elements and given a choice, which value would you try to implement in a workplace first? Give your reasons.

2. If the organisation was meeting their primary and secondary accountabilities but the individuals collectively were not, what could be some reasons for this situation? What would you do about this as a manager?

---

3. If employees in a company were generally meeting their primary and secondary responsibilities in the model for any of the values and related values, but the organisation was not meeting its responsibilities, what could happen? What are some reasons for this situation occurring?

4. In reality, individuals and organisations meet some and not all primary and secondary accountabilities. What is likely to be the outcome under these circumstances? Can you give an example of this situation from your experience as a manager?

■ Top 10 Key Points from Chapter 14

1. The purpose of the strategic framework for change is to give managers, project teams, and management researchers a structure for each of the eight values.

2. The structure illustrates and explains the interdependency between the values in the model with respect to the employment relationship.

3. The related values for the value of Flexible Deployment are Customer Focus, Performance Focus, Human Spirit and Work, Commitment, and Learning and Development.

4. The related values for the value of Customer Focus are Human Spirit and Work, Learning and Development, and Open Information.

5. The related values for the value of Performance Focus are Flexible Deployment, Customer Focus, Human Spirit and Work, Commitment, Learning and Development, and Open Information.

6. The related values for the value of Project-Based Work are Flexible Deployment, Performance Focus, Commitment, Learning and Development, and Open Information.

7. The related values for the value of Human Spirit and Work are Flexible Deployment, Customer Focus, Performance Focus, Commitment, Learning and Development, and Open Information.

8. The related values for the value of Commitment are Flexible Deployment, Customer Focus, Performance Focus, Project-Based Work, Human Spirit and Work, and Open Information.

9. The related values for the value of Learning and Development are Flexible Deployment, Customer Focus, Performance Focus, Project-Based Work, Human Spirit and Work and Open Information.

10. The related values for the value of Open Information are Flexible Deployment, Customer Focus, Performance Focus, Human Spirit and Work, Learning and Development and Open Information.

Chapter 1

Adamson, S.J. (1997). Career as a vehicle for the realisation of self. *Career Development International*, 2(5), 245–253.

Albrow, M. (1997). *Do organisations have feelings?* London: Routledge.

Baker, T.B. (2000). Not just a job! *Management Today*, 12, 20–22.

Baker, T.B. (2005). *Towards a new employment relationship model: Merging the needs and interests of individual and organisation.* Retrieved May 30, 2008, from http://adt.library.qut.edu.au/adt-qut/uploads/approved/adt-QUT20051006.150037/public/02whole.pdf

Beaumont, P.B., & Harris, R.I.D. (2002). Examining white-collar downsizing as a cause of change in the psychological contract: Some UK evidence. *Employee Relations*, 24(4), 378–389.

Boswell, W.R., Moynihan, L.M., Roehling, M.V., & Cavanaugh, M.A. (2001). Responsibilities in the 'new employment relationship': An empirical test of an assumed phenomenon. *Journal of Managerial Issues*, 13(3), 307–327.

Bridges, W. (1994). The end of the job. *Fortune*, September, 50–57.

Burack, E. (1993). *Corporate resurgence and the new employment relationship: After the reckoning.* Westport, CT: Qurum Books.

Capelli, P., Bassi, L., Katz, H., Knoke, D., Osterman, P., & Useem, M. (1997). *Change at work: How American industry and workers are coping with corporate restructuring and what workers must do to take charge of their own careers.* New York: Oxford University Press.

Coulson-Thomas, C.J. (1998). Careers, development and the future of the organisation. *Career Development International*, 3(1), 13–17.

De Meuse, K.P., Bergmann, T.J., & Lester, S.W. (2001). An investigation of the relational component of the psychological contract across time, generation, and employment status. *Journal of Managerial Issues*, 13(1), 102–118.

Drucker, P. (1992). *Managing for the future.* New York: Harper Row.

Eldridge, J., Cressey, P., & MacInnes, J. (1991). *Industry sociology and economic crisis.* Hemel Hempstead: Harvester.

Fairholm, G.W. (1997). *Capturing the heart of leadership: Spirituality and community in the new American workplace.* Westport, CT: Praeger.

Frame, R.M., Neilsen, W.R., & Pate, L.E. (2000). Creating excellence out of crisis. In C.H. Bell, W.L. French, & R.A. Zawacki (Eds.), *Organisation development and transformation: Managing effective change* (pp. 411–423). Boston: Irwin McGraw-Hill.

Fuchs, M. (2002). Changing employment relations, new organizational models and the capacity to use idiosyncratic knowledge. *Journal of European Industrial Training*, 26(2/3/4), 154–164.

Gee, P.G., Hull, G., & Lankshear, C. (1996). *The new work order: Behind the language of the new capitalism.* St Leonards, Australia: Allen and Unwin.

Grimmer, M., & Oddy, M. (2007). Violation of the psychological contract: The mediating effect of relational versus transactional beliefs. *Australian Journal of Management*, 31(1), 153–173.

Grint, K. (1997). *Fuzzy management: Contemporary ideas and practices at work.* Oxford, UK: Oxford University Press.

Guest, D.E., & Conway, N. (2002). Communicating the psychological contract: An employer perspective, *Human Resource Management Journal*, 12(2), 22–39.

Handy, C. (1989). *The age of unreason.* Boston: Harvard Business School Press.

Herriot, P. (1992). *The career management challenge: Balancing individual and organizational needs.* London: SAGE Publications.

Hosking, D.M., & Anderson, N. (Eds.). (1992). *Organizational change and innovation: Psychological perspectives and practices in Europe.* London: Roultedge.

Kissler, G.D. (1994). The new employment contract. *Human Resource Management, 33,* 335–352.

Leans, C.R., & Feldman, D.C. (1992). *Coping with job loss: How individuals, organizations, and communities respond to layoffs.* New York: Macmillan/Lexington.

Maguire, H. (2002). Psychological contracts: Are they still relevant? *Career Development International, 7*(3), 167–181.

Morrison, E.W., & Robinson, S.L. (1997). When employees feel betrayed: A model of how psychological contract violation develops. *Academy of Management Review, 22,* 226–256.

Nelson, L., & Tonks, G. (2007). Violations of the psychological contract: experiences of a group of casual workers. *Research and Practice in Human Resource Management, 15*(1), 22–36.

Neusch, D.R., & Siebenaler, A.F. (1998). *The high performance enterprise: Reinventing the people side of your business* (2nd ed.). New York: John Wiley.

Noe, R.A. (1999). *Employee training and development.* Boston: Irwin/McGraw-Hill.

Noer, D.M. (1997). *Breaking free: A prescription for personal and organizational change.* San Francisco: Jossey-Bass.

Organisation of Economic Cooperation and Development. (1996). *The OECD job strategy: Technology, productivity and job creation.* Paris: Author.

Robinson, J.P. (2000). *What is the new economy?* Retrieved October 17, 2008, from http://www.aces.edu/crd/workforce/publications/9-22-00-new-econ-defined.PDF

Robinson, S.L. (1996). Trust and breach of the psychological contract. *Administrative Science Quarterly, 41,* 574–599.

Roehling, M.V., Cavanaugh, M.A., Moynihan, L.M., & Boswell, W.R. (2000). The nature of the new employment relationship(s): A content analysis of the practitioner and academic literatures. *Human Resource Management, 39,* 305–320.

Schein, E.H. (1965). *Organizational psychology.* Englewood Cliffs, NJ: Prentice-Hall.

Shore, L.M., & Tetrick, L.E. (1994). The psychological contract as an exploratory framework in the employment relationship. *Trends in Organizational Behaviour, 1,* 91–109.

Simonsen, P. (1997). *Promoting a development culture in your organization.* Newbury Park, CA: Davies-Black.

Sims, R. (1994). Human resource management's role in clarifying the new psychological contract. *Human Resource Management, 33,* 373–382.

Chapter 2

Atkinson, P. (2000). The strategic imperative: Creating a customer-focused organisation. *Management Services, 44*(10), 8–11.

Beaumont, P.B., & Harris, R.I.D. (2002). Examining white-collar downsizing as a cause of change in the psychological contract: Some UK evidence. *Employee Relations, 24*(4), 378–389.

Cassar, V. (2001), Violating psychological contract terms amongst Maltese public service employees: Occurrence and relationships. *Journal of Managerial Psychology, 16*(3), 194–203.

Denis, J.-L., Lamothe, L., & Langley, A. (2001). The dynamics of collective leadership and strategic change in pluralistic organizations. *Academy of Management Journal, 44*(4), 809–837.

Grimmer, M., & Oddy, M. (2007). Violation of the psychological contract: The mediating effect of relational versus transactional beliefs. *Australian Journal of Management, 31*(1), 153–173.

Guest, D.E. (1998). Is the psychological contract worth taking seriously? *Journal of Organizational Behaviour, 19,* 649–665.

Guest, D.E., & Conway, N. (2002). Communicating the psychological contract: An employer perspective. *Human Resource Management Journal, 12*(2), 22–39.

References

Hyman, J., & Mason, B. (1995). *Managing employee involvement and participation.* London: SAGE Publications.

Jordan, M.H., Schraeder, M., Field, H.S., & Armenakis, A.A. (2007). Organizational citizenship behaviour, job attitudes, and the psychological contract. *Military Psychology, 19*(4), 259–271.

Kahn, R.L. (1974). Organizational development: Some problems and proposals. *Journal of Applied Behavioral Science, 10,* 485–502.

Kissler, G.D. (1994). The new employment contract. *Human Resource Management, 33,* 335–352.

Lankhuijzen, E.S.K., Stavenga de Jong, J.A., & Thijssen, J.G.L. (2006). Psychological career contract, HRD and self-management of managers. In J.E. Streumer (Ed.), *Work-related Learning* (pp. 309–331). Dordrecht, Netherlands: Springer.

Llewellyn, N. (2001). The role of psychological contracts within internal service networks, *The Service Industries Journal, 21*(1), 211–227.

Maguire, H. (2002). Psychological contracts: Are they still relevant? *Career Development International, 7*(3), 167–181.

Marks, A. (2000). Caught in the cross-fire – the complexity of psychological contracts in teamworking. *Management Research News, 23*(9–11), 106–108.

Morrison, E.W., & Robinson, S.L. (1997). When employees feel betrayed: A model of how psychological contract violation develops. *Academy of Management Review, 22,* 226–256.

Nelson, L., & Tonks, G. (2007). Violations of the psychological contract: experiences of a group of casual workers. *Research and Practice in Human Resource Management, 15*(1), 22–36.

Noe, R.A. (1999). *Employee training and development.* Boston: Irwin/McGraw-Hill.

Pate, J., & Malone, C. (2000). Enduring perceptions of violation. *Human Resource Management International Digest, 8*(6), 28–31.

Pate, J., Martin, G., Beaumont, P., & McGoldrick, J. (2000). Company-based lifelong learning: What's the pay-off for employers? *Journal of European Industrial Training, 24*(2/3/4), 149–157.

Pavlou, P.A., & Gefen, D. (2005). Psychological contract violations in online marketplaces: Antecedents, consequences, and moderating role, *Information Systems Research, 15*(4), 372–399.

Pickard, J. (1993). The real meaning of empowerment. *Personnel Management,* November, 28–33.

Schalk, R., & Roe, R.E. (2007). Towards a dynamic model of the psychological contract, *Journal for the Theory of Social Behaviour, 37*(2), 167–182.

Schalk, R., & Freese, C. (2007). The impact of organizational changes on the psychological contract and attitudes towards work in four health care organizations. In K. Isaksson, C. Hogstedt, C. Eriksson, & T. Theorell (Eds.), *Health effects of the new labour market* (pp. 129–143). Stockholm: Springer.

Shore, T.H., Bommer, W.H., & Shore, L.M. (2008). *An integrative model of managerial perceptions of employee commitment: Antecedents and influences on employee treatment.* Retrieved April 24, 2008 from http://www3.interscience. wiley.com/journal/117902498/abstract

Sparrow, P.R. (1996). Transitions in the psychological contract: Some evidence from the banking sector. *Human Resource Management Journal, 6,* 75–92.

Tekleab, A.G., & Taylor, M.S. (2003). Aren't there two parties in an employment relationship? Antecedents and consequences of organization-employee agreement on contract obligations and violations. *Journal of Organizational Behaviour, 24*(5), 585–608.

Thompson, J.W. (1995). The renaissance of learning in business. In S. Chawla, & J. Renesch (Eds.), *Learning organizations: Developing cultures for tomorrow's workplace* (pp. 85–99). Portland, OR: Productivity Press.

Weiners, B. (2004). Ricardo Semler: Set them free. Retrieved June 1, 2008, from http://www.cioinsight.com/c/a/ExpertVoices/Ricardo-Semler-Set-Them-Free/2/

Chapter 3

Bridges, W. (1996). Leading the de-jobbed organization. In F. Hesselbein, M. Goldsmith, & R. Bechhard (Eds.), *The leader of the future, new visions, strategies, and practices for the next era* (pp. 11–18). San Francisco: Jossey-Bass Publishers.

Cummings, K.J., & Kreiss, K. (2008). *Contingent workers.* Retrieved June 3, 2008 from http://www.cdc.gov/niosh/ blog/nsb021 908_contworker.html

Kanter, R.M. (1995). Mastering change. In S. Chawla, & J. Renesch (Eds.), *Learning organizations: Developing cultures for tomorrow's workplace* (pp. 71–83). Portland, OR: Productivity Press.

Noer, D.M. (1997). *Breaking free: A prescription for personal and organizational change.* San Francisco: Jossey-Bass.

Performance Management Company (1992). *Square Wheels.* Retrieved June 4, 2008 from http://www.squarewheels.com/mainpage/s wsmain.html

Szablowski, P.A. (2000). Customer value and business success in the 21st century. *Managed Care Quarterly, 8*(2), 11–33.

Thompson, J.W. (1995). The renaissance of learning in business. In S. Chawla, & J. Renesch (Eds.), *Learning organizations: Developing cultures for tomorrow's workplace* (pp. 85–99). Portland, OR: Productivity Press.

Wigand, R., Picot, A., & Reichwald, R. (1997). Information, organization and management: Expanding markets and corporate boundaries. Chichester, UK: John Wiley.

Chapter 4

Baker, T.B. (2005). *Towards a new employment relationship model: Merging the needs and interests of individual and organisation.* Unpublished doctoral dissertation, Queensland University of Technology, Brisbane.

Carmeli, A., Sternberg, A., & Elizur, D. (2008). Organizational culture, creative behaviour, and information and communication technology usage: A facet analysis. *CyberPsychology and Behaviour, 11*(2), 175–180.

McNamara, C. (2008). *Organizational culture.* Retrieved June 4, 2008 from http://www. managementhelp.org/org_thry/culture/ culture.htm

McShane, S., & Travaglione, T. (2005). *Organisational behaviour on the Pacific rim.* Sydney, Australia: McGraw-Hill.

Chapter 5

Atkinson, P. (2000). The strategic imperative: Creating a customer focused organisation. *Management Services, 44*(10), 8–11.

Carnoy, M. (1998). The changing world of work in the information age. *New Political Economy, 3*(1), 123–128.

Casey, B., Keep, E., & Mayhew, K. (1999). Flexibility, quality and competitiveness. *National Institute Economic Review*, April, 70–81

Cole, K. (2005). Management theory and practice (3rd ed.). French's Forest, Sydney: Pearson Education Australia.

Cook, J. (1998). Flexible employment: Implications for gender and citizenship in the European Union. *New Political Economy, 3*(2), 261–277.

Greene, B. (2000). Independent contractors: An attractive option? *New Zealand Journal of Industrial Relations*, June, 183–204.

National Association of Citizens Advice Bureaux. (1997). *Flexibility abused — A CAB evidence report on employment conditions in the labour market.* London: Author.

Chapter 6

Adams, J.S. (1976). The structure and dynamics in behaviour in organizational boundary roles. In M. D. Dunnette (Ed.), *Handbook in industrial and organizational psychology* (pp. 1175–1199). Chicago: Rand McNally.

Atkinson, P. (2000). The strategic imperative: Creating a customer focused organisation. *Management Services, 44*(10), 8–11.

Bathie, D., & Sarkar, J. (2002). Total quality marketing (TQM) — A symbiosis. *Managerial Auditing Journal, 17*(5), 241–245.

Berry, L.L., Parasuraman, A., & Zeithaml, V.A. (1988). The service-quality puzzle. *Business Horizons, 31*(September–October), 35–43.

Bommer, W.H., Johnson, J.L., Ricj, G.A., Podsakoff, P.M., & MacKenzie, S.B. (1995). On the interchangeability of objective and subjective measures of employee performance. A meta-analysis. *Personnel Psychology, 48*(3), 587–605.

Brighton, S. (2000). Customer information: Integration before management. *Call Centre Solutions, 19*(4), 52–54.

Brocklebank, E. (2000). A matter of convergence. *Bank Systems and Technology, 37*(9), 5–7.

Greenguard, S. (2002). When customer-focus is king. Retrieved June 8, 2008 from http://www.allbusiness.com/ businessplanning/business-structures-incorporation/203272-1.html

Heiss, J. (1990). Social roles. In M. Rosenburg, & R.H. Turner (Eds.), *Social psychology: Sociological perspectives* (pp. 94–129). New Brunswick: Transaction.

Homburg, C., Workman, J.P., & Jensen, O. (2000). Fundamental changes in marketing organization: The movement towards a customer-focused organizational structure. *Academy of Marketing Science Journal, 28*(4), 459–478.

Nancarrow, C., Rees, S., & Stone, M. (2003). New directions in customer research and the issue of ownership: A marketing research viewpoint. *Journal of Database Marketing and Customer Strategy Management, 11*(1), 26–31.

Rogers, B. (2003). What gets measured gets better. *Journal of Targeting, Measurement and Analysis for Marketing, 12*(1), 20–25.

Sebastianell, R., & Nabil Tamimi, N. (2003). Understanding the obstacles to TQM success. *The Quality Management Journal, 10*(3), 4–5.

Troyer, L., Mueller, C.W., & Osinsky, P.I. (2000). Who's the boss? A role-theoretic analysis of customer work. *Work and Occupations, 27*(3), 406–427.

Wright, J.N. (2002). Mission and reality and why not? *Journal of Change Management, 3*(1), 30–45.

On the interchange ability of objective measures of employee performance. *Personnel Psychology, 48,* 587–605.

Borman, W.C., & Motowidlo, S.J. (1997). Task performance and contextual performance: The meaning for personnel selection research. *Human Performance, 10*(2), 99–109.

Burke, P.J. (1991). Identity process and social stress. *American Sociological Review, 56,* 836–849.

Motowidlo, S.J., Borman, W.C., & Schmit, M.J. (1997). A theory of individual differences in task and contextual performance. *Human Performance, 10*(2), 71–83.

Noe, R.A., Hollenbeck, J.R., Gerhart, B., & Wright, P.M. (1994). *Human resource management: Gaining a competitive advantage.* Burr Ridge: Irwin.

Noer, D.M. (1997). *Breaking free: A prescription for personal and organizational change.* San Francisco: Jossey-Bass.

Schein, E.H. (1980). *Organizational psychology.* Englewood Cliffs, NJ: Prentice Hall.

Sturman, M.C., Trevor, C.O., Boudreau, J.W., & Gerhart, B. (2003). Is it worth it to win the talent war? Evaluating the utility of performance-based pay. *Personnel Psychology, 56*(4), 997–1017.

Thoits, P.A. (1992). Identity structures and psychological well-being: Gender and marital status comparisons. *Social Psychology Quarterly, 55,* 236–256.

Welbourne, T.M., Johnson, D.E., & Erez, A. (1998). The role-based performance scale: Validity analysis of a theory-based measure. *Academy of Management Journal, 41*(5), 540–56.

Chapter 7

Andrew, J.P. (2006). *Senior executive innovation survey.* Retrieved June 9, 2008 from http://www.bcg.com/publications/files/2006_Innovation_Survey_report.pdf

Baker, T.B. (2005). *Towards a new employment relationship model: Merging the needs and interests of individual and organisation.* Unpublished doctoral dissertation, Queensland University of Technology, Brisbane, Queensland.

Bommer, W.H., Johnson, J.L., Rich, G.A., Podsakoff, P.M., & Johnson, D.L. (1995).

Chapter 8

Ashforth, B.E., & Mael, F. (1989). Social identity theory and the organization. *Academy of Management Review, 14*(January), 20–29.

Baker, W. (1992). The network organization in theory and practice. In N. Nutria, & R. Eccles (Eds.), *Networks and organizations* (pp. 397–429). Boston: Harvard Business Press.

Carney, M. (1998). The changing world of work in the information age. *New Political Economy, 3*(1), 123–128.

Cross, R.L., Yang, A., & Louis, M.R. (2000). Boundary activities in boundary less organizations: A case study of a transformation to a team-based structure. *Human Relations, 53*(6), 841–857.

Devine, D.J., Clayton, L.D., Philips, J.L., Dunford, B.B., & Melner, S.B. (1999). Teams in organizations: Prevalence, characteristics, and effectiveness. *Small Group Research, 30*(6), 678–711.

Hackman, J.R. (2002). *Leading teams: Setting the stage for great performances.* Boston, MA: Harvard Business School Publication.

Parker, G.M. (1994). Rewarding cross-functional teamwork. Retrieved June 12, 2008, from http://www.winstonbrill.com/bril 001/html/article_index/articles/101-150/article131_body.html

Scott, W.R. (1992). *Organizations: Rational, natural, and open systems.* (3rd ed.). Englewood Cliffs, NJ: Prentice-Hall.

Sethi, R. (2000). Superordinate identity in cross-functional product development teams: Its antecedents and effect on new product performance. *Academy of Marketing Science Journal, 28*(30), 330–344.

Sheridan, J.H. (1996). Lessons from the best. *Industry Week, 245*, 13–20.

Stewart, T. (1994). Managing your company's most valuable asset: Intellectual capital. *Fortune,* October, 28–33.

Symon, G. (2000). Information and communication technologies and network organization: A critical analysis. *Journal of Occupational and Organizational Psychology, 73*(4), 389–414.

Yan, A., & Louis, M.R. (1999). Migration of organizational functions to the work unit level: Buffering, spanning, and bringing up boundaries. *Human Relations, 52*(1), 25–47.

Zhang, O., & Cao, M. (2002). Business process reengineering for flexibility and innovation in manufacturing. *Industrial Management and Data Systems, 102*(3/4), 146–153.

Chapter 9

Alderfer, C. (1969). An empirical test of a new theory of human needs. *Organizational Behaviour and Human Performance, 4,* 142–175.

Ashmos, D.P., & Duchon, D. (2000). Spirituality at work: A conceptualization and measure.

Journal of Management Inquiry, 9(2), 134–145.

Bertram, E., & Sharpe, K. (2000). Capitalism, work, and character. *The American Prospect, 11*(20), 44–48.

Beyer, J. (1999). *Culture, meaning, and belonging at work.* Chicago Academy of Management Meeting Proceedings. Chicago.

Brandt, E. (1996). Corporate pioneers exploring spirituality peace. *HR Magazine,* April, 82–87.

Brown, E.D. (2008). *Employee engagement — Not just a buzz word!* Retrieved June 15, 2008 from http://ericbrown.com/ category/ organization

Buckingham, M., & Coffman, C. (1999). *First, break all the rules: What the world's greatest managers do differently.* New York: Simon and Schuster.

Burton, H., & Farris, D. (1999). Work and development. *International Labour Review, 138*(1), 5–30.

Conger, J.A. (1994). *Spirit at work.* San Francisco: Jossey-Bass.

Hamel, C.K., & Prahalad C.K. (1994). *Competing for the future.* Boston: Harvard Business School Press.

Herzberg, F. (1966). *Work and the Nature of Man.* New York: World Publishing.

Isaksen, J. (2000). Constructing meaning despite the drudgery of repetitive work. *The Journal of Humanistic Psychology, 40*(3), 84–107.

Lester, S.W., & Brower, H.H. (2003). In the eyes of the beholder: The relationship between subordinates' felt trustworthiness and their work attitudes and behaviors. *Journal of Leadership and Organizational Studies, 10*(2), 17–25.

Maslow, A.H. (1954). *Motivation and personality.* New York: Harper.

Noer, D.M. (1997). *Breaking free: A prescription for personal and organizational change.* San Francisco: Jossey-Bass.

Sennett, R. (1998). *The corrosion of character: The personal consequences of work in the new capitalism.* New York: Norton.

Tang, T.L., Furnham, A., & Davis, G.M. (2003). A cross-cultural comparison of the money ethic, the protestant work ethic, and job satisfaction: Taiwan, the USA, and the UK.

International Journal of Organization Theory and Behaviour, 6(2), 175–186.

Terkel, S. (1995). *Working.* New York: Ballantine.

Wheatley, M.J. (1992). *Leadership and the new science.* San Francisco: Berrett-Koehler.

Zohar, D. (1997). *Rewiring the corporate brain: Using the new science to rethink how we structure and lead organizations.* San Francisco: Berrett-Koehler.

leader-member exchange: A social exchange perspective. *Academy of Management Journal, 40*, 82–111.

Wooden, M., & Sloan, J. (1998). Industrial relations reform and labour market outcomes: A comparison of Australia, New Zealand and the United Kingdom. Retrieved June 18, 2008 from http://www.rba.gov.au/PublicationsandResearch/Conferences/1998/WoodenSloan.pdf

Chapter 10

Capelli, P. (2000). A market-driven approach to retaining talent. *Harvard Business Review,* (Jan.–Feb.), 103–111.

Eisenberger, R., Fasolo, P., & Davis-La Mastro, V. (1990). Perceived organizational support and employee diligence, commitment, and innovation, *Journal of Applied Psychology, 75*, 51–59.

Johnson, L.K. (2005). Rethinking company loyalty. Retrieved from http://hbswk.hbs.edu/item/5000.html.

Meyer, J.P., & Allen, N.J. (1991). A three-component conceptualization of organizational commitment, *Human Resource Management Review, 1*, 61–89.

Meyer, J.P., & Herscovitch, L. (2001). Commitment in the workplace: Toward a general model. *Human Resource Management Review* 11, 299–332.

Schein, E.H. (1978). *Career dynamics: Matching individual and organizational needs.* Reading, MA: Addison-Wesley.

Shore, L.M., & Wayne, S.J. (1993). Commitment and employee behaviour: Comparison of affective and continuance commitment with perceived organizational support. *Journal of Applied Psychology, 78*, 774–780.

Stephens, G.K., & Feldman, D.C. (1997). A motivational approach for understanding career versus personal life investments. In G. R. Ferris (Ed.), *Research in personnel and human resource management* (pp. 333–378). Greenwich, CT: JAI.

Tech Republic (2008,). *Diagnostic tool for assessing employee commitment.* Retrieved June 19, 2008 from http://downloads.techrepublic.com/thankyou.aspx

Wayne, S.J., Shore, L.M., & Liden, R.C. (1997). Perceived organizational support and

Chapter 11

Aktouf, O. (1992). Management and theories of organizations in the 1990's: Towards a critical radical humanism? *Academy of Management Review, 17*(3), 407–431.

Anderson, J.R. (1995). *Learning and memory: An integrated approach.* New York: Oxford University Press.

Argyris, C. (1964). *Integrating the individual and the organization.* New York: Wiley.

Bandura, A. (1997). *Self-efficacy. The exercise of control.* New York: Freeman.

Barrie, J.R., & Pace, R.W. (1999). Learning and performance: Just the end of the beginning — a rejoinder to Kuchinke. *Human Resource Development Quarterly, 10*(3), 293–296.

Berger, P.L., & Luckman, T. (1966). *The social construction of reality.* New York: Doubleday.

Elliott, C. (2000). Does HRD acknowledge human becomings? A view of the UK literature. *Human Resource Development Quarterly, 11*(2), 187–195.

Fisher, D., & Torbert, W.R. (1995). *Personal and organizational transformations: The true challenge of continual quality improvement.* New York, McGraw-Hill.

Kincheloe, J.L. (1995). *Toil and trouble: Good work, smart workers, and the integration of academic and vocational education.* New York: Peter Lang.

Kohlberg, L., & Mayer, R. (1972). Development as an aim of education. *Harvard Educational Review, 42*(4), 449–496.

Kellie, D. (1999). Human resource development: Improving performance at Catering corporation. In J. Griffiths, B. Lloyd-Walker, & A. Williams (Eds.), *Human resource management* (pp. 378–379). Melbourne: Prentice Hall.

Kuchinke, K.P. (1999). Adult education towards what end? A philosophical analysis of the concept as reflected in the research theory, and practice of human resource development. *Adult Education Quarterly, 49*(4), 148–160.

Lawler, E.E. (1992). *The ultimate advantage: Creating the high involvement.* San Francisco: Jossey-Bass.

Lawler, E.E., Mohrman, S.A., & Ledford, G.E. (1995). *Creating the high performance organization: Practices and results of employee involvement and total quality management in fortune 100 companies.* San Francisco: Jossey-Bass.

Maitland, I. (1994). The morality of the corporation. *Business Ethics Quarterly, 4,* 445–458.

Nader, L. (1984). *The handbook of human resource development.* New York: Wiley.

Rummler, G.A., & Brache, A.P. (1990). *Improving performance: How to manage the white space on the organizational chart.* San Francisco: Jossey-Bass.

Stryker, S., & Statham, A. (1985). Symbolic interaction and role theory. In G. Lindsay, & E. Aronson (Eds.), *The handbook of social psychology.* (3rd ed.). New York: Random House.

Watkins, K.E., & Marsick, V.J. (1993). Sculpturing the learning organization: Lessons in the art and science of systemic change. San Francisco: Jossey-Bass.

Chapter 12

Campbell, D.J. (2000). The proactive employee: Managing workplace initiative. *Academy of Management Executive, 14*(3), 52–66.

Guest, D.E., & Conway, N. (2002). Communicating the psychological contract: An employer perspective, *Human Resource Management Journal, 12*(2), 22–39.

Denis, J-L, Lamothe, L., & Langley, A. (2001). The dynamics of collective leadership and strategic change in pluralistic organizations. *Academy of Management Journal, 44*(4), 809–837.

Hyman, J., & Mason, B. (1995). *Managing employee involvement and participation.* London: SAGE Publications.

Pickard, J. (1993). The real meaning of empowerment. *Personnel Management*, November, 28–33.

United States Chamber of Commerce (2008). Southwest's secret to a positive corporate culture: Its employees. Retrieved June 24, 2008 from http://www.uschamber.com/bclc/profiles/southwest.htm.

Chapter 13

Baker, T. B. (2005). *Towards a new employment relationship model: Merging the needs and interests of individual and organisation.* Unpublished doctoral dissertation, Queensland University of Technology, Brisbane, Australia.

Blake, D. (2001). *Skroo the rules: What the world's most productive workplace does differently.* Melbourne, Australia: Information Australia.

Christie, D.J. (2005). *HIPSYS user's handbook: An easy reference guide to HIPSYS.* Retrieved June 28, 2008 from http://www.hipsys.com

Margerison, C., & McCann, D. (2009). *Team Management Systems Model.* Retrieved June 1, 2009, from http://www.tms.com.au/tms03.html

9 781921 513206